Whimsical Tales
of
old Wanganui

Whimsical Tales of old Wanganui

Murray Crawford

Rangitawa
PUBLISHING

Whimsical Tales of old Wanganui published by Rangitawa
Publishing, Feilding New Zealand 2018

ISBN978-0-9951046-3-1

www.rangitawapublishing.com
rangitawa@xtra.co.nz

A safe but sometimes chilly way of recalling the past is to force open a crammed drawer. If you are searching for anything in particular you don't find it, but something falls out at the back that is often more interesting.

J.M. Barrie

<u>CONTENTS:</u>

<u>*A word from Alzheimers Whanganui:*</u>

Dementia in New Zealand is a major and growing health challenge. There has been a marked increase in the number of people with dementia over recent years – from nearly 50,000 in 2011 to over 62,000 in 2016. Over that period the costs associated with dementia are estimated to have increased by 75% - from over $950m in 2011 to nearly $1680m in 2016. In today's dollars the figure could reach $2.7b by 2030. It's predicted that by 2050 there will be over 170,000 New Zealanders who will have some form of dementia.

Alzheimers Whanganui Inc began in 1986 as a small informal group of carers meeting at the Wanganui District Health Board. It became an Incorporated Society in 1990 and gained Charities Commission registration in 2007. The organisation has grown significantly since its inception over 30 years ago and now supports people affected by Alzheimers throughout the Whanganui, Rangitikei, Taihape and Waimarino regions.

Alzheimers Whanganui is governed by a board which employs four part-time staff – a manager, office manager and two diversional therapists/community support staff. We are backed by a team of wonderful volunteers who assist with activities such as group outings, administration tasks, education and fundraising.

As a not-for-profit organisation with no guaranteed income, Alzheimers Whanganui relies upon the generosity of the community for the funds required to meet the growing need for our services. These involve working with the person with dementia, supporting the main carer and extended family/whanau, and the provision of advocacy services when required. The aim is to strengthen the family by providing an understanding of dementia and supporting the person with dementia by focusing on what they are still able to do rather than what has been lost.

All profits from the sale of this book will be used to provide services to families affected by Alzheimers throughout the Whanganui, Rangitikei and Waimarino districts.

Wendy Paterson: Manager, Alzheimers Whanganui.

<u>*Prologue:*</u>

Who would have thought that one of Wanganui's most popular doctors had no formal medical qualifications? Or that a judge advocated the torching of our former courthouse. Why was an insignificant gorse fire the catalyst which intensified the rivalry between our two daily newspapers and led to over 100 years of insults and journalistic mud-slinging? How many people know that our recent "h" debate was played out over 100 years ago, with many of the same arguments for and against? Did our early firemen deserve the oft-presented image of a bunch of bumbling Keystone Cops? How long ago were kangaroos hopping around the district? And why did an impoverished domestic servant who eked out a miserable existence in broken-down hovels on the outskirts of town attract such paternalistic attention from the powers-that-be?

The following series of sad, quirky, humorous, inspirational and outrageous tales from the past does not pretend to be a definitive account of our town's history. It is simply a collection of stories taken from our early newspapers, in particular the *Evening Herald* (later the *Wanganui Herald*) and the *Wanganui Chronicle*, aimed at giving readers a glimpse into the way our forebears lived their lives, which in many ways (apart from advances in technology) may not have been so much different from ours as we like to think. They too grappled with issues such as dangerous footpaths, burglaries, council bureaucracy, postal delays, missing newspapers, teenage immorality and parental irresponsibility to mention just a few. We tend to look at them askance - bewhiskered men and grim-faced women whom we imagine lived in a dull monochrome world with little inspiration or excitement. We are sometimes disdainful of their perceived attitudes and ways of doing things, while failing to recognise that had we lived in their times, we too would probably have

14

held those same views and responded in a similar manner to the situations they faced, in accordance with the perceived wisdom of the day. In like manner future generations will no doubt snigger at (or regard with horror) the so-called enlightened views which we pride ourselves as possessing in today's allegedly sophisticated world. At least our forebears knew how to roll up their sleeves and get a job done, without the encumbrance of interminable and multifarious public opinion surveys and consultation exercises which are deemed so necessary today, thus transforming vast tracts of sandhills and swampland into the pretty, celebrated city we now enjoy.

So if readers find themselves chuckling at the foibles and idiosyncrasies of our Victorian and Edwardian ancestors, but at the same time begin to feel a kinship with those whose blood, sweat and tears helped provide the comforts and rights we take for granted in this "different country" of the 21st century, the author will be well satisfied.

Most of these stories, presented only very loosely in any form of chronological order, have appeared as a regular series in the *River City Press* under the same title as this book. Others have been published occasionally in the *Wanganui Chronicle,* usually to commemorate anniversaries of historical events such as Wanganui's own 9/11 disaster, or to highlight matters of topical interest such as the aforementioned "h" debate or "buy local" campaigns. (There is indeed nothing new under the sun). Most appear as stand-alone stories although some, notably those of the *Fire Brigade,* the *Hewett* story, *Little Gib* and *Granny Dalton* are presented as a series.

The author hopes others will derive as much pleasure reading this collection of historical literary all-sorts as he did in researching and compiling them. They have been arranged in such a way as to be savoured as a pick-and-mix, to enjoy on the run or – for the voracious reader – to be scoffed in one sitting.

****

Readers will note that the names of our city and river have been variously spelt Wanganui or Whanganui in accordance with the era in which they occur – usually the former due to the historical nature of this book. Places such as Queens Park and Cooks Gardens may be alternatively spelt as Queen's Park/Cook's Gardens, also according to the context in which they appear.

Some articles use phrases such as *"this month"*, *"lately"* or *"this year"* and relate to the time the original article was published. In such cases an accompanying note, dates, information within the article or the reader's memory will give an indication as to the times referred to.

For the convenience of readers unfamiliar with pre-decimal currency the *"£"* symbol represents a pound, *"s"* a shilling and *"d"* pence.

If words such as *"honour"* or *"colour"* appear in quoted newspaper texts without the customary *"u"* and without the required [sic] to indicate a spelling mistake, it's because it isn't – a spelling mistake, that is. It seems the dropping of the *"u"* was not unusual in newspapers of the time and was certainly the option favo(*u*)red by the *Herald,* at least in its earlier years.

Most articles have been expanded from the original now that word-count restrictions no longer apply, or where new information has since come to hand.

Although primarily dealing with early Wanganui issues, this book seeks to reflect the thinking, values and attitudes on matters common throughout the colony.

The reader should not be surprised if occasionally the same quote or anecdote appears more than once. It may be because separate articles containing the quote were published by both *RCP* and the *Chronicle,* it may be relating to a different subject, or it is simply an indication that the author is fast approaching the time when he will require the services provided by the very worthy organisation benefiting from the funds derived from this publication.

Newspaper references are from *Papers Past: National Library of New Zealand - Te Puna Mātauranga o Aotearoa,* which has provided a wonderful resource for historians and genealogists. This volume should be regarded as a mere dipping of the toes into the vast ocean of information which is now readily accessible online, which leads to the question, "How does one know when to stop, when there are so many stories yet to be rediscovered?" Perhaps the answer lies in the possibility of a sequel, should our local newspapers continue to humour the author by tolerating his ramblings in their esteemed journals.

Thanks must go to both *River City Press* and the *Wanganui Chronicle* for their agreeing to the compilation of these articles. Also to the *Whanganui District Library (NZ)* and H&A Print (*Memories of Old Wanganui)* for permission to reproduce several of the photographs contained herein, and the *Whanganui Regional Museum* for permission to reproduce the Sandown image.

Every effort has been made to trace copyright of the images used that are not attributed.

"There was once a man who had never been to Wanganui"

So begins a 1925 promotional brochure, aimed at giving readers *"a bird's-eye view"* of New Zealand's River City.

"He was a New Zealander," it continues, *"who travelled the world in search of the perfect hometown. He'd seen the colour and glare of the East, the lights and life of England, the story-book towns of the Continent, Switzerland's quaint villages, America's temples of modernity and towns which are the pride of Canadian hearts.*

He'd seen all these and marvelled – but came back to New Zealand. One day he realised he'd never been to Wanganui. He shrugged his shoulders – and came. He is here yet, and will remain. He had found 'the perfect hometown.' Have you?"

Pretty cheesy, huh? But wait - there's more! In the tradition of all good bodice-rippers it hints darkly of forbidden desires.

"This is a book of temptation," we are cautioned, *"because to know Wanganui is to want her! She is a city who twines her way around your heart. Her traditions and history fire the imagination, her success is infectious, her future is bright with the certain success of her citizens! Here is a city of twenty-five thousand people which was a precarious, peril-threatened settlement only sixty years ago! A city which is architecturally ahead of almost any other town in the Dominion. A modern city with electric light, gas, tramways, beautiful buildings, parks, wide streets, harbour and schools unsurpassed. A city to be proud of even in this age of marvellous cities!"*

****

The above literary gem was *"issued in the interests of Wanganui by the Wanganui Chamber of Commerce"* and published by the *Wanganui Chronicle Co., Ltd.* It describes *"a city of romance, success and vast possibilities"*, outlines our *"prudent policy of persistent progress"* and boasts of *"energetic people who are building good citizens for the Dominion."*

Full marks for trying must go to the Wellington advertising company which produced the script for this brochure, but while it would have failed to make the cut today it "ticked all the boxes" nearly a century ago - just a year after our township had passed the threshold of achieving city status.

But 1925 marks the end point of our *"Whimsical Tales"* series. Let us then take a look at a selection of anecdotes, observations and milestones in our history which led to this momentous pinnacle. (Which should not be taken to infer that we've been going downhill ever since).

Wanganui - ahead of most other towns in the Dominion

A cliff by any other name.......

Who was the first European to discover Wanganui? We will probably never know for certain, but an intriguing possibility is recorded in the 6 May, 1891 edition of the *Wanganui Herald*, which if proved, would rewrite our colonial history and indeed have a massive impact upon English history and literature as we know it.

The first European to discover Wanganui, according to an early scribe, was none other than William Shakespeare. Sceptical? Then read on:

"It has always been a vexed question as to whom rested the honour of being the first discoverer of Wanganui," wrote a correspondent who went by the nom de plume of *Marksman*. *"By many of the older settlers it is claimed that Shakespeare is entitled to this distinction, and in proof of this assertion they proudly point to the cliff overhanging the river, which bears the name of that memorable and eventful occasion. It is further contended that it was on this identical hill that he composed his great masterpiece Macbeth, and there is considerable colouring as proof of this assertion, as many namesakes and descendants of the Scottish king are still found settled over portions of the Rangitikei district, whilst *Macduff still survives and runs the largest coach factory in Wanganui."*

Note: Shakespeare is believed to have written *Macbeth* about 1606, placing his purported discovery well before 1642, the year Abel Tasman reached our shores.

(Many less imaginative historians, apparently unaware of the above account, subscribe to the belief that Shakespeare's Cliff was named by Wanganui settler John Nixon because it reminded him of the historic Shakespeare Cliff that dominates the entrance to Dover Harbour in England).   A further twist to the story is this letter which followed up the *Herald's* article: *"Sir, It is most annoying to us historians to find any reference to that great fraud – Shakespeare. There never was no such person; neither did he ever own a cliff, either in Wanganui or on the Kentish coast. No such cliffs exist, or ever did, or ever will. These cliffs really belong to Mr Bacon, Esq., so for the future we trust they will be called by their proper names. I am, dear sir, ONE WHO KNOWS ALL ABOUT IT."*

But what we do know is that the first *recorded* visit to Wanganui by a European is that of a gentleman by the name of Joseph Rowe, whose tale could perhaps go under the subtitle of "The Headless Oarsman." Mr Rowe brought his little vessel to shore at Landguard Bluff in 1831, only to find himself in a spot of bother with the locals. One of them apparently recognised his cousin's facial features amongst Rowe's cargo – a boat-load of shrunken Maori heads. The upshot of the whole business was that Mr Rowe's head was then separated from his shoulders as utu and his body, now of no use to its former owner, served up for the evening meal. Ironically, 1831 was the year that the British government ruled the trade in human heads illegal – not that anyone took much notice for many years.

* An obituary in the *Wanganui Chronicle* (5 September, 1914) for Miss Fanny MacDuff, stated that her father, Mr W. MacDuff, *"carried on business in Wanganui as a coachbuilder for many years."*

Was the Bard the first European to discover Wanganui?

Colonial capers

Early newspapers often ran *Local & General* columns reporting interesting, humorous and sometimes quirky news items. Here are a few snippets from the *Chronicle* and *Herald*.

"McDowell's premises were burglariously entered on Monday evening and several pieces of stuff were abstracted therefrom."

"Mr Wicksteed has had a narrow escape. He rode quite close to two mounted natives and only became aware of their friendly intentions by being fired at by one with a revolver, whilst the other dismounted for a steadier shot. Mr Wicksteed did not wait to ask their reasons for this conduct."

"A misguided youth saw fit to sound the Fire Bell on Saturday, which had the effect of producing considerable consternation in various quarters. Before the sound had died away, firemen Palmer and Turnbull appeared fully equipped, several people assembling at the Albion corner. The lad, the cause of the commotion, had cause to regret his inquisitive phrenological development, and will probably restrain his inquiring disposition in future."

"If the gentleman at the Phoenix Hotel does not pay for the hat he lost at billiards at Queen's Birthday, he will hear more about it."

"The Glassblowers gave their farewell exhibition last night. A committee of ladies awarded the prize pipe to a well-known businessman as being, 'the plainest man in the hall'."

"Monday next is Whit Monday and the banks in Wanganui will close their doors all day. There is no one class of the community equal to the banking people in strict observance of ecclesiastical times and seasons."

"Today being the festival known as Ash Wednesday, is kept sacred by the dealers in bullion."

"It is a practice on New Zealand railways to allow church men to ride ½ fare, and one of the cloth wrote asking the manager, 'if he could embrace his wife also.' The manager replied that he thought he could, but did not want to say positively until he had seen the parson's wife, as he was 'a little fastidious in his tastes.'"

"John Hayes was fined £1, with costs, for driving a vehicle with tyres narrower than provided for in the by-laws."

"A youth of horsey proclivities, riding a three-legged chestnut nag, made rather an exhibition of himself yesterday, trying to jump his apology for a steed over the furze bushes at the top of Guyton Street near Churton's Creek. It is a pity some more useful occupation could not be found for him."

"A question of privilege was raised in the police cells the other night. An inebriate was singing to the annoyance of another inebriate. 'Shut up or go outside,' remarked the annoyed one. 'Shut up yourself,' was the indignant response. 'I have as much right to be here as you have.'"

"James McCann, for having no visible means of support, was sentenced to three months' imprisonment with hard labour."

"A near-sighted Irishman, about to fight a duel, 'insisted that because of his disadvantage he should stand six paces nearer to his antagonist than the latter did to him.'"

*"If some patriotic individual would walk around and whitewash the corner posts of the streets in the suburbs, he would offer a national benefit. Some of them are positively dangerous, especially on dark nights. Only a few nights ago, an unfortunate female ran full butt against the post on the corner of *Nixon and Guyton Streets, the sensations of which collision may be imagined. Seriously, some are notoriously dangerous."*

"The residents of Nixon Street have to thank the Foreman of Works for having diminished the dangers of their nightly peregrinations by ordering the painting of the corner post in proximity thereto. Such can now be distinguished even on the darkest night."

* When Wanganui East merged with the Borough of Wanganui, Nixon Street, (to avoid confusion) was renamed Nelson Street, but the then lower end of Nelson Street was named Cook's Street. It would have been at the corner of Cooks and Guyton that the *"unfortunate female"* came off second best following her altercation with the post.

Wicksteed – Streets ahead of attackers

Colonial complaints

One of ratepayers' most common complaints is the state of our roads and footpaths, so spare a thought for our town's early inhabitants. Here are a few examples of what they had to put up with.

"A valuable draught horse fell into the open drain in Glasgow Street on Saturday night last and was killed."

"Sir, When the Town Board found they could not get money from the Provincial Government to repair the River Bank, they slapped on 50% to the general rate. This money was paid months ago and the River Bank is still crumbling away. Will the board's surveyor kindly tell us what has become of the money. Yours, Hard-Up Ratepayer."

"Complaint has been made to us of the inattention shown to the requirements of the streets in the upper portion of the town, particularly Liverpool Street. The footpaths in these streets afford anything but satisfaction to the residents in the localities interested, and a little attention on the part of the Borough authorities would not be misplaced."

"For the convenience of pedestrians some street improvements have become an almost imperative necessity, as for ladies to cross the Avenue and the Quay, and in many other places also, the terribly muddy condition of the roadway is such as to cause the effort to be a most unpleasant and arduous undertaking."

"RIDGWAY STREET: From the Rutland Chambers to Miller and Graham's corner is the dread of pedestrians, especially female ones, at night. Inequalities abound, and pools exist, whereupon a punt service could be established. Surely the Foreman of Works must have seen the condition of the footpath in the much used street referred to. For a load or two of gravel the residents and the public would render him a unanimous vote of thanks."

"Sir, Yesterday afternoon, just about the time when children were coming home from school, some half-dozen head of cattle, driven by three or four stockmen, fairly took possession of Wilson Street,

tearing through private properties, smashing gates and fences and scattering men, women and children in every direction, seeking refuge from the charge. Anything more reckless, dangerous and improper I have never seen permitted in the streets of a town. It is a miracle some poor child was not trampled or gored. If the streets are to be converted into cattle runs, it is better that the citizens should be made aware of it, so that they may know where and when to expect the stampede. If a repetition of the practice I refer to is sanctioned by the authorities, I feel sure some serious or fatal accident will result. It is anything but a pleasant sight for parents, who expect their children on the way from school, to see pedestrians flying before a charge of horsemen and maddened cattle, which destroy property and terrify the residents with impunity."

"We understand it is very likely that the police will take steps against Henry Williams for driving cattle through the town yesterday morning."

"That very dangerous hole at the corner of Wicksteed Street near the Phoenix Hotel, to which we alluded on a previous occasion, still remains unattended to. As we said before, the dangerous opening is in a frequented portion of the street, and it is simply miraculous that some serious accident has not occurred before now. Horsemen are almost hourly rounding this corner, often at a rapid rate, and nothing is surer, than that should a horse put his foot in the cavity thus formed, a severe accident to both horse and rider would be the inevitable result. Would it be too much to expect the occupants of the premises in close proximity thereto to place a box or barrel over the opening as a temporary protection until the Corporation should see fit to effect the necessary repairs."

"If he (the pound-keeper) has any desire to fill his establishment, we would recommend him to take an assistant and ride round Glasgow Street, London Street, the top of the Avenue (where the gardens of private residences are favorite hunting grounds for wandering horses and cattle), Liverpool and Wicksteed Street, and he will reap a rich harvest. The law appears to have quite lost its terrors to the owners of wandering animals – if indeed the word terror can be applied to a trifling fine, without costs and Magisterial

apology for inflicting it."

"Several parts of this street (Guyton) require the attention of the Foreman of Works. On both sides of the Avenue, both roadway and footpath are a series of inequalities, as awkward to the spring of vehicles as to the nerves of pedestrians, especially on dark nights. Could not Mr Gilmour effect an amelioration of the state of things now complained of."

"Guyton Street is now frequently used as a convincing speed ground on which to test the merits of horses. Yesterday two equestrians might have been seen doing a gallop on this thoroughfare. The safety of the public should surely be a prior consideration to the superiority of speed and endurance claimed by owners of horses, who could find room beyond the suburbs for turf amusements."

"We are requested to call the attention of the Municipal Authorities to a fact which may possibly have slipped from memory, viz., that there is, within the Borough of Wanganui, such a thoroughfare as Alexander Street, and further that the said thoroughfare is in a disgraceful condition at present. Should any doubts arise to the reliability of the foregoing statements, a correspondent suggests that the Foreman of Works, when he has an hour or so to spare, should personally inspect the locality indicated and report as to the state thereof to the Borough Council. If convenient, such official inspection to be made after two or three days' rain, such as fell last week."

The Harrison Street drain:

"A gentleman of our acquaintance has lost a valuable retriever dog through falling into the Harrison Street drain, where he was discovered yesterday morning."

"Perhaps it has never occurred to many that there is a great distinction between drains and drainage, and if there are those inclined to dispute the fact, let them go down Harrison Street and 'snuff the gentle breeze', which is wafted over an excavated drain running along that street, when they will feel for once convinced, if they have a nerve in their nostrils .... There are plenty in and

about Wanganui that make an impression similar to what was produced on the student at Cologne who, on putting his head out of his bedroom window, was met with 50,000 different smells. We urge upon the 'authorities', (whoever they are) in these matters to look after the public health."

"The Harrison Street drain, of great celebrity, requires the immediate attention of the Town Board. A short time back some alterations were made in the drain, and this morning the covering of the drain had fallen in for more than halfway across the street, a large volume of water running so that if any person should fall in, he must inevitably be drowned and there is nothing to prevent such a catastrophe after dark, which would be more likely than otherwise to anyone traversing the street." (Herald).

"Nocturnal peregrinations in the vicinity of this ditch are attended with danger to a greater or lesser extent. On Thursday night, two gentlemen unexpectedly found themselves struggling at the bottom of its slimy depths, much in the same predicament as Jack and Jill, except that the pail of water was not the end and object of their research. In other respects, the history as told in the old familiar ballad repeated itself. Pedestrians should exercise due care when promenading about, especially at night." (Chronicle).

"Even Councillor Nathan is not a bad fellow, though he did make a mess of the Harrison Street drain."

Swallowed up by the Glasgow Street drain

The Hewetts (Part 1): Brunswick farmer beheaded

Last month (February, 2015) marked the 150th anniversary of an event which shocked the Wanganui community, causing its inhabitants to once again wonder about the future of their town.

Wanganui had, the previous year, been spared the threat of attack when local Maori defeated the Hau Hau at Moutoa Island but discontent simmered. Captain James Hewett, ex-army and local militia member had received permission to tend his farm at Brunswick, while his family sought refuge in town. On the night of February 9, 1865 he was alerted by barking dogs and went outside to investigate, confident that as a friend and employer of local Maori he would be safe. He was met by a hail of gunfire and as he lay dying he ordered his farmhand, James Deegan, to try to escape. "Save yourself!" he cried. "I'm done for." While making his getaway Deegan tripped on a fence wire and lay low in the long grass, thus eluding his pursuers. He eventually made his way back to town and brought the tragic news of his employer's death to Mrs Hewett. The *Chronicle's* correspondent (10 February) reported that the attackers must have been disturbed at some point because they left behind weapons and ammunition. He rued the fact that men could not be spared to pursue them, *"as it is said they have carried off a cask of rum, and, if so, they are probably lying drunk not far off."*

Kowhai Ngutu Kaka, who later became prominent in the Hau Hau movement under Titokowaru, claimed to have been one of those responsible for the attack. Reminiscing in an article in the *Herald* (13 February, 1884) nearly twenty years later, he admitted his part in the killing.

"We called Dr Hewitt [sic] out of his house one night when all was still. He came out with his man-servant to see who it was calling to him, and then we seized him and cut off his head for our

Niu (pole)."

Hewett's head, along with those of other colonials including Captain Thomas Lloyd, was then carried on a pole around the North Island for use in a Hau Hau recruitment drive and as a means of communicating with the war gods.

"It was a very nice religion," said Kowhai Ngutu Kaka, although he confessed to not understanding, *"the apparent gibberish we gave utterance to."*

It was not until many years later that Mrs Hewett found out why her request for a lock of her husband's hair was not granted, although eventually the remains of his head (and heart which was also removed) were recovered by missionary William Williams and interred with his body in the Sandhills (now Heads Road) Cemetery. The dedication of a new epitaph on his grave was held at a ceremony in 1990, commemorating the 125th anniversary of Hewett's death. A sword, used by Hewett's father Colonel William Hewett at the Battle of Waterloo, was prominent at the ceremony. It had been lost for many years, but was eventually discovered at the Hawera Museum, returned to Mrs Hewett and is with the family to this day.

A tree still standing at the site of the Brunswick homestead, contains the remains of an iron bedstead which was thrown into it and was visible for many years, when the house was ransacked and burned by the Hau Hau. Ellen sold the property and returned to England to educate her four children, before returning with them to New Zealand. She died in an Auckland rest home in 1926 and is buried at Purewa Cemetery.

James Hewett

Ellen Hewett

The Hewetts (Part 2): Laundry day, pioneer style

Our previous article featured the killing of Brunswick farmer James Hewett (known to his family as "Jem") during the Hau Hau uprising of the 1860s. Hewett had brought his 15 year-old bride Ellen to Toi Farm in about 1860. The following is Ellen's account of laundry day, from her book *Looking Back*.

"Before our deep well was dug we were obliged during a hot, dry summer, to cart our soiled clothes about a mile from the house, where there was a spring at the bottom of a deep gully. First we rolled a large iron boiler down the gully, then came the clothes in bundles and then we ourselves followed, hanging on to the branches of trees till we reached the stream at the bottom.

It was lovely under the shelter of the palm and fern trees, but it was not easy getting the washed clothes hauled up again in the tubs. My husband did not like losing a day from farm-work to help, but it was inevitable until the deep well was made, which was, of course, a great improvement, and rendered us independent of the droughts, and also masculine aid at the arduous operation of washing."

After the wet clothes were carried back to the homestead they were spread over gorse bushes to dry, with Ellen no doubt hoping they wouldn't be blown off into the mud or targeted by overflying birds.

The well was eventually dug, but it was located several hundred yards from the house and was 100 feet deep, requiring a windlass to haul up each bucket of water.

"It was hard work, especially on clothes-washing day," said Ellen, who also described another luxury her husband provided for her.

"A lean-to, built at the back of our small bedroom, served for a bathroom. A hole was bored through the floor over a small drain-pipe, and over this was placed a large wooden tub with a hole in it, and a big cork which served as a plug."

Unfortunately the Hewetts lost the house shortly afterwards

32

in a fire, (the first of three to destroy their home).

"There was no water in the well, and having had a long spell of dry weather it was quite impossible to save our pretty little home, although the men worked hard to save it until they fell exhausted to the ground."

Wash-day featured strongly on the occasion of the Hewett's second house fire. Ellen records that her sister and a friend were staying and had been helping all day with the laundry.

"It was a very big wash, and we put the clothes on to the furze fence, which surrounded our garden, excepting a few things left in the tubs to finish the next day."

Because their domestic/nurse-girl's carelessness had led to the first fire, Ellen was in the habit of taking away her candle each night, but confessed to being so tired she just called out to the girl to be careful in putting out her light. At about midnight she was awoken by a strange sound and alerted her husband, who slipped on some clothes and went to investigate.

"On opening the kitchen door he uttered an exclamation of horror. Then I heard a loud bang and all was silent. It was an awful moment! I thought my husband had been killed."

Ellen decided she must face the danger, but on entering the kitchen found it full of smoke and her husband dragging something along the floor.

"This proved to be the nurse-girl, half stupefied by the smoke. Her bedroom, which led out of the kitchen, was a mass of flames. The three men, who had come with their scythes the day before to cut the hay, had been aroused and were soon putting out the fire with the clothes I had left in the rinse-tubs. There is nothing like wet clothes for putting out a fire; but it is rough on the clothes! The men smacked the clothes against the walls and ceilings and soon the fire was out – at least, so we thought. The nurse-girl, in spite of my warnings, had left her candle burning and the bedclothes had caught fire."

When they judged it safe the family returned to bed, but

were later woken by a frantic banging at the bedroom window. It was one of the farm-hands who had awoken from a dream that the house was again on fire, went to investigate and found his dream had come true. Everyone escaped safely, but virtually nothing of the house and its contents remained, apart from some drawing room furniture.

"We were in our very scanty night-clothes. The men were sent to one side of the gorse-bush to dress, whilst the women used the other side as our dressing room. My young friend and my sister were the most presentable; they had even saved their crinolines, which were indispensable in those days.

Fortunately for me and my husband, we had a few clothes drying on the gorse fence; these were quite dry as the sun rose early, it being mid-summer. My pink print dress looked funny, rough-dried and crinkled up with starch, but by means of several pullings at the hem it came down to my heels. I had stockings, but no shoes. Fortunately, there were no holes in the stockings.

Also, fortunately, I had just washed a pair of my husband's white duck unmentionables, or he would have had none to put on, as all the clothes in our bedroom were burnt. So he wore them rough-dry off the gorse hedge and his shirt in the same condition. And he too had only socks, no shoes."

The sorry party, miserable and hungry, then made its way to town, pulled by a skitterish horse in a broken-down cart. At the top of a steep hill the horse bolted, taking the terrified occupants of the cart on a helter-skelter ride around sharp bends with steep drops until James managed to steer the horse into a swamp at the bottom of the hill. Leaving his exhausted passengers, who were too weary to move or even speak, in the shade of a flax-bush, he rode the rest of the way into town to bring help in the form of several officers of the 57th Regiment, one of whom convulsed with laughter at the forlorn sight which greeted him.

"How thankful we were at last to arrive in the little town and to receive the kindly welcome of friends eager to help us!" wrote Ellen.

"My husband's spirits were always tip-top. He had said on his way into town to a man who was riding past, 'If you get into town before we do, please call at Mrs McDonough's house and tell her we are burnt out and have lost everything but our appetites!'"

So ended another Hewett washday.

Outdoor laundry

The Hewetts (Part 3): A child bride faces down danger

Our two previous articles looked at aspects of the lives of the Hewett farming family who lived at Brunswick. Besides the rigours of pioneer life the Hewetts constantly faced the threat of attack from hostile Maori. The first was during a time of unrest when a group of twenty workers struck while thatching a farm building. They demanded more money for the toi-toi they were cutting which grew on their own land nearby.

"Jem objected, as he knew he was giving them full payment and insisted upon them finishing their work according to agreement. They refused and tried to prevent our man from going with the horse and cart for another load of toi-toi," wrote Ellen.

A tussle ensued but eventually Hewett prevailed and got the cart moving again. Afraid and standing holding her new-born baby on the doorstep, Ellen tried to go with her husband but he told her to return. One of the aggrieved workers tried to push past her, but she would not allow him into the house, then relented when he said he just wanted a light for his pipe.

"Instead of that he took two lighted pieces of wood, which he brandished about. The other natives gathered all the ignitable stuff they could into a high heap against our dwelling-house and were about to set fire to it. For an instant I prayed to God to give me courage and strength; then I rushed past them and jumped onto the heap, sat down, spread my dress out as far as it would go and with hands stretched out I dared them to come near me!

I could not speak Maori, but they understood and were astonished, and I do not know what would have happened but for the intervention of some Maori women who had come to cook for the men and who, when they saw me do this, came running up to me with beaming eyes and laughing faces, uttering exclamations which I did not understand, but patting me on my shoulders. This, which was, of course, their way of saying 'Well done!' amused the men, and the wife of a chief who was there ordered them all to shake hands with me, which they did as I sat in state upon the heap they had intended as a funeral pyre for our home!

The scene changed rapidly; the men who a moment before looked so ominously angry were now smiling and shaking hands with me. I suppose it struck them as strange to see such a young girl confronting twenty men without showing any fear. At any rate it 'fetched' the Maori women and brought them all to my side, so that I was a sort of heroine in their eyes."

When Ellen's husband appeared again with his horse and cart the women ran to him in great excitement to tell him what his *"picannine wahine (child wife), had done to defend his property."*

Ellen Hewett records several other occasions when she and her children nearly lost their lives before losing her husband to the Hau Hau in 1865, but writes, *"Life has been very full for me of work amongst my children and grandchildren and in works of philanthropy. My three years of Gospel-Temperance work among the Maoris was, I believe, the most successful of all. The Maoris realised that I, as well as themselves, had suffered during the war and they never failed to appreciate, in the most responsive way, all my efforts on their behalf."*

Ellen Hewett in her old age (with great-grandson James Paterson)

Wife wanted – must have nice legs

"WANTED BY A GENTLEMAN, A WIFE," began an advertisement in the *New Zealand Colonist & Port Nicholson Advertiser* (5 August, 1842). *"She must possess affable manners, an agreeable person and a temper as good as may be; money not so much an object as economical habits; accomplishments would be desirable, but are not a great object. The advertiser would prefer a lady not much given to talking. This would form a desirable opportunity for a lady not long arrived in the colony, the advertiser having a great objection to colonial habits and manners. The gentleman is a young man of genteel manners, good temper, well educated and of good exterior. N.B. - No Widow need apply. To prevent unnecessary application, thick legs and large feet are a decided objection."*

"We think," opined the editor, *"that in the present scarcity of marriageable ladies in Port Nicholson, the above advertisement might have been inserted by many of our fashionable young men in Wellington."*

But the situation (certainly in New Plymouth) had improved 30 years later according to the *Evening Herald* (4 April, 1873), when it advised any young man seeking a mate to knock on the first door in that town he came to.

"The chances are that he will find at least three eligible young ladies, and it is his own fault if he does not soon get a wife; and a good one too."

The *Herald* hastened to add that it should not be inferred that New Plymouth ladies couldn't get married. It was just that there were so many of them that they were, *"committing matrimony to an alarming extent."*

Another lonely heart from 1842 sought a handsome lady, about middle size and not too stout, with engaging manners, sweet temper and affable disposition. He described himself as being in the prime of life, rather handsome, possessing an income of £200 per year and promising the greatest secrecy to all applicants, although probably revealing his own identity by advertising under the unlikely moniker of "Mr Nosnah", which of course reads Hanson when spelled backwards.

But finding a wife in colonial New Zealand was usually a challenge as men outnumbered women by a substantial margin for many years. One startling suggestion – made to the *Oamaru Times* - was to make marriage compulsory as a means of populating the country, and seen by its proposer as preferable to retaining the services of a paid immigration agent. How his scheme would have worked in practice was not explained, but it reminded the editor of the tale of a Scottish border laird – the father of an aesthetically challenged daughter. Having captured a notorious fugitive, the laird ordered him to to marry *"Muckle-mouthed Meg"* or be hanged. Fortunately for the victim he had seen the intended bride *sans* veil, so wisely chose *"the halter for the altar"*.

However, steps were made to remedy the imbalance of the sexes, as revealed in this *Herald* article of 30 July, 1902: *"The colonial marriage market is likely to liven up speedily. It is announced by the People's Journal that the Yorkshire Ladies' Council of Education at Leeds is training young women for the position of wives in the colonies. The training is in cookery, laundry work, needlework, household accounts, first aid and household management. For those anxious to become thoroughly equipped for life in the colonies the council has arranged a three months' course in dairy work and poultry keeping."*

Sadly, not many years later, the Great War's terrible harvest on European battlefields played a part in correcting the imbalance which social engineering had struggled to achieve. *"But look at the great mass of marriages that take place over the whole world,"* the *New Zealand Gazette & Wellington Spectator* had warned many years previously (4 January, 1843). *"What poor, contemptible affairs they are! A few soft looks, a walk, a dance, a squeeze of the hand, a popping of the question, a purchasing of a certain number of yards of white satin, a ring, a clergyman, a stage or two in a hired carriage, a night in a country inn and the whole matter is over. For five or six weeks two sheepish looking persons are seen dangling on each other's arm, looking at water-falls, or making morning calls, and guzzling wine and cake; then everything falls into the most monotonous routine; the wife sits on one side of the hearth; the husband on the other; and little quarrels, little pleasures, little cares and little children gradually gather round them. This is what ninety-nine out of one hundred find to be the 'delights' of matrimony."*

So the idea of compulsory wedlock, thereby circumventing the disruptive influence of romance, may not have been a bad one after all. Perhaps the one-out-of-a-hundred unions to escape the *Gazette's* gloomy prediction was that of the gallant groom, newly married to *"a little undersized beauty."* In response to comments regarding her dimunitive stature he replied, *"She would have been taller, but is made of such precious materials that nature could not afford it."*

Thick legged ladies need not apply

The new ideal in husbands

The above headline appeared in the *Chronicle* (1 November, 1919) subtitled, *"Adventurous Suitors Now Cupid's Favourites"*. The article was written by an appropriately named Hilda Love who opined that, *"The man with the safe, sure job has no longer the pull in courtship."*

This was at a time when surviving soldiers were returning from the battlefields of Europe to young women who, in the absence of young men, had learned to be enterprising and independent. Previously, according to Hilda, the safe, sure job used to be one of the best passports with which a man would come to the girl of his choice.

"'He's steady!' said the maiden to her secret self, while that secret self obediently put away its dreams of a bold adventurous lover. So she took the man with the yearly increase of salary, a yearly holiday, a yearly insurance and everything cut, dried and secure for the years ahead. This man had the pull in courtship. His attractive but adventurous brother was turned down in favour of the less enterprising but steady suitor. The latter occupied the highest pedestal in the matrimonial market. Wise mothers encouraged his worship.

That was before the demobbed maid of the new age returned from her war work, surveyed the old idol and decided that his carefully assured future brought no joy to her spirit. The man of enterprise, the man who is not afraid to leave the old rut, who is willing to take a chance in making good on his own – this is the man who gets her attention. Her newly awakened love of adventure responds to his enterprising spirit, his ambitions meet with instant sympathy. Here is her ideal combination of romance and adventure. Heart and head answer to his wooing.

The thousands of war brides who have crossed the waters are evidence of the attraction of the adventurous husband. Thousands of other young couples are but waiting their passages to the new lands where they hope for the greater opportunity that may come to spirits unafraid. Gone forever are the heart-breaking farewells of other days when the man left the girl behind while he went to make a home.

'I'm coming with you,' says our modern maid, eager and enthusiastic. 'We'll have this adventure together!'

One mother tried to understand why her daughter had refused a comfortably situated bank clerk.

'You evidently do not love him!' she declared when her daughter attempted to explain.

'No, but I could,' retorted the girl, 'if only he had more adventure in him. That monotonous career ahead of him quite contents him. A motor-bike and a house of his own will be the end of his adventure. I couldn't marry a man who lacks the confidence to do the things I would do. I should have to take the lead. I want a man who'll take the lead himself and let me be there and help too.'

That girl is now on her way to the Fiji Islands, the wife of a demobbed man she knew in her schooldays, who is making a bid for the life he always wanted. When she made the outburst to her startled parent she voiced the sentiments of her widowed and single sisters in her demand for an enterprising husband. It is the result of the enlarged vision of war years, of their knowledge of the heights to which youth can climb when endowed with 'push and go.'

Every woman in her heart loves a fighter. The war girl has the fighting spirit. She put up her own little show during the dark days. That is why the man who steps out from the old secure commercial shelter where circumstances and not inclination placed him, and fights for his own real niche, gains her admiration. Side by side with him she will fight for a place in the sun.

Everywhere there is evidence that women are backing the demobbed man who wishes to make a new venture, are helping him to snap the old chains. Women's timorous dread of the unknown formerly smothered adventure in many a man, glued him to the uncongenial job. The banishment of fear is one of the war's most marked effects on women. Hers is now the helping, not the restraining hand. The adventurous husband has come into his own. The girl of the war days sees in him the mate that meets her require

-ments as a man and a lover. And, thank goodness, she is usually discerning enough to differentiate between the purely restless adventurer and the man who is honestly out to make good. But this latest spirited edition of Britain's daughters is not likely to sit down and pity herself should the reality prove less rosy than the pictures. She takes the chance of love and life boldly and well she may, for Fate has dowered her with the Spirit of Adventure and Romance, those twin gifts which give the world gay hearts and great lovers."

Go Hilda!

Little Gib (Part 1): A popular Wanganui doctor

One of our first doctors was immensely popular among our early inhabitants, although his qualifications may have been a little dodgy. Not much is known of George Henry Gibson's early years and he appears to have had no formal medical qualifications, although it's believed he may have completed an apprenticeship with a doctor in England.

Gibson arrived in Wanganui in 1859 and according to friend James Woon became *"perhaps the most widely known, popular and sought after of all those* (doctors) *residing in Wanganui."*

Known amongst his more intimate acquaintances as "Little Gib", he arrived in Wellington from England as medical officer in charge of a group of immigrants, but had spent time in the early 1850s on the Australian goldfields and could tell many a good story about them.

"I don't think he made a pile whilst there," said Woon, *"or if he did he must have parted with it, for when he came to Wanganui he was somewhat 'hard up'."*

Gibson was persuaded to come here by Captain Benjamin Trafford, following the unexpected death of the colonial surgeon George Rees. "Little Gib" accompanied the captain to Wanganui, taking up residence with him and fellow officers of the 65th Regiment.

"He soon made headway in his profession and became a great favourite with all and sundry – the ladies especially – as he was of a most genial disposition, could sing a capital song and possessing a beautiful voice was much sought after in social circles."

Dr Gibson was described as a *"good all-round man"* and took part in most of the community's activities, particularly horse racing. The one activity he avoided was politics, which he detested. Gibson was appointed Medical Officer at the Colonial Hospital (sited near St George's Gate on what is now Somme Parade) with a salary of £75, later doubled.

44

According to Woon, *"Doctor Gibson's kindness, goodness, liberality and charity were boundless and many a poor man and woman had occasion to bless him. In his role as Colonial Surgeon he was reckoned very skilful, having performed many difficult and critical operations."*

Dr Gibson set up his home and surgery in Victoria Avenue where the former National Bank premises now stand, but a tragedy occurred when he began to develop the area. He had contracted builder William Aiken to construct a fence along the rear of the property, but a sandbank collapsed, burying a worker.

"In spite of the eager efforts of a number of persons who rushed to the spot, more than twenty minutes elapsed before the man could be extricated, and he was then to all appearance dead. He is a carpenter, but even Mr Aiken did not know his name." (Chronicle: 18 October, 1865).   Good business for Mr Aiken, who was also an undertaker.

Earlier that year Dr Gibson had attended to the Hewett family from Brunswick when farmer James Hewett had been murdered by some of his former workers, new recruits to the rising Hau Hau religion. Readers will recall that Hewett's head had been impaled upon a pole and used to promote the movement around the North Island and to communicate with the war gods. In accordance with Victorian custom, Hewett's widow Ellen asked Dr Gibson for a lock of her husband's hair, a request he was unable to comply with. It was not until many years later that Ellen discovered the reason why, as much of the detail of her husband's dreadful end was kept from her. She was even persuaded to abstain from attending his funeral, staying instead with friends away from the sights and sounds of his final farewell.

Dr George (Little Gib) Gibson

Little Gib (Part 2): Smallpox scare

Dr George Henry Gibson, whose early years in Wanganui were outlined in our previous article, attended to a suspected smallpox patient in February, 1869. In his position as Colonial Surgeon and Health Officer at the Colonial Hospital he declined to admit the patient for obvious reasons. A meeting of local magistrates resolved to isolate the man at the racecourse for treatment under Gibson, who then advised the public to avoid crossing Churton's Creek or approaching *"the land known as the Wanganui Racecourse and Cricket Ground."* But Walter Buller (Resident Magistrate), who was out of town when the decision was made, over-ruled these arrangements and had the patient removed from the racecourse, concerned that Gibson, who also had a private practice in town, might put his own patients at risk. To confuse the matter further, both men's notices to the public appeared in the same newspaper - Dr Gibson's dated the 6th and Mr Buller's dated the 9th, were printed one above the other in the 9 February, 1869 edition of the *Evening Herald.* The *Herald,* which gave the man's name variously as Francisco and Francesco, considered the RM's decision would *"relieve the public anxiety upon the subject. Under Mr Buller's directions every precaution has been taken to prevent the spread of the disease and it was entirely owing to that gentleman's absence from town that the proper precautions were not taken sooner. A considerable expense is being incurred on the responsibiiity [sic] of our Resident Magistrate who, no doubt, looks to the Government to recoup him."*

Under the Harbour & Quarantine Regulations Act 1868, Mr Buller declared the South Spit a quarantine ground and decreed that a yellow flag be hoisted from sunrise to sunset to caution *"all masters of vessels and others"* against approaching, except by authority of acting Health Officer Dr Best (recently recovered from battle injuries).

Dr Best was paid £1 per day to tend to the patient. He was given blankets, a tent, a servant and two assistants and ordered to remain in quarantine himself for 21 days. After seeing the patient safely into a canoe to be transported to South Spit, he and his servant crossed over in another vessel but the sick man never arrived. After enduring an overnight drenching in a wild storm, Best went in search of the patient, eventually finding him at Putiki – still in the canoe and exposed to the rain. His two intoxicated "carers" had abandoned him, but were located and made to convey him to the quarantine station.

"Poor Francisco has received already enough kind treatment to have killed a dozen men," lamented the *Herald*, *"simply because there was no board of health in Wanganui and because no one knew what to do before the return of the Resident Magistrate."*

The patient died soon after and was buried in the sandhills, bringing an end to a matter which must have put a black mark against Dr Gibson's good record thus far. Dr Best also came in for criticism by the *Herald* - some justified, some perhaps not: *"We cannot understand the action of Dr Best, who must have seen whether the men were in a fit state to take charge of the canoe and ought to have initiated enquiries when he found his patient had not arrived."* (The latter not so easy when caught in a blinding rainstorm).

Two months later Dr Gibson's house was nearly destroyed in a fire which swept up the Avenue, but action by men of the 18th Royal Irish Regiment (which had recently re-occupied the Rutland Stockade) and the volunteer fire brigade, brought it under control, *"the palings communicating with Dr Gibson's house having been pulled down."* The sandhill at the rear of the property (which featured in our previous article and caused the death of a worker) was also credited with having checked the fire.

Resident magistrate Walter Buller

Little Gib (Part 3): A dismal diagnosis

Dr Gibson had carved a niche for himself in the society of Wanganui's fledgling township. He was popular in community circles, proved himself to be a competent physician and had risen to the position of Colonial Surgeon and Health Officer at the Colonial Hospital, securing a 100% pay rise following his initial appointment to the position.

Unfortunately, soon after the smallpox scare of the previous episode, the dimunitive doctor was forced to make a hurried return to England to receive treatment for a life-threatening ailment. Plans were hastily set in motion to hold some sort of farewell appropriate to the occasion and to acknowledge the esteem in which Gibson was held by both colleagues and the local citizenry. A public meeting was held with the purpose of setting up the necessary committee which would arrange a complimentary dinner to take place on the eve of the doctor's departure for England.

"Dr Gibson, from his long residence in Wanganui, and many amiable qualities, has numerous friends who would like to do him honor, if the means were placed at their disposal." (*Herald*: 18 May, 1869).

Unfortunately, the meeting was hijacked by a group the *Herald* labelled *"a few of the right stamp"* who *"commenced the process of selection by making the tickets at 25s each. The honor of the affair will thus be lost in a most foolish attempt to keep the dinner confined to the 'forty'. Surely the price of the ticket does not contain the amount of respect to be shown,"* complained the *Herald,* pointing out that an excellent public dinner had recently been given for Sir William Fox, the tickets for which were only 10s each.

"The public have at least as high an opinion of Dr Gibson and would equally honor him if they were not virtually excluded. When we want to pay our respects to a townsman, in order that those

respects may be worth anything, they should come from all classes of the community."

A *Herald* subscriber, writing under the *nom de plume* "Consistent," while agreeing with the idea of a farewell dinner, demanded to know why a petition collecting signatures for a testimonial for Gibson was circulating around town, when no such testimonial was presented to Sir William.

But then a public notice appeared in the *Herald* (19 May) reading: *"Dr. Gibson's medical adviser, having intimated to the committee that the impaired state of the doctor's health will not permit of an appearance at any public demonstration, the committee have decided to abandon the proposed dinner for Friday evening next. They have further decided on convening: A PUBLIC MEETING THIS EVENING, to take into consideration the best means of testifying to the general esteem in which Dr Gibson is held."*

The meeting, duly held in the Oddfellows' Hall, with Mr Thomas Powell Esq. in the chair, was reported by the *Herald* the following day.

"(Mr Powell) said they had met there that evening to show their appeciation of a gentleman who, as a citizen, a friend, and a public benefactor, had won the esteem of everyone who knew him; he might truly say that Dr Gibson never lost a friend or made an enemy. He was now about to leave for England, his health requiring that he should have the advice of the highest talent in his profession and he hoped that in twelve or eighteen months the doctor would return amongst them improved in health, and as good a man as he ever was (applause)."

A letter from Gibson's medical partner, Dr Robert Earle, was then read to the meeting. It confirmed Gibson's poor state of health and expressed his desire *"to leave as quietly as possible,"* a desire the committee was not about to let him get away with while they had anything to do with it. Attendees patiently waited while members drew up the following valedictory address: *"We, the undersigned inhabitants of the town and district of Wanganui, having heard with regret of your approaching departure for England on sick leave, cannot allow you to part from us without expressing in the most sincere terms our appreciation of your past services in your professional capacity, and our sense of your many social qualities as a friend and fellow colonist. The marked success which has attended your long professional career in this place, the readiness with which you have at all times endeavoured to alleviate suffering and distress among all classes of the community, and the unvarying liberality which has ever characterised you, alike call for our united and heartfelt recognition. Reluctant as we are to part with one whose face has always been so familiar and welcome in every household, we earnestly pray that your visit to England may be attended with the happiest results, and that under God's blessing you may return to this country with fully established health."*

It was then proposed that a subscription be taken up and a purse of sovereigns be presented to Dr Gibson, *"as a slight proof of regard and appreciation of his professional and private worth."*

After a short squabble as to whether the contents of the purse should be dedicated towards some particular object, *"such as the purchase of a piece of plate when the doctor arrived home,"* the motion was carried without qualification. Another committee was formed to *"carry the matter to completion"*, then the meeting was finally declared over, although the organisers came in for some less-than-flattering comments from the press about the sloppy way in which it had been handled.

"The committee that called the meeting, having no proposals of any kind to submit, threw the meeting into confusion and damped enthusiasm. Everyone was of opinion that Dr Gibson was worthy of some mark of respect, and it was for those who called the meeting to have brought forward resolutions which had been previously drawn up. This is the proper way of doing such things; and the convenors of public meetings generally might, by adopting the practice, facilitate greatly the transaction of business."

The *Herald*, however, had more positive words to say about

52

"The Gibson Testimonial" (24 May, 1869). "The testimonial to Dr Gibson has been numerously signed and will be ready for presentation by tomorrow. The engrossing of the testimonial reflects the greatest credit on Mr G.F. Allen and Mr Blaydes. In the left hand corner there is a photograph of the Moutoa monument, underneath which is an excellent likeness of the Doctor, and a little lower still the Colonial Hospital. In the right hand corner there is a photograph of the steamer Wanganui lying in the river opposite Shakespeare's Cliff. The photography is by Mr Harding, from larger photographs in his possession reduced to the proper size, and is faithfully and artistically executed. Around the testimonial there is a scroll with holly fern entwined and representing the union of England and New Zealand. The writing is in the mediaeval style and is tastefully illuminated. The testimonial presents a very artistic appearance, and is worthy of the position it will occupy as an heirloom."

Mr Harding also produced reproductions of the original, the *Herald* (27 May, 1869) adjudging them *"very faithful representations,"* while expressing confidence that *"many will be glad from their esteem of Dr Gibson to possess a memento of one who has won the golden opinions of all."*

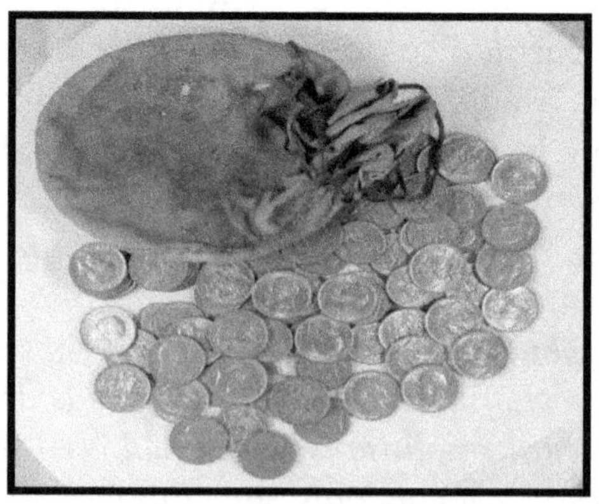

A parting gift for Dr Gibson

Little Gib (Part 4): Chance meeting leads to reconciliation

While seeking medical help in England, Dr Gibson sought out Ellen Hewett, whose husband had been murdered and beheaded by the Hau Hau four years previously. Readers will recall that Mrs Hewett had returned to her homeland to further her children's education. Some time later she was visited by a third ex-Wanganui resident at the home of her parents-in-law in Folkstone where she was residing but her *visitor, a former army officer, was unaware that Gibson was in England. Ellen expressed surprise that he *"had not heard of the arrival in London of one of our most popular men, Dr Gibson. But,"* she added sadly, *"Dr Gibson's life hangs on a thread. Do go and see him. You will find him greatly changed by a severe illness. He came to Folkstone to see me when he first arrived, but I was sure then that he was dying."*

A few days later Ellen was overjoyed to receive a note from Gibson which read: *"I write to thank you for bringing together two old friends and for thus healing an estrangement just at the right time, before one of us passed away into another world. Come and see me when you are in London."*

She accepted the invitation and was pleased to see him well cared for by his landlady, who suggested she send a clergyman to see him - a tactic which had far from the desired results, as Ellen discovered at a chance meeting with Gibson one day at Tonbridge Junction Railway Station whilst changing trains.

"Don't send any more parsons to see me," he berated her, *"and don't write me any more religious letters!"*

(Ellen had undergone a radical religious conversion while in New Zealand and claimed to have conversed with her husband in a vision after his death).

"He tried to say more," writes Ellen of Dr Gibson, *"but a fit of coughing came on and I had to make a rush for my train. I threw*

myself into one of the corner seats and sobbed uncontrollably."

She attributes what followed next to three fellow passengers (two charming girls and an elderly lady) who, on learning the cause of her distress, prayed for the ailing (and now cantankerous) doctor, turning the remainder of her railway journey into *"a little bit of heaven"* which, she believed, lead to a change of heart on Gibson's part.

Ellen was convinced their prayers had been answered as Gibson revived sufficiently to show an interest in religion although at first, according to Ellen, he protested.

"It is of no use; I have been thinking over everything. I have neglected God all my life and lived for whatever pleasure I could get out of the world. It would be mean to turn to Him now when there is nothing left. No, it is too late."

But, according to Mrs Hewett, he relented and the words of the popular hymn *"O Lamb of God, I come,"* were always on his lips.

"When he was dying," she records, *"he looked up with such a smile and said, 'Delightful.'"*

* Another friend and regular visitor was Dr Isaac Featherston, former Superintendent of Wellington; then in London as Agent General for New Zealand.

"Old Feathery" - a friend and visitor

Little Gib (Part 5): Sad news from Home

The message was short and to the point: *"We regret to learn by mail that Dr Gibson is dead."* (*Herald:* 11 October, 1870).

More detail was forthcoming the following day: *"GIBSON,- On the 5th of August at Ramsgate, G.H. Gibson, Esq., Surgeon. Late of Wanganui. Aged 48 years."*

A lengthy tribute to Gibson featured in the same edition: *"There are few in Wanganui but will hear with profound regret of the death of Dr Gibson. For sixteen years a resident of Wanganui, he had commanded the respect of all classes. His urbanity, good-fellowship and open-handed charity had endeared him, perhaps more than any other man in the community, to those who knew him, and, by sympathetic contact, to hundreds who had only heard of his name. There never was a loss by death more generally and keenly felt than this, among the people of a young settlement. The doctor had written to Dr Earle but three days before his death, perfectly conscious that his end was rapidly approaching, conveying his last farewell to the people of Wanganui, and expressing the only regret that lay at his heart, that he could not die and be buried in the place where he had spent the best and happiest years of his life. Dr Featherston visited his old friend a short time before his death and found him sinking beneath the infirmity for which he had sought relief by a visit to England. As a last hope Dr Gibson went to Ramsgate, a place celebrated for its salubrious and exhilerating climate, and here he breathed his last, in the 48th year of his age. Many years may pass and many changes come, but the memory of Dr Gibson will not cease to be cherished by those who knew his worth. He will not soon be replaced as a genuine and noble-hearted friend and physician."* Within a matter of days suggestions were circulating as to what would be the most suitable form of memorial to Dr Gibson: *"It has been suggested that the most appropriate manner of paying our respect to the memory of the late Dr Gibson would be to erect a marble tablet in the English Church."* (*Herald:* 14 October, 1870). *"We thoroughly agree with the suggestion and hope the initiative will be taken by some person. The public would consider it a privilege to contribute to the memory of the Doctor."*

Another public meeting was called, the chair again occupied by Thomas Powell, who went on record as saying that he would not advocate for large sums to be spent, but would allow the community to join in contributing to the memorial. Resident Magistrate Walter Buller, (who had over-ruled Dr Gibson in the matter of quarantine during the small-pox scare) moved the meeting's first resolution – that it record the extreme sorrow for the loss sustained by the town and district through the death of Dr Gibson and that a public memorial be erected for the man who was *"respected by all, loved by many and hated by none. (Applause)."* A twenty-five man committee was then elected to carry out the resolution (yes, you read correctly – 25) but with power to add to that number if necessary! Then came a discussion as to where the monument should be located.

It was first proposed that it be erected in the general cemetery (Heads Road). Then came an amendment that it should be in the churchyard of Christ Church which was Wanganui's first public cemetery, the site now occupied by the renovated Selwyn Buildings in Victoria Avenue. This was initially favoured by the meeting *"on the grounds that the churchyard, being in the centre of the town, the monument should be erected in the most conspicuous place,"* although some still favoured the cemetery due to its non-sectarian character, no doubt influenced by the belief that Dr Gibson was not a religious man. However the deadlock was broken with the suggestion that the memorial should be erected in front of the Colonial Hospital (which stood on what is now Somme Parade, near St Georges Gate), to which all previous proposers and seconders of resolutions and amendments withdrew to support the new resolution. Seconded by Mr John Ballance and carried unanimously. A vote of thanks was also passed to Mr Ballance who had been the first to suggest a monument to the memory of Dr Gibson.

"A vote of thanks having been proposed and carried, the meeting, which adopted the resolutions with enthusiasm and unanimity, dissolved." (Herald: 19 October, 1870).

Christ Church, Victoria Avenue - suggested first site for Gibson Memorial

Little Gib (Part 6): His monument erected, but..........?

The project quickly gathered momentum. On the following Friday evening a meeting of the committee was held, this time at the Rutland Hotel. (The Oddfellows' Hall was all well and good for public meetings, but a hotel allowed participants to get more involved in the "spirit" of an occasion). Another committee was formed, this one comprising a mere five members, all of whom attached their names to a subscription list which was then opened to the general public. The *Herald's* report the following day carried this curious statement: *"Several monument designs were inspected, and without deciding in favour of any, the preference was given to one, which will probably be selected."*

The venture appears to have faded from public attention for a time as members of the seemingly over-weighted inaugural task force no doubt fell over each other as they went about achieving their stated aim, although it did not go unnoticed in Nelson, whose newspaper had compared the public-spirited action of the Wanganui populace to that of its own.

"The Nelson Colonist," gloated the *Herald* (14 November, 1870), *"noticing the proposed monument to the memory of Dr Gibson, compares the action of the people of Wanganui with that of the people of Nelson; asking how long it will be before Nelson does its duty in that respect to the memory of its departed Superintendent, Mr Rolleston,* (corrected in the next day's edition to Robinson) *who was drowned while doing his duty for the new gold-fields of the West Coast. It is seldom Wanganui does anything for which it gets credit from other places."* Not all were in agreement with the idea of a monument. A regular contributor to the *Herald* at this time, whose articles appeared under the heading *"JOTTINGS"* wrote: *"A considerable time ago, a subscription was got up for the purpose of erecting some sort of monument to the late Dr Gibson. It is always a pleasing thing to*

*see people keeping in remembrance their departed friends, and showing by some 'In Memoriam' token, whether in the form of a sarcophagus, or an humble chaplet of fresh-culled flowers that, although gone, they are not forgotten. Dr G. was a worthy man, 'a jolly good fellow,' who kept a good table and had many friends. But that he should have a monument by public subscription any more than nine-tenths of our departed friends is more than I can understand. *Dr Rees was a settler of long standing, and, although of a reserved disposition and bearing, he was an honourable man and possessed many good qualities, as many can testify. And now, as everybody knows, Wanganui is richer by £300 per annum, thanks to his thoughtful generosity. Had Dr Gibson left a similar legacy to the hospital, his posthumous popularity would have made the proposition of a monument more welcome."*

Despite such objections the monument to Dr Gibson was finally erected, although in the best of bureaucratic traditions it took nearly four years for the 25-man committee (and its various sub-committees) to accomplish, long enough for memories to have faded sufficiently to merit just the following notice in the local press. The *Chronicle* (9 February, 1874) reported: "*THE LATE DR. GIBSON.- The monument in memory of this gentleman, purchased by the inhabitants of this place, has been erected in the Hospital grounds; it is a simple one, but sufficient to show to new comers the fact that the worthy Doctor was appreciated by the Wanganui public.*"

But whatever happened to it and what was inscribed on it? The old Colonial Hospital was torched in 1897 in a spectacular public commemoration of Queen Victoria's Diamond Jubilee and the Central Baths later built on part of the site. The area today is privately owned, but having tracked Dr Gibson to this point I felt he was owed one final act of public recognition. The memoirs of fellow early settler and friend of Gibson, James Garland Woon, (who gave the cause of Gibson's death as consumption) state that the memorial was "*subscribed for, and placed in its former and present position by Dr*

60

Earle, Dr Gibson's partner for several years, and a few of his more intimate and cherished friends." (Only partly correct, for as we have seen it was also originally funded by public subscription). The *"present position"* would have been common knowledge when Woon penned his memoirs around the turn of the 20th century, but have the years – and weeds – obliterated it from the public memory?

With help from the obliging staff at the Alexander Heritage Library and due to the "monumental" project by genealogist June Springer to record details of headstones in the Heads Road Cemetery I found some answers.

There appears to be no record of the original inscription, but cemetery files reveal that the following was inscribed at the time of its relocation: *"George Henry Gibson for many years Colonial Surgeon at Wanganui, died at Ramsgate, England, 1870. This monument was removed from the site of the Old Wanganui Hospital in June 1898 by a few of the late Dr Gibson's surviving friends."*

A peaceful walk through the *Heritage New Zealand*-listed cemetery led me to the grave of Dr Robert Earle, who succeeded Gibson as Colonial Surgeon in Wanganui, and to whose family plot the monument had been relocated to. Unfortunately vandals have desecrated it and the top portion, which probably contained both inscriptions, no longer exists, while the middle slab lies on its side between the base and a neighbouring rock wall.

The 150th anniversary of Dr Gibson's death will fall in 2020. Perhaps a fitting tribute would be to repair his monument with the above inscription or, now that council is said to be in the process of installing a plaque identifying the site of the Colonial Hospital, transfer the refurbished monument back to its original site for that purpose.

*Dr George Rees (1818-1858) bequeathed large sums to educational   institutes in Wanganui. Whanganui City College's "Rees House" is named after him.

Dr Gibson's memorial as it is today

62

The burglar's diary

In former times the local newspapers published what must have been a very valuable tool for any enterprising burglar. The general public was regularly kept up to date with the comings and goings of those who moved in the higher circles of society, in much the same way as alleged celebrities are looked up to today. The following excerpts are a smattering of the weekly gossip:

"Mrs Morice has been on a visit to her parents, the Premier and Mrs Seddon. She leaves shortly for Christchurch, where she will be the guest of her sister Mrs Bean (the Vicarage) for a week."

"Mr and Mrs Harry Robinson (Castlecliff) are spending a holiday in Sydney. Mr Robinson is the popular guard for the Castlecliff Railway Co."

"We trust that the trip to the Hot Lakes district will be beneficial to Mr J.G. Swan, and that he will come back quite his old self."

"Mr R.J. Clinton, of St Johns Hill, has just spent a delightful holiday in Palmerston, Pahiatua and surrounding districts. He was accompanied by Mrs Clinton. They returned home on Friday."

"The many friends of Mr and Mrs W.F. Russell will be pleased to hear that both have much enjoyed their trip. They safely reached the end of their journey by the Manawatu on Saturday."

"Mr Brent, of Bathgate Homes, Rotorua, is on a visit to Wanganui, renewing old acquaintances."

"By the through train on Saturday, Mr Arthur Sherriff and his bride arrived in Wanganui and were right warmly welcomed by many friends."

"Mr Empson returned yesterday from Wellington. We regret to say that he is seriously ill and is at present lying in at Miss Hook's private hospital."

"Mr and Mrs Ewen Campbell of Wiritoa, who have been on a visit to the old country, returned by the P.S. Manawatu on Sunday."

"Earl Dundas and his son have been staying in Wanganui for a day or two at the Rutland Hotel and left for Wellington by the 1.20pm train yesterday."

"Mr and Mrs Peake left for Wellington last night. They go Home (to England) in the Aorangi and expect to be away about a year."

Rich pickings for the well-read entrepreneur

The dust fiend

Letters to the *Chronicle* lately have complained of dust problems in Whanganui East caused by logging trucks. Our early residents would have rejoiced to have had so few problems when it comes to dust and mud. The following letter appeared in the 2 January, 1879 edition of the *Chronicle*: *"Sir, Water, water, everywhere, yet not a drop to water the streets. 'Where are the water carts today?' was the cry on Tuesday. Nobody seemed to know where the water cart was, but everyone was loud in his declamation of the Council, or whoever is responsible for that respectable machine. A worse day for dirt could not have been, but the responsible parties allowed the goods of tradesmen and ratepayers to be damaged, citizens to be half-blinded, the town to get a bad name and everyone to be rendered uncomfortable and half-choked. Surely if water is laid on and a cart made expressly for the purpose of watering the streets, it would not be too much to see it out on dusty days. On Monday it was raining – out comes the water cart and carefully supplements the rain, making the streets almost impassable with mud. Perhaps someone will explain. I'm certain I can't. As it is I am quite ashamed to subscribe my name. I am, Aqua Westmera."*

The situation clearly had not improved two years on, as this item in the same journal of 16 November, 1881 reveals: *"The dust in the streets yesterday forenoon was quite unendurable and the question, 'Where are the water-carts?' was in everyone's mouth, when the flying clouds permitted them to speak. The carts turned up in the afternoon and much improved matters, though they were unable to lay the dust for more than a few minutes together."*

The device *"Aqua Westmera"* referred to was a horse-drawn water tank used to sprinkle the roadways, although its effectiveness was doubtful given his and other correspondents' criticisms that it only temporarily held the *"dust fiend"* at bay. The problem was caused largely by the sandy nature of the ground the township stood upon and was exacerbated by the two massive sandhills which enclosed it – Rutland Hill (Queen's Park) and Cook's Gardens. That our roads at the time were unsealed added to our forebears' distress, particularly at times of high winds and over 20 years later there was no end in sight, as these two snippets in the *Herald* within a month of each other show: *"The unwelcome presence of the 'Dust Fiend' and the absence of the very necessary water carts were the subjects of common topic in town today."*

"The 'Dust Fiend' was again rampant throughout the town today, much to the detriment of business generally and emphasizing the aimed prosecution of the suggested scheme to abate a nuisance so inimical to the interests of the town."

A further article in the same paper gives more details of the aforementioned suggested scheme: *"At last, after years of persistent advocacy by prominent citizens, a more up-to-date method of treating the tar and using it on our streets. A large tar-treating and asphalt-mixing plant is to be erected at the gas works. It is intended, the mayor says, to make a commencement this week in asphalting the Avenue, the first section to be undertaken being between Ingestre and Guyton Streets."*

However Wanganui, like that other famous city, was not built in a day so street watering and tar-sealing had to go hand in hand for some time to come, according to a decision by the Borough Council three months later. For street watering it recommended the cheaper option of using lake water rather than pumping it from the river. The area in question to be watered was from Guyton Street to Taupo Quay, plus a few chains of each cross street. It was estimated that to do this for 100 days during summer would take 11½ million gallons, equal to three days' town supply. The council was of the opinion that drawing from the lake would have to be resorted to for the summer of 1902/03, but from then on the permanent asphalting of city streets would be a much better use of ratepayers' money.

The council also recommended (subject to agreement from Avenue shopkeepers) that a fee of 6d to 1s a week (according to the size of shop frontages) be imposed to finance a gang of men and horses to sweep footpaths and streets from daybreak until 8.30am. Two men would also be employed full-time to collect horse-droppings, which were considered by some to be a greater source of trouble than dust. The scheme was fine-tuned after it was implemented, banning shopkeepers from sweeping dust from their shops into the water channels. *"At present this is a great nuisance,"* stated a council report, *"and is often done immediately after the cleaning cart has swept the channel."*

Advances in tarsealing methods saw a gradual abatement of the problem, although dust caused headaches for years to come, particularly with the advent of the motor car, according to the *Herald,* (9 December, 1909).

"The dry spell is creating dust which the cars are beginning to raise in considerable clouds, indicating that it might be as well to give the track a coat of tar. The trouble in doing such a thing, however, is that all the traffic immediately takes to the track, but perhaps some day we may see a start made with tar-painting streets for their whole width."

Should the council bring back one of these for our long-suffering East-side residents?

Coach service to New Plymouth established

This month (January, 2016) marks the 145th anniversary of the first commercial coach journey from Wanganui to New Plymouth. For today's travellers, it is a pleasant drive of a couple of hours, but in those days it was an almost insurmountable journey due to unforgiving terrain, dangerous river crossings and the uncertain intentions of Titokowaru and his followers.

The enterprise was first signalled in December of 1867 when a Mr Davies proposed a regular Cobb's Coach service to Patea which was shelved due to "many difficulties". (Read "native uprisings"). However the 4 January, 1871 edition of the *Wanganui Herald* advised readers that Mr William Henry Shepard had been buying likely coach horses at the Rutland sale yards.

Three days later the *Taranaki Herald* announced that a Cobb's coach would arrive in New Plymouth on the 12th. (Cobb's Coaches was an Australian company, but its good name was blatantly appropriated throughout New Zealand, in much the same way that "Stryans" have in turn over the years purloined many an iconic Kiwi innovation – or music star). *"All who have travelled by their coaches must admit that there is no line in the colony better horsed, or boasting of more careful drivers,"* crowed the *Taranaki Herald* on the back of the Aussies' reputation.

The coach duly left Wanganui from the Rutland Hotel at 6.00am on January 11 with no less a passenger than Premier William Fox (accompanied by orderly), among others. They arrived at Hawera at 8.00pm, then resumed their journey at 3.30am the following morning. The Waingongoro River was found to be high but Mr Shepard *"gathered up the reins and telling the passengers to jump out if necessary, gave a terrific yell and rushed the river, the horses taking the coach up the cutting in excellent style."*

At one point the coach was mired in mud, requiring the united efforts of the passengers, *"including the Hon. Mr Fox, who took his part as well as the rest, to drag it out."* The coach eventually arrived in New Plymouth at 9.15pm, over three hours late due to the difficulties encountered. It was met by large cheering crowds, while bunting and flags hung from buildings and flagpoles.

"ARRIVAL OF COBB'S COACH. ENTHUSIASTIC RECEPTION:" declared the *Taranaki Herald*, (14 January, 1871). *"We do not ever remember seeing the town so gay as it appeared on Thursday last, as bunting was floating in the wind in all parts of it. Across Brougham-street the flags were arranged in numerical order from the Commercial Code of Signals, so as to signify 'Welcome to New Plymouth,' with the American Flag in the centre. The flags on the signal-staff were also symbolically arranged, 'Glad to see you safely arrived.' There was a string of flags across the Devon-street, at the White Hart Hotel, and also between Fort Eliot and the Custom House. The Taranaki Hotel was covered with bunting and an ensign was hung from a window over the Post Office."*

A large, excited crowd had gathered at about 4.00pm to witness the coach's arrival, remaining until dark but eventually dispersing when there was no sign of it. A group on horseback rode out to meet it, but when it had still not appeared by 8.00pm, most returned. But soon afterwards the news came through: *"Messrs. Shepard & Co, with their coach, were close to town! Shortly after nine o'clock the cheers to be heard along the Great South Road made it known that the coach was near at hand, when it quickly made its appearance. As the coach approached the Post Office the cheers became deafening and a call for three cheers for the Hon. Mr. Fox and Hon. Mr. Gisborne were vociferously responded to. Messrs. Shepard & Co. were also cheered."*

A slap-up dinner was put on for the conquering heroes - apart from Mr Fox who was *"too fatigued with the journey."*

Then followed the usual long list of speeches and toasts, most speakers assuring their audience that they would keep their contributions short out of consideration to the weary travellers, but failing to keep their promises. Mr Shepard was presented with a congratulatory address engraved on parchment extolling his momentous accomplishment, while expressing the hope that *"the undertaking may prove successful to you commercially and that we may long continue to welcome you as visitors to this town."*

Mr Shepard responded modestly by saying that while he was not much of a speaker, *"he supposed he could drive a coach as well as most,"* and that he thought the time was not far distant when he would be able to drive right through to Auckland.

Unfortunately that would be for another to accomplish. Mr Shepard was killed in October of the same year when he went to meet a coach arriving at Patea carrying his wife. After taking over the reins the harness broke, throwing him into the surf and under the wheels. But the service he had initiated opened up a regular passenger, luggage and mail run between Wanganui and New Plymouth.

Cobb's Coaches were a regular sight on the colony's roads

Kangaroos at Okoia!

One of New Zealand's first Acclimatisation Societies was established in Wanganui in 1864. The aim of the societies was to enrich the surrounding countryside with birds and animals introduced from around the world, usually in the belief that the local fauna was deficient, but also to satisfy the nostalgia of settlers by enabling them to encounter species they were familiar with from home.

We now know that the unregulated release of many of these species was disastrous, all the more so because of the ideal conditions they were released into, which allowed them to thrive. The following article appeared in the 30 September, 1867 edition of the *Herald*, enthusiastically promoting the ideals and activities of the society.

"The Acclimatisation Society have received some fine kangaroos, pigeon and quail which they intend disposing of by auction. We have no doubt Mr Finnimore will have a large company on Wednesday as all must view such sales with special interest. The Society has displayed so much enterprise and spirit in introducing into the district foreign animals and birds that it has attained to great celebrity, not only in this but in some of the neighbouring colonies. We cannot exaggerate the benefits which the Society have, and are conferring upon Wanganui and the whole province, but their work has only commenced and it lies with the public whether their efforts in the future will be attended with complete success. The society have also received from Sydney 100 carp, which they purpose to distribute in the lakes around Wanganui."

The Mr Finnimore referred to was auctioneer William Finnimore, who placed this advertisement in the *Herald: "Wm Finnimore has received instructions from W.F. Russell Esq., Treasurer Acclimatisation Society, to sell by public auction on Wednesday next at his rooms, Taupo Quay at 11 o'clock – 1 Pr Pet Forest Kangaroos, 1 Pr Tasmanian Kangaroos, 5½ Pr Wonga Wonga Pigeons, 6 Pr Colonial Quail."*

The animals were sold to local landowners in the hope they would be released around the district. Fortunately for today's motorists the kangaroos failed to establish themselves and the last local reported sighting of one was at Okoia in 1869, although wallabies were more successful and survive on Kawau Island and in parts of South Canterbury to this day. But not everyone was enamoured with the society's efforts. The *Chronicle's* "*Own Correspondent*", who probably wisely wrote anonymously, blasted the society for the damage done by introduced species.

"If there is any body of man who deserves the curses of farmers it is the Wanganui Acclimatisation Society. It is difficult to think of any animal they have introduced which has not turned out a nuisance. As I write, sparrows in scores on the roof are chattering, skirmishing and fouling the gutters, while the fruit-buds and early fruit are attacked by swarms of these pests and their brethren and other hard-beaked birds. Quails eat our strawberries, pheasants dig up our newly sown maize and potatoes. Weasels (we have the Government to thank for them) kill our hens and ducks and turkeys."

Labelling the societies and the Government the true pests "*Own Correspondent*" concluded, "*I wonder the Acclimatisation Society don't import wolves, cobras and rattlesnakes. They would probably do less harm than the other pests they have billeted upon us.*" (*Chronicle:* 3 December, 1891).

Not all were of that opinion. After starlings were released by the society a Wanganui farmer, who previously had voted all small birds a nuisance and whose turnips were yearly in danger of being consumed by caterpillars, had this to say: "*They literally gorged on those caterpillars and devoured every one of them.*" Another agreed, saying that he could not grow anything before the sparrows were released as caterpillars devoured everything, but now they were under control.

It should be mentioned, of course, that the proliferation of caterpillars was caused by the rapid depopulation of native birds which was due to rapid deforestation. The *Chronicle* (4 March, 1881) reported on a startling invasion of caterpillars which it admitted *"sounded like a Yankee yarn: Yet such a thing actually took place on our local railway a few days ago. In the neighbourhood of Turakina an army of caterpillars, hundreds of thousands strong, was marching across the line bound for a new field of oats when the train came along. Thousands of the creeping, crawling vermin were crushed by the wheels of the engine and suddenly the train came to a dead stop. On examination it was found that the wheels of the engine had become so greasy that they kept on revolving without advancing – they could not grip the rails. The guard and the engine-driver procured sand and strewed it on the rails and the train made a fresh start, but it was found that during the stoppage caterpillars in thousands had crawled all over the engine and over all the carriages, inside and out."*

But still there were grumblings. A letter to the *Chronicle's* editor (19 August, 1884) under the heading *"THE SPARROW NUISANCE"* and signed by *"A Sufferer"*, suggested that the member of the Acclimatisation Society who was foolish enough to vote £100 for the importation of sparrows should now offer three prizes; the first £50, the second £30 and the third £20 to those who at the end of three months produced the largest number of sparrows' heads.

"The nuisance has already become a very serious one," he declared, *"and if not checked at once, and in a most decided manner, will threaten to ruin all those whose livelihoods are gained by orchards and gardens, to say nothing of the great damage and almost ruin to grain crops."*

Fish & Game Councils, established under the Conservation Act of 1987, eventually replaced Acclimatisation Societies.

Aussie invaders failed to take over

Guy Fawkes – it'll never become popular in New Zealand

"Remember, remember, the fifth of November,
The Gunpowder treason and plot."

How could we not remember – albeit for different reasons than celebrating the dastardly, but thwarted designs of Guy Fawkes and his fellow conspirators in trying to reinstate a Catholic king on the English throne over 400 years ago.

Because these days each anniversary of the event brings a proliferation of calls to abolish what is labelled an outdated custom with no relevance to today's society; although the contrary could earnestly be argued, given that Mr Fawkes is sometimes toasted as "the last man to enter Parliament with honest intentions."

But today's objectors should not mistakenly consider themselves to be the vanguard of some relatively modern anti-fireworks ginger group. The *Evening Herald* (5 November, 1869) stated: *"We are glad to find that this anniversary is not likely to become a Colonial institution, and that the particular form of loyalty which exists in crackers loses its zest and fervour by being transplanted."*

(For the benefit of the *Herald's* *"many aboriginal readers,"* a brief explanatory note was given). Meanwhile the *Chronicle* slammed the celebration as *"senseless"* and hoped it would soon become a thing of the past.

There were numerous accounts of the dangers of fireworks in the hands of larrikins. A horse and rider were injured when crackers were thrown during a parade, a boy lost sight in one eye when struck by a rocket and a housemaid had a narrow escape when a *"bunger"* exploded in her face.

"It is high time such wicked, wanton pranks were stamped out and that the lives of women and children should not be at the mercy of hoodlums who think it a 'lark' to throw a lighted firework in the faces of passers-by," railed the *Herald,* while the *Chronicle* called

for *"legitimate pyrotechnic displays under proper control,"* along with the exercise of common sense and prosecution of offenders.

In 1886, the Grand Orange Lodge in Auckland requested that Protestant ministers preach thanksgiving sermons in memory of deliverance from the Gunpowder Plot but the Church of England bishop, reminding the lodge of its reverence for Holy Scripture, pointed out that stirring up feelings of resentment among New Zealand Catholics, (who probably abhorred Fawke's actions as much as lodge members themselves), was not the best way to foster tolerance among Christians, although that did not stop Orange Lodge "Gunpowder Plot" marches for years to come. And the *Chronicle*, editorialising over yet another recently-celebrated *"relic of barbarism"* stated: *"It is quite possible that the majority of Catholics have too much good sense to be insulted by the letting off of bungers and crackers,"* (supplies of which could be obtained locally from Wong Chong, 153 Victoria Avenue).

The *Chronicle* also claimed that Fawkes would *"squirm in his grave were it possible for him to see the hideous representations of his historical 'phiz', from which Wanganui juveniles perpetrate on the 5th of November. A more or less ugly mask clapped on to the top of a hurriedly stuffed sugar bag, a pair of dangling ill-formed legs and equally clumsy arms, and Guy Fawkes is himself again! Time was when boys knew how to build a decent dummy, and when they took the time to learn the lines and tune of the popular ditty."*

(Thankfully, limited column space spares me the shame of relating my own boyhood attempts at "Guying", while seriously mangling the aforementioned ditty and extorting pennies and ha'pennies from sleepy-eyed Koromiko Rd residents). During World War I the emphasis of Guy Fawkes changed. Instead of earning money for fireworks, children began collecting for the Belgian Relief Fund, with the results of their efforts published in the local "blab-sheets". One youngster, Jack Allpress, devoted his proceeds to the purchase of smokes for soldiers on active duty. Imagine his delight when he received a letter from the front, thanking him for the *"big parcel of tobacco and cigarettes you so kindly sent."*

And for 1915 celebrations, *"a guy with a flattering likeness to Kaiser Wilhelm was burned with enthusiasm, accompanied by a devout wish that the original would some day have a similar, but possibly more torrid experience."*

Unpopular figures have been burned in effigy with enthusiasm down through the ages so instead of an outright Guy Fawkes ban, perhaps we should follow the splendid example of our forebears by simply redirecting the focus of our attention to whomsoever most deserves our disapprobation at any given time.

Guy Fawkes – Gunpowder Plot celebrity

Wanganui Bridge: (1871-1969)

With three road bridges to choose from, we think nothing of crossing the Whanganui River these days and consider ourselves seriously inconvenienced if one of them is closed temporarily for maintenance.

Spare a thought then for our early settlers whose only means of "crossing over" was to rely upon obliging Maori to ferry them. The situation improved with the introduction of ferry services, one of which operated from Market Place to Purua Creek and another from the foot of Victoria Avenue to Campbelltown, the eventual site of the Wanganui Bridge; (the epithet "Town" added to distinguish it from later usurpers). But so erratic and unreliable was the ferry service that a commercial hub which served the Campbelltown residents was necessary.

The first bridge to span the river was thought by some to have been originally intended for India. Others said France, although such claims have been refuted. It was designed specifically for the Wanganui River by British civil engineer George Robert Stephenson, known also in New Zealand as the designer of the Lyttleton Rail Tunnel. Its metal components were constructed by Kennards of London and shipped out for assembly in Wanganui.

The construction of a bridge was first proposed in the 1850s when surveying and roadbuilding throughout the colony began in earnest. In 1856 a delegation of prominent citizens petitioned the Superintendent of Wellington Province, Dr Isaac Featherston, on the matter and received a favourable reply. Visiting Wanganui the following year, the superintendent not only promised a bridge, but expressed the hope that he would personally open it within eighteen months. Featherston was a little optimistic, although he was back here in 1859 to drive in the first pile. Thirty more went in before work stopped – firstly because of contractual problems, but later due to a massive flood which washed away the Whangaehu Bridge, preventing the transport of the necessary timber.

Rumblings of discontent followed, such as this letter to the *Wanganui Chronicle* in February, 1866. *"Sir, Cannot anything be done to facilitate the crossings of passengers, horses, etc. over the river? There is little chance of us getting a bridge for many a year and are we to put up with the same style of ferry we had years ago? It is a common thing to wait for an hour for the punt to take a horse across. Trusting you will agitate the matter. I am:- A Sufferer."*

Meanwhile disagreements over the best site, concerns over upriver access, worries of earthquake risks and finally the viability of the township itself due to the Hau Hau uprising delayed the project. But amongst all the gloom came this snippet of cheering news from abroad: *"The Queen is still in Balmoral, but her health is much improved."*

Even more cheerful was another little snippet of news which appeared in the local press, advising residents that the lowest tender for the construction of a bridge, that of Mr McNeil for £12,850, had been accepted and that he had two years to complete the contract. *"We shall shortly be hearing the ring of hammers and seeing in reality the long talked of bridge rising before our eyes."* However, further objections were made on the grounds that the proposed swing span would seriously impede wharf operations, particularly in view of the expectation of a greatly increased volume of trade, *"if the reported discovery of a rich gold field in this neighbourhood should prove correct."*

But by this time the project was gathering momentum. Public notices advised residents that: *"The bridge is an iron truss bridge supported with iron cylinders. The length of the bridge is about 600 feet with a swing span. The iron material of the bridge is supplied and now lies at Wanganui,"* although some were eager to see the materials put to a more immediate and practical use.

"Cannot the bridge material, lying uselessly on the beach (Taupo Quay), *be turned to some account in the shape of blockhouses, which could be erected in the suburbs of the town,"* suggested one (*Herald:* 8 December, 1868), an idea that was echoed by others.

Foundation Stone Laid:

Once objections were over-ruled and as the Hau Hau threat receded, preparations were made for the laying of the foundation stone. Featherston and Premier Sir William Fox were welcomed to Wanganui on 9 November, 1869 with a long-winded speech from Resident Magistrate Walter Buller, followed by three rounds of "three cheers" (including one for Her Majesty), then the visitors were off to their hotel for some welcome refreshments while an impatient crowd gathered, although kept in good humour by the heroic efforts of the Fife & Drum Band. Finally at 3.00pm the dignitaries emerged, led by the Wanganui Cavalry which paraded down St Hill Street then greatly amused the crowd by performing a turn, which aimed the horses' rear ends towards the Freemason's Hall in perfect time to herald the appearance of the masons in all their ritualistic finery. The cavalcade then marched to the ceremonial site at the foot of the Avenue where firemen stood with hooked poles, ready to repel any overly-enthusiastic bystanders. Various mementos were placed within a cavity in the foundation stone, which was then lowered into place.

Featherston began his speech by announcing: *"Although I have this satisfaction now, it is marred by the shame and humiliation I feel at having performed this same ceremony years ago."* Although acknowledging that delays were due to unforseen circumstances he continued, *"Whenever I cross the Wanganui River, that gaunt pile which I had driven seems to stare me in the face and reproach me with not erecting its companion .... that pile has haunted me night and day ...... and I believe it will remain there, taunting me with its presence until the new bridge is erected. I trust that the first thing done when the bridge is commenced will be to*

80

remove that obnoxious pile."

He did, however, remind his listeners that while the previous wooden bridge had been abandoned, a handsome iron structure would instead be erected. An unscripted portion of proceedings was the prediction by an old kuia that the wrath of the gods would fall upon anyone who bridged the mighty Wanganui.

Official Opening Ceremony:
Fast forward to two years later (29 November, 1871) when the bridge was officially opened. Featherston is no longer Wellington Superintendent, so the honours go to Governor Sir George Bowen. The vice regals had arrived the previous day, although the occasion was marred when one of the horse team provided by stable-owner Mr Gordon was frightened by a military salute. Lady Bowen declined to step into Mr Gordon's carriage, *"preferring to walk as a far more safe method of proceeding."* However a knight-in-shining-armour, coach-builder Mr McBeth, placed his buggy at her disposal, *"thus she was not suffered to walk the whole distance."*

Preparations for the opening were meticulous, including practise runs over the bridge by the Volunteer Fire Brigade's "Star of Wanganui" fire engine, pulled by four horses belonging to stable-owner Mr Smiley who, *"tooled them over and round one or two blocks in fine style."*

But it wasn't just a gathering of colonials. *"The natives, of whom there were plenty in town, were attired in strange and fantastic costumes."* Te Keepa Rangihiwinui (Major Kemp) was there in military uniform, *"wearing the State sword presented to him by Her Most Gracious Majesty and apparently felt, as he should be, proud of the gift."*

The dusty roads were well watered by the Fire Brigade – uneccessarily as it transpired, for a sudden deluge soaked parade participants who had gathered at Market Square, but soon there was *"old Sol peeping down, seeming to enquire if his services would be of any avail in remedying the damage done by the rain."*

Crowds filled a specially erected grandstand, many spectators lined the roadways while others spilled out from upper floor windows – some even gathered on the hill above Campbelltown. Mr Gordon had provided a new horse team which appeared to satisfy Lady Bowen, then what was probably the grandest parade ever witnessed in Wanganui commenced. It comprised about 14 military units and bands made up of over 300 men, joined by the Fire Brigade, bridge committee and reception committee.

Then came the tedious bit as dignitary after dignitary regaled the crowd with their oratorial skills, real or imagined. The Bridge Committee chairman, soon-to-be mayor W.H. Watt, noted with great pride that the project had been completed *"without one single melancholy or painful remembrance."* In other words, no-one had been killed or seriously injured, an achievement he attributed to the contractor Mr McNeil. Her Majesty the Queen and long-deceased consort Prince Albert were of course given due and lengthy credit for their contribution to the project then finally, no doubt to onlookers' great relief, the Governor declared the bridge open. But then a statement from Major Kemp sparked another round of speeches, culminating with the Governor's declaration that *"the bridge now united the two banks of the river as symbolic of uniting the dwelling place of the Pakeha with that of the Maori,"* adding that, *"the desire of the Queen was that the two races should grow into one, with equal laws and privileges."*

After countless "three cheers" all round, the vice-regal couple boarded their carriage which then led the commonalty over the bridge, stopping briefly for a photographer to record the occasion for posterity. After more "three cheers" the *Herald* noted that *"the multitude, to who the title of the 'great unwashed' would certainly not be applicable, began to search the town for means to refresh the inner man,"* providing a golden harvest for the town's many pub owners. At 2.00pm the Governor held a *lĕvee*, individually receiving gentlemen in his room, while Lady Bowen did likewise for the ladies.

Celebration time:

Then came the ball, the culmination of months of concerted effort by a 33-man committee. Tickets were offered for sale at £1/1s, giving each holder: *"The privilege of admitting 1 lady. Each additional lady, 10/6d."*

"The Oddfellows' Hall had been most tastefully decorated for this the ladies' own particular sphere of conquest," the *Herald* declared. *"Walls were gaily festooned with flags and evergreens, while the stage was a marvel of ornamental work."* The caterers were praised for the provision of a sumptuous feast, although the musicians may have fallen short, gaining merely the following faint praise: *"The music was provided by the Marton Band who, on the whole, gave every satisfaction."*

There were more speeches, many toasts and no doubt much slurring of speech as the night wore on, along with a suggestion that the new bridge be called *"The Lady Bowen."* (Hic)! Mr McNeil rounded off all the grandiloquence with a rebuff to those who had predicted that he would never be able to complete the contract, then said, *"Mr Watt has told you of so many of my good qualities that I never knew I possessed until now, but if I say any more you will find out he has been flattering me. But I am sure the ladies would rather be in the ballroom than hearing any more twaddle about myself!"*

The *Herald* reporter raced off to write up his report which he finished thus: *"The oratorial portion of the proceedings having been happily concluded, the company returned to the ballroom, and the mazy dance was resumed with vigour and continued till the small hours of the morning."*

"We suppose," the editor opined, *"the festivities are at an end and the opening of the Wanganui Bridge has become an event of history. By next week the relaxation will be over. The bridge will*

then be looked upon from a more utilitarian point of view, while expectations will be transferred to other public works in contemplation and progress."

Then when it came to wrapping up all the pomp and ceremony the *Herald* had this to say of the speech-writer after the Governor's departure: *"The committee evidently got hold of a practised hand, one who would not hesitate to lay the butter on thick, and he suited the occasion very well. To say scarcely anything at all in a great many words, and to make the greatest possible parade of meaning to say a great deal in a few words, are an admitted principle in the preparation of these singular productions of clever wordmongers. Congratulatory addresses always deal largely in commonplace generalities, abound in effusive praises and have a hollow sound, consequently the world has pretty well agreed to attach no importance at all to them."*

But this was no criticism – in fact it was quite the opposite. The *Herald* was merely acknowledging what was common practice on such an auspicious occasion, but using it as a good excuse to do what it never lost an opportunity of doing – to goad the *Chronicle,* which had that morning dismissed the *"prosiness and inflated phraseology"* of the speeches. Perhaps we could conclude this account of the building of the Wanganui Bridge by noting, "They knew how to work back then. But they also sure as hell knew how to party!"

Sir George and Lady Bowen

Laying of Wanganui Bridge foundation stone

More stories of the Wanganui Bridge

The bridge's swing span was installed for the purpose of allowing vessels to supply various upriver enterprises. When gas, water and telephone services crossed the river via the bridge they were installed in such a way as to enable them to be disconnected whenever the span was activated. This caused delays of up to half an hour each time the span was opened, leading to much frustration. But even before then long delays occurred, as evidenced by the following *Chronicle* report from 23 June, 1874.

"For exactly half an hour yesterday was the traffic over the bridge suspended, during which time the St Kilda was being taken through. Considerable inconvenience was caused thereby and a perfect crush of horsemen, traps and carts waited impatiently for the bridge to be closed again so as to permit the resumption of traffic. Surely some means could be devised by which these delays would not occur. Ten minutes at the outside should be abundant time for any steamer to occupy in passing through."

The article acknowledged, however, that in this particular case the extended delay was not the fault of the lessee of the bridge. Apparently a *"well-known steeple-chaser"* had caused a security problem. He became so impatient that he jumped his horse over the safety bar and trotted on until he was prevented by a closed gate from travelling any further. However, locals must have fumed over regular and long holdups. The following article appeared in the *Chronicle* on 18 March, 1893. *"Bridge traffic was completely suspended at noon yesterday by the crossing of a large flock of some 4,000 sheep. They were in the charge of four drovers and were on their way to pasturage at Waitotara."*

The last time the swing span was opened is believed to have been in 1902, when the *Huia* delivered heavy bridge material for the repair of the Aramoho Railway Bridge. Just prior to the

86

opening of the Dublin Street Bridge in 1914 the Town Bridge was declared a closed structure by the Borough Council, although there was a celebrated (and heavily censured) prank many years later by a local radio personality who announced to the public that the span was to reopen. A large crowd gathered to witness the historic event, but eventually dispersed disappointed.

The Wanganui Bridge served its city well and older members of the community could tell many a story about it. Indeed, the author well remembers with great trepidation negotiating a small truck over its narrow carriageway when learning to drive, just missing opposing traffic on one side while trying desperately to avoid rearranging Messrs Kennard's fancy ironwork on the other. However, seventy years after its construction it was becoming increasingly clear that the bridge was inadequate for the needs of the growing town. In Chapple & Veitch's *History of Wanganui* (1939) the authors predicted: *"The time is coming when it will have to be replaced by a stucture more suited to modern needs."*

Thirty years later the bridge was demolished and a new one built, but one thing is certain – the celebrations and festivities attending the opening of the Whanganui City Bridge nowhere near matched the heights and enthusiasm of the inauguration of the original.

Suicide bridge

"The Wanganui Bridge has attained a notoriety pertaining to well known and favourite places for suicides," declared the *Taranaki Herald* (13 April, 1872).

Well, hardly. The bridge had only been open a few months, but dramatic headlines sell newspapers – in this case proclaiming, *"BODIES OF UNFORTUNATES FOUND – ROMANTIC STORY REVEALED AT INQUEST."*

The usual crowds of rubberneckers gathered to show ghoulish interest when news of the tragedy first emerged. It all began with the testimony of a young lad who had seen a couple standing on the carriageway talking as he crossed the bridge on the night of Good Friday. As he approached they crossed to the other side and continued their conversation. When he reached the toll-house, situated on the town end, he heard a heavy splash, turned around and saw they were no longer there. The boy told the toll collector what he had witnessed, describing the couple's appearance as best he could. The splash was also heard from a vessel which was moored at the wharf and a small boat was sent out to investigate. All the searchers recovered was a gentleman's "bell-topper" white hat and a lady's white straw hat, which were found floating on the water. Witnesses also reported hearing weak cries, apparently from someone in the water. An immediate police search was commenced, but was initially unsuccessful due to tide flows at the time. The hats were identified as belonging to a Richard Crossing and Mrs Crossing, recent arrivals from Sydney, who had been seen that evening at the Red Lion Hotel. Mr Crossing was described as a stout elderly individual *"about fifty-five years of age"*, and his wife about twenty. By the time their bodies were recovered several days later, more information had come to hand revealing *"a painful story"* at the subsequent inquest.

The New South Wales *Police Gazette* of 13 April, 1872 had

issued a warrant for the arrest of Richard and Bella Crossing, suspected of involvement in the murder of an illegitimate child, the offspring of Bella Crossing, although no body had been found. Descriptions of the pair coincided with sightings of the Crossings in Wanganui. It also emerged that Isabella was not the wife of Richard but his niece and that they had been engaged in an adulterous relationship in Mudgee, Australia. Shortly after they arrived here, Crossing – a relatively wealthy man – began negotiations to purchase a farm at Brunswick, but a letter from the Australian authorities concerning the inquest of the now-discovered body of the child disrupted his plans and the couple apparently decided that the best solution for all concerned was to escape the hangman's noose by ending their lives.

A suicide note, which partly blamed himself and partly his wife back in Mudgee for not being understanding enough of the situation, was read at the inquest, along with instructions as to how his estate should be divided. He lamented the fact that while he left Australia under the assumed name of John Evans, he used his real name after his arrival in Wanganui to ensure his children would not lose any inheritance due to them.

"If I had stuck to that," he wrote, *"I should have been right."*

A further poignant note to one of his sons read: *"Dear James, I send my watch to you by Robert.* (His servant and distant relative). *"I hope you will take care of it and think of your ill-loved – FATHER. Goodbye all. March 28th, 1872. May the Lord have mercy on us."*

A letter from Isabella also left instructions as to the dividing up of her possessions. The jury at the inquest returned a verdict *"found drowned"* in the case of Isabella. For Richard the coroner strongly urged the jury to return a verdict of *"felo de se"*, an archaic, legally unforgiving term meaning *"felon of himself"* and usually applying to suicides. In early times it meant forfiture of assets to the monarchy and a shameful burial without benefit of clergy. However, after considerable debate the coroner accepted the following verdict: *"That the deceased, Richard Crossing, whilst in a state of temporary insanity, committed suicide by throwing himself from the Wanganui Bridge and was drowned."*

So ended a tragic tale, but while the bridge may have been the means of some to end their lives, it failed to gain the notoriety which the *Taranaki Herald* had predicted.

Wanganui Bridge - photo taken in the same year as the Crossing suicides

Be afraid – be very afraid

Possessing an appropriate surname sometimes lends an air of credibility to one's profession. Graves, for example if one is a sexton. Or Nicks, if one happens to be a police officer. So perhaps one of our early borough councils looked for more than just the usual job qualifications when it appointed its new Inspector-of-Just-About-Everything, bringing not only credibility but also a stamp of authority to the position.

"The name's Fear. George Fear!"

Mr Fear lost no time in gaining a reputation equal to his moniker, as Wanganui automobile owners soon discovered: *"Speeding motorists have evidently met their Waterloo,"* declared the *Wanganui Herald,* (30 September, 1921). *"The inspector is about to introduce a batch of over 20 to the Magistrate at an early date, with most of the alleged offences committed in Dublin Street and the upper end of Victoria Avenue. In the meantime Mr Fear is spending a good deal of overtime after fresh scalps."*

But the formidably named inspector had more than errant motorists in his sights. *"Mr Fear,"* continued the *Herald,* *"stated that he has now been authorised by the Council to proceed with the 'Keep to the left' campaign for pedestrian traffic. This is a reform that is long overdue in Wanganui to bring it into line with other towns where the regulation is enforced. The local campaign will not start until Mr Fear has everything in readiness. Sign boards will be placed along footpaths to catch the eye and advertisements will appear simultaneously in the local papers. The police will be asked to assist in directing attention to the new regulations."*

Pedestrian regulations, however, were nothing new. A letter to the *Herald* (26 June, 1871), expressed anxiety about impending plans to prohibit perambulators on the Wanganui Bridge walkway. *"A Mother"* asked if she would have to choose between carrying her baby across the bridge or leave it behind, imploring the editor to use his influence, *"so that the hard hearts of the Bridge people may be softened."*

But wait. There's more! *"Heads of families and nurse girls particularly would do well to bear in mind that they render themselves liable, after the first of January, to the pains and penalties of the Police Offences Amendment Act, attaching to wheeling perambulators on all sidewalks of cities, towns, and boroughs. The local police, it is understood, will rigidly enforce the Act.* (*Herald,* 31 December, 1884).

The announcement prompted the following letter to the editor. *"Sir, Am I mad or am I dreaming, that perambulators are to be banished from the footpaths and that my wife or servant, when wheeling out the baby, must tramp in the gutter?"* (In defence of bureaucrats of the day, it should be noted that footpaths generally were much narrower back then and perambulators were not easily manoeuvred).

But a much greater threat to public safety came with the introduction of the horseless carriage and as early as 1907 two motor car drivers appeared before the magistrate charged with reckless driving. Arthur Lewis was accused of driving around the Guyton Street corner into the Avenue at a speed of 10 miles per hour. (The speed limit around corners was 8mph). Lewis claimed it was not more than seven, that his car was under control, there was little traffic and that he had made a wide sweep, leaving room for horses and other vehicles. His case was dismissed, the magistrate ruling that while it was very close to the border line it was not advisable to press such cases unduly hard. But Thomas Atkins was not so fortunate. Alleged to have rounded the same corner at 14mph, he was charged with *"furious driving"* and fined £5 plus costs. His Honour noted that the defendant was *"a somewhat confirmed offender".*

By 1913 the increasing numbers of automobiles on the roads were causing concern. *"MOTORISTS IN THE AVENUE",* headlined the *Chronicle,* (25 April). *"HOW TO STOP FURIOUS*

DRIVING". The article complained about, *"the manner in which motorists practically take charge of the Avenue."* It recommended that the matter come under police control, where it eventually ended up and has remained ever since – without (George) Fear or favour.

Not on the footpath, ladies

Nymphs of the pavement

In 1868 (16 June) an outraged *Herald* subscriber had this to say about the world's oldest profession operating in a respectable Wanganui neighbourhood.

"Sir,- If there is nothing more disgusting than another in a respectable neighbourhood, it is the existence of a house of ill-fame, which I have every reason to believe exists in a certain part of this town, situated only a short distance from the new Presbyterian Church. The place has been a great plague to the public for a long time, and I think it quite time something was done to remove it. It is a rendezvous for the lowest in Wanganui, both by night and day. I have had occasion to pass there at nearly all hours of the night and on one occasion in particular, about 3 o'clock on a Sunday morning, there was singing, screaming, swearing and fighting going on, enough to shock any person. It is a part of the town the police do not think it necessary to visit, although the existence of the place is well known to them. The authorities are surely sufficiently powerful to have it removed from such a respectable and prominent part of the town as Victoria Avenue. If the police would only make it their business to visit that locality at nights, they would be able to obtain sufficient proof to warrant laying information against the offenders, and it would not be the first time two of the three women have figured at the Police Court. Trusting something will be done to make the place less offensive to passers-by, and that I am not taking up too much of your valuable space. I am, Sir, Amicus."

A more indulgent writer (Charitas) responded. Referring to the *"certain house of ill-fame pretended to have been discovered in Victoria Avenue,"* Charitas was convinced the matter had been greatly exaggerated, pointing out that acts of gross ignorance, violent quarrels, improprieties and curses occurring amongst people of lower classes did not constitute a house of ill-fame, as everyone knew that such things were only too common with people who drink. There were only three or four women living there with their husbands, who engaged in what he called *"pure little family jollification."* Charitas claimed to have had no personal interest in the alleged house of ill-fame, only wanting its inhabitants to maintain their good name. He seemed to have had quite an intimate knowledge of the "families" who lived there so perhaps he had more than a casual interest in refuting the charges levelled by Amicus – or perhaps not.

The situation concerning brothel-keeping in Wanganui had clearly not changed much fifteen years later. An article in the *Chronicle* (12 May, 1883) described the plight of a landlord who had *"the fortune, or misfortune to own a house in that not very savoury locality, the east side of Market Square."* The house had been empty for a long time and the owner despaired of finding a tenant, *"beginning to think that a fire was not such an unmixed evil after all."*

To his delight, however, he was paid a visit by a well-spoken stranger from Patea. The man inspected the premises, declaring them to be admirable for his purposes and made no attempt to haggle over the rent, but when he volunteered the information that he was a married man the owner, himself a married man with children, felt obliged to point out that his immediate neighbours were *"a very long way off being the cream of respectability."*

The gentleman from Patea shook his head and heaved a deep sigh at the wickedness of the world, but signed the rental agreement and moved in his furniture. But to the landlord's disgust he soon learned that he had let his house to the agent of *"certain nymphs of the pavement, compared with whom the next door neighbours were angels of light."*

The pleasant spoken Patea gentleman was suddenly nowhere to be found, but had left on the premises *"a choice assortment of human beings,"* who the landlord would have given a month's rent to get rid of – if only he knew how. He was reported as saying he would rather have the house empty – and virtuous!

Reports continued to surface in the local press, calling the authorities' attention to brothels operating around the town, including the following which caused quite a stir when it appeared in the *Herald* on 30 November, 1886.

"Complaints reach us of the presence of a house of ill-fame in Niblett Street, which is a cause of annoyance to the respectable portion of the residents in that vicinity. The house, we are informed, is the property of a person who takes a leading part in religious matters here. Surely this cannot be true? A man who reads the gospel in public on Sunday would hardly have the effrontry to call at a brothel for his rent on Monday, at least we should think not."

On the 4th of December the *Herald* published a disclaimer from a Dudley Eyre, who had been asked if he was the owner of the property in question. Mr Eyre denied owning any property in or near Niblett Street and suggested the complainant go further afield to find the proprietor.

The preacher referred to must have been a *Herald* subscriber for, according to a subsequent story, he promptly put matters right, having apparently been unaware of the purposes his property had been put to.

Early settler C.S.Niblett would have been horrified to know the goings-on in the street named after him

To merge, or not to merge

An exchange of views over the pros and cons of media mergers (*Chronicle*, 3 February, 2017) was a rather genteel affair compared to the gloves-off approach of such matters over a century ago, particularly when it came to competition between our two main local newspapers. (Correspondent Brit Bunkley argued against a proposed merger between *Fairfax* and *NZME*, while *Chronicle* editor Mark Dawson pointed out the advantages).

The *Wanganui Chronicle* (regarded as conservative in its views) began publication in 1856, followed in 1867 by the liberal *Evening Herald* – (founder/editor John Ballance, later New Zealand premier). Unfortunately few pre-1874 copies of the *Chronicle* survive, but an attempted arson at the *Chronicle* office in 1868 sparked a round of accusations and denials between the two, with the *Herald* concluding *"that if a conflagration had been the result, it would have been the first ray of any kind that has proceeded from that dismal abode for many, many months."* (4 February). Competition between the two papers remained spirited, although a hint of what was to come appeared with the arrival of a third competitor.

"We will be happy to welcome the new paper if it exhibits a closer acquaintance with the usages of respectable journalism than that displayed by the present Chronicle proprietry," declared the *Herald* (14 October, 1870).

But it was a gorse fire that really sparked an ongoing conflagration between the two main papers, whipping up a firestorm of bitter rivalry and barbed insults which lasted for over a hundred years and could be attested to by old hands to this day, although they may be unaware of its origins. It all began on a pleasant St Patrick's Day holiday in 1873, with a regatta taking place on Taupo Quay. *"What little bunting Wanganui can sport was hung out to do duty for the occasion and assisted in giving the town a gala appearance,"* observed the *Herald,* (17 March).

What happened next missed that day's deadline, but appeared in the *Herald* the following day: *"In the midst of the sport yesterday the dread alarm of fire was raised, causing a stampede of horsemen and vehicles in the direction of the supposed conflagration."*

Dense smoke billowed from Plymouth Street and it was thought that either the mayor's residence (Sandridge Hall) or the Church of England parsonage was ablaze. Fire Chief Robinson ordered brigade volunteers to prepare for action, but they were not required.

"The advance guard found Mr W.H. Watt engaged in deliberately burning furze in the street," complained the *Herald.*

His Worship's response? *"People are having their fun on the Quay and I'm having mine here!"*

A series of claims, counter-claims, explanations, denials and insults followed before the *Herald,* under the heading, *"THE LAST ESCAPADE OF HIS WORSHIP'S",* quoted the Constabulary Force Ordinance Act: *"Any person setting fire to the bush scrub or flax within the limits of any town shall be liable to a fine of not more than Forty, nor less than Five shillings and shall compensate any person damnified thereby."*

The *Herald,* after reminding readers that Mr Watt had committed an identical offence twelve months previously, then demanded action from the authorities: *"In the interests of the public safety we call upon the police, without fear or favor, to perform their duty. There need be no fear of lack of evidence. Mr Watt admitted the burning in the presence of half-a-dozen highly respectable witnesses, amongst them the Captain of the Fire Brigade. If from fear of Mr Watt's position they hold back from their public duty, from doing what they are paid to do, they are not worthy of their hire."* (21 March).

The *Herald* appears to have dug further into regulations pertaining to such matters for it then waved (figuratively) the

Municipal Corporation Act in Mr Watt's face, quoting Section 5, Part VII: *"Every person who wilfully sets fire to any inflammable matter whatsoever in the open air without having given notice in writing to the occupiers of the land adjoining ....and also to the Town Clerk of his intention so to do ...... shall forfeit a sum of not exceeding five pounds."*

"The lawmakers should be the last to be the law breakers," thundered the *Herald*. *"The Mayor should figure in the Police Court."*

A letter to the *Herald's* editor, responding to a missive from Mr Watt, (unfortunately now lost to history) to the *Chronicle*, slammed the mayor's *"vulgar slang..... disgracing the Council of Wanganui, first for the tone in which it is written; next for attempting to justify the conduct of fire raising, simply because it was on his own property. Mr Watt ought to know that persons cannot do as they like at all times with their own property – or why the Inspector of Nuisances? Are we to be thus roasted in our beds because Mr Watt says, 'Its [sic] my property I was burning?'"*

Even the *Herald's* reporter felt compelled to write a letter to his own paper in answer to the mayor's letter to the *Chronicle*, in which Mr Watt appears to have back-tracked over his earlier admission and accused the *Herald* of having *"told three lies."*

"Mr Watt's statement that the burning furze on his own property and not on the public street proves him to be a person of fine distinction, and adept at that interesting science of 'splitting straws'," wrote the reporter. *"Possibly by a few inches the street was avoided. Nice distinction to base an 'unqualified denial' upon."* Like a dog with a bone the *Herald* would not let the matter go. *"The police have not taken the slightest action,"* it complained. *"Their conduct appears utterly inexplicable, if it is not to be imputed to fear of offending Mr Watt, who is a member of the Provincial Executive, under whose authority the police are placed. Let the public, therefore, from these and surrounding circumstances, judge of the social, political, and moral state of the Mayoralty in Wang-*

nui." (24 March, 1873).

But when the *Herald* labelled the mayor a delinquent and accused him of lying, the matter took a more serious turn. *"The proprietor of this journal,"* (John Ballance) *"has been served with a writ at the instance of Mr W.H. Watt, at which damages are laid at £1,000 and special damages for journeys to Wellington at £100, arising out of certain letters and articles which have appeared in the Herald. The libel is said to be contained in expressions which are said to have injured that gentleman's reputation."*

A statement informed readers that the *Herald's* solicitor had been instructed to defend the case and that no comments would be made which would prejudice a fair and impartial hearing and decision, although it published this statement on 17 April. *"The following telegram appeared in our contemporary this morning: 'In the case of Watt v. Ballance, an attempt will be made to change the venue to Christchurch.' Watt's party are actively working. Why attempt to change the venue to Christchurch? Does the plaintiff think he would not receive a fair trial in the midst of his fellow townsmen?"*

The usual delays occurred, *"purely of a technical nature,"* observed the *Herald, "but, happily for the gentlemen of the long robe, attended with costs."* Mr Watt's request was denied and the matter eventually scheduled for October in the Wanganui Supreme Court but his Honour, after perusing the jury list, pointed out that the names of both the complainant and defendant appeared on it, theoretically enabling them to adjudicate their own case! Once that was sorted both counsels conferred, then requested the case go instead to arbitration, albeit reluctantly on Ballance's part. His Honour happily agreed, opining that a jury trial *"would have been accompanied by serious evil in the community,"* which he then congratulated for having escaped such a scandal. Deliberations duly took place at the Rutland Hotel, with John Bryce (M.H.R) representing Ballance and former premier Sir William Fox for Watt. With a third arbitrator they found in favour of Watt, awarding him £50 damages, plus costs. Both men claimed victory – Watt, for having won and Ballance because it was such a paltry sum. *"Fifty pounds from £1,100 is a salve for his wounded reputation,"* declared Ballance, *"an indication of the estimation in which he is held."*

Mr Watt lit no more illegal gorse fires but hedged his bets by – wait for it; buying the *Chronicle!* Former *Chronicle* owner William Hutchison, a supporter of Mr Watt, then became mayor, both men effectively swapping roles. The friction between the two newspaper magnates then moved up a level. Ballance became a Member of the House of Representatives, but lost his parliamentary seat to Watt in 1881 by a margin of four votes (a group of Ballance supporters failing to make it to the polling booth in time when their coach broke down). Three years later Ballance took the seat back from Watt by a large majority. Meanwhile the insults flew and charges such as, *"The Chronicle has out-Heroded Herod,"* and *"The Herald's political mission is to misrepresent and is too old a sinner to be reformed now,"* became common-place.

Unfortunately what was once such splendid entertainment for the reading public finally ceased with the demise of the *Herald* as a daily in 1986. So ummm ...... I think I'll side with Brit on this one.

William H. Watt

John Ballance

Journalistic one-upmanship

As mentioned in the previous story, competition between our two daily newspapers ceased with the demise of the *Herald*. But until then the intense rivalry between the two papers ranged from cleverly crafted insults to gloves-off belligerence, with the latter being stepped up a notch or three as a result of the aforementioned Ballance/Watt stand-off. Here is a selection of some of the heavy artillery the papers brought to bear against each other for over a hundred years.

Herald vs *Chronicle*: *"The contemptible Chronicle. One of the most dastardly, cowardly, contemptible and unjournalistic attacks ever made on the Herald by the Chronicle – a journal which has ever been noted for mudslinging of the most vicious kind, was made in its column this morning."*

"Mrs Harris. This illustrious lady informs us, through her friend Mrs Gamp, that she is tired of the Chronicle and desires to open a correspondence with ourselves."

"Similar pleasure to the Chronicle's was felt by the mob which compelled Pontius Pilate to send Jesus of Nazareth to the place of crucifixion."

"Of course it is not to be expected that the ignoramuses of the Chronicle should know much about science."

"No doubt many of our readers have watched the desperate struggles of a fly, stuck in a pot of treacle, to extricate itself from its unpleasant predicament. The present desperate wrigglings of the Chronicle remind us very much of the efforts of the bluebottle to extricate itself from its treacly slough."

"Assertions made so daringly by the Chronicle as the most unblushing lie ever published in that unscrupulous journal."

"Like the Kaiser, the Chronicle is often in a hurry and like most people in a hurry, it sometimes forgets to make sure."

"Good Sir Chronicle. This caps all the native absurdity of your character. This chronic love of telling untruths is always breaking out!"

102

"The Wanganui Chronicle was always paltry, but never was its utter regard of fair play more completely displayed than in the report it gave this morning of Mr Hogan's meeting.................. No doubt the Chronicle thought that by suppressing some facts and entirely distorting others, on the very morning of the election, it would have a free hand, and meet with no opposition in its wilful perversion of the truth. That was always characteristic of it."

"When our contemporary takes in hand the congenial work of censuring and spitefully maligning the present Ministry, it is not expected to stick very closely to facts, and therefore we may be excused if we do not reply on all occasions when its prejudice gets the better part of its common sense."

"For many years the Chronicle has held undisputed sway in the devious art of misrepresentation."

"We can assure him (Chronicle editor) we care nothing for his abuse; his weak and absurd effusions are already measured, and the Chronicle is what it has ever been, a paper without ability, conscience, or the respect of any class in the community. An apology is due to our readers for any allusion to a paper of the status of the Chronicle, which has become a hopeless mass of twaddle and abuse, and is a disgrace to colonial journalism."

"No matter what form the Chronicle takes, it is impossible to add either to the quality or quantity of its own brain department."

<u>Chronicle vs Herald</u>: *"The Wanganui Herald suggests that the volcanic activity of Ngaruhoe [sic] and the prevalence of 'la grippe' may be due to the fact that the planets Jupiter and Saturn are close together. We congratulate the Herald on its new departure from the plan of blaming the alleged 'Tory' press for all existing evils."*

"The Wanganui Herald criticising the London Times is about equal to a whitebait finding fault with a whale."

"The Herald is as tricky as its political chief.......... We never before heard of even the lowest journalistic hack doing anything so mean, so utterly contemptible. Is the Herald laying down a new rule in journalism?"

"Last evening the Herald was in a tantrum again. One has difficulty in knowing where the paper stands politically."

"Our evening contemporary is really funny..........We suppose that what the Herald says in its leading column is meant to be in a serious strain. It should be, but our contemporary is so queer that one never knows how to take it. The older it gets, the funnier it gets."

"Those whom the gods wish to destroy they first make mad. The Herald is very mad."

"The Herald says the clapper on the fire-bell is loose. How would it have it? Tight?"

"The Herald has bungled somewhat badly in its tactics. It has left its game too late."

"The Evening Herald, it seems, has been much disturbed in mind lately, and it has been visited by unpleasant dreams."

"The Evening Herald is evidently a firm believer in the line, 'Fear not to lie. It will seem a lucky hit,' and provided it can say something malicious of the Chronicle, it cares not whether the statement be true or falte [sic]."

Of course the rivalry comprised more than single salvos, with replies compiled and fired off once each editor had read his contemporary's edition for the day. One such round began with the *Chronicle* (20 January, 1879) suggesting that the Herald owner and editor Mr Ballance had his hand in the Government Treasurer's pocket: *"Mr Ballance, proprietor of the Wanganui Herald, being an intimate and highly esteemed friend of the Colonial Treasurer, came in for a good haul from the Colonial Chest on Saturday. One insertion of the notification from the Public Works office tots up the nice little total of fifteen pounds."*

Mr Ballance must have been rubbing his hands in glee at the opportunity of silencing his competitor with his reply that evening: *"The only special feature about the Public Works announcement that appeared in our issue on Saturday, and which has so enraged our contemporary, is the fact that by law the Government were compelled to give two insertions. One was inserted in the Government Gazette, and the other in the journal*

104

possessing the largest circulation in the Wanganui District. The public interest therefore has been best observed by the course adopted, the pitiful whine of the Chronicle notwithstanding."

Perhaps the *Herald* was smarting from recent *Chronicle* comments which referred to the evening paper as *"an unprincipled organ of the present Ministry,"* alleging it *"misrepresented the facts, spread deliberate falsehoods, made untruthful statements and printed pure fabrication."* The *Chronicle's* editor referred to *"our exceedingly sharp-witted contemporary's guesses,"* its *"childish braggdocia"* and condemned the *"tergiversation of the subsidised journal."*

Over twenty years later they were still at it, with neither paper able to refrain from what appears to be little more than a playground squabble.

"Our contemporary is jubilant," announced the *Chronicle*, (14 January, 1902). *"It has found a subscriber at the foot of Mount Ruapehu."*

Apparently a Waiouru resident had forwarded an order to the local chemist wrapped in an advertisement clipped from the *Herald. "'This proves,' says our delighted friend, 'that the Herald is as well read in the back blocks as it is in the town.' We rejoice to know that our contemporary is happy, and, with a view to filling the cup to the brim, we may add that a correspondent informs us that his butcher yesterday left the morning sausages wrapped up in a Herald article on, 'Tuberculosis and how to cure it!'"*

Unfortunately a typo in the *Chronicle* gave the *Herald* cause to crow loudly in return, pointing out that its *"facetious morning contemporary"* was evidently *"quite oblivious of the fact that yesterday's issue* (dated the 13th) *of his own journal was post-dated to the 31st of the month."*

In fact it was post-dated to the 131st of January and, seemingly unnoticed by the *Herald,* the same edition of the *Chronicle* was predated to 1901 on page 4!

Perhaps the *Herald's* observation from our previous story,
that of having *"a closer acquaintance with the uses of respectable*

journalism than that displayed by the present Chronicle proprietry," applied equally to both papers.

Over a century of journalistic sparring

Liberals vs Conservatives

Despite the constant mud-slinging between the two dailies, both papers often conducted "friendly" sporting fixtures, although it should be noted that they were probably played by lesser staff, with editors and managers likely enjoying brandy and cigars while underlings spilled their blood in true gladiatorial style. Rugby, cricket, soccer, rowing and golf were regular events and contested *"in a gentlemanly and sportsmanlike manner"* if post-match write-ups can be believed, although serious bias is evident in both papers. In an account of a rugby match played in 1892 the *Chronicle* refers to itself in capitals and its rival in lower case. The *Herald* does the same but vice versa of course, and while the *Herald* trumpets its win with the headline *"Herald v. Chronicle: Victory for the Herald Team"*, its defeated rival merely states, *"Herald v. Chronicle"*.

The match was played at the Recreation Ground (referred to as the "Rec" - now Spriggens Park) on a Tuesday afternoon (28 June). According to the *Chronicle* it was one of the largest attendances seen for some time although it conceded *"the full number could not be exactly estimated owing to the misty state of the weather, which obscured everything outside fifty or sixty yards' range."* The reporter lamented the fact that there was no band in attendance to enliven the proceedings, *"but this was well counterbalanced by the brilliant and dashing game between the two teams."*

The *Chronicle* team had marched onto the field at 3.30pm sharp to the cheers of the spectators, then it was the *Herald's* turn to receive the crowd's ovation. *"The latter, however, were driven to the ground in a handsome brake, whose foaming steeds were handled by a well-known knight of the ribbons."*

Once the theatrics were done, both teams got down to business. *"No time was lost to set the ball in motion and a better thirty men it would be hard to conceive could ever grace a football ground. Each man in well-known colours looked the picture of physical strength and just as the whistle was blown by Umpire O'Leary commenced one of the best contests ever witnessed."*

The game was evenly contested for the first five minutes, according to the *Chronicle's* reporter, making it difficult to determine which was the better team. *"The loud cries of the bookmakers, however, settled this question by making the Heraldites the favourites. Nor were those of the CHRONICLE lacking supporters, for the bets were as freely taken as laid. By some ding-dong play the ball was taken in the Herald's territory and there it stayed for fully 20 minutes, when an opening occurred which gave the captain of the Herald team a chance, and he was not slow to avail himself of it and carried the ball in a dashing manner over the CHRONICLE'S line, amidst the deafening applause from the enthusiastic onlookers. The try was not converted although a good attempt was made, leaving the half-time score at 2-0 to the Herald."*

After partaking of some refreshments the players *"attended the referee's whistle in splendid fettle to contest the second spell. Determination was plainly stamped on each man's face, but those of the CHRONICLE wore the expression of 'do or die', and with this will they set to work to make themselves level with their opponents."*

There were descriptions of *"closely packed scrums, good dribbling, neat passing and dashing runs ....Then the cries from the spectators proclaimed their numbers by, 'Go it Herald, well done,' and 'Good boys CHRONICLE, you'll dish 'em yet.'"*

Then suddenly Jones of the *Herald* scooped up the ball and carried it over the opposition's line. *"This time the scene was terrific, although the concourse of people could not be seen, their enthusiastic cheers resounded with so much volume as to be almost deafening,"* with the *Chronicle's* supporters joining in the applause in true sportsmanlike manner. Again the try was unconverted.

"The game became furious, the CHRONICLE team playing splendidly .... and Jones, of the CHRONICLE, getting the ball, dashed through the whole fifteen of the Herald team and carried it over the Herald's line with a couple of the team hanging on him,

amidst the wildest scene imaginable. Now the cheers rose to a sound like the rush of a mighty cataract and 'Go it CHRONICLES,' 'Well played,' and 'Good boy Jones,' were intermingled with the uproar."

Then the *Herald* scored another try, this time the conversion *"successfully launched over the bar,"* making the score 9-2 to the *Herald,* where it stayed until full time which was called shortly afterwards.

"The game was one that had to be seen," enthused the *Chronicle* reporter, *"for the play was of that sort that baffles description."*

The *Herald's* account was much more matter-of-fact and analytical than the *Chronicle's* euphuistic report, but like its opponent it gave credit where credit was due. Conversion misses were described as *"failing to increase the score"* while a success was conversely written up as *"this time increased the score"*. Striking the uprights was labelled a *"poster"*, while a tackled player was referred to as having been *"grassed"*. Tries were plainly worth two points apiece in those days, so the *Herald's* one conversion must have counted for three to bring its score to nine.

The customary after-match function was held, a celebration the typesetters must also have attended for the *Chronicle's* coverage of the event referred to itself on one occasion as the *"Chronile"*, the opposition as the *"Hearld"* and the whistle-blower as the *"refree."* (Hic)!

Which of these mutually contemptuous journalistic enterprises was the better newspaper probably depended upon the reader's personal bias and political persuasion, but one thing is clear – that on 28 June, 1892 the *Herald* was the better rugby team on the day.

But an insidious scourge was already creeping into the game. Just a week before it was played two letters to the editor, under the heading, *"BETTING ON FOOTBALL MATCHES"*, appeared in the *Chronicle*. One, while commending the success of a newly formed club, slammed the *"deadheads and hangers-on"* its popularity had attracted. It was a class of person, the writer warned, that *"tends to demoralise and permeate with a spirit of gambling."* The second letter, under the *nom de plume "FAIR PLAY"*, was much less given to excess verbiage and came straight to the point: *"Sir,- I have heard, on very good authority, that the practice of betting is being indulged in to a great extent among our local (Wanganui) footballers. I am applying for insertion in your paper for the purpose of making the Rugby Union authorities acquainted with the fact, so that they may take immediate steps to put a stop to this evil practice. I think sir, that you will agree with me in saying that until measures are taken to eradicate betting, in any shape or form, over our Cup matches, the position that football holds among the leading pastimes of the day will be on the decline both morally and physically, and finally no conscientious man will be able to take any part in the game."*

It is plain, from accounts of the *Chronicle* v. *Herald* match, that very little weight was attached to the letter writers' opinions.

"Good boys, CHRONICLE, you'll dish 'em yet!"

The flowers of speech

It's hard to imagine that the profane language articulated so freely in public places today would have seen offenders hauled up before the courts in colonial times. An early *Chronicle* court report (12 May, 1883) states, *"Information was laid against Fanny Preston (a notorious woman of ill-fame) and George Chamberlain, (a well-known horsey character), for using abusive language. The woman is charged with having dropped the flowers of speech in question as far back as the 20th of April, while the man's alleged offence is so recent as Sunday last."*

The Police Offences Act of the time states: *"Any person who sings any song or ballad, writes or draws any indecent or obscene word, figure or representation or uses any profane, indecent or obscene language in any public place.......... shall on conviction be liable to imprisonment with hard labour for any time not exceeding one year."*

The *Wanganui Herald* (30 January, 1885) was confident that based on convictions already secured (with fines not optional), *"our streets and public places will be freed from the hideous obscenity of language and moral disfigurements, which now make them at times quite unfit for ladies and children to pass through."* The *Herald* noted that the courts had powers to commit particularly gross acts to a higher court, *"where on committal the offender, in addition to imprisonment, may be ordered to be once or twice privately flogged to the extent of twenty-five lashes at each whipping. The 'cat' is the only cure for some bad cases of obscenity."* The *Herald* hoped that the effect of the Act would be to *"purify the moral atmosphere of the public streets and places of the colony,"* although the "fairer sex" whom the Act was designed to protect were often the worst offenders and those who were convicted discovered that custodial sentences applied equally to them as to the "sterner sex". A "lady" by the name of Nellie Corney, was overheard by a police officer using some particularly choice language *"between the hours of one o'clock and two o'clock in the morning,"* and sentenced to three days' prison with hard labour.

But it became apparent that the Police Offences Act was not having the desired effect, as this piece in the *Herald* (18 January, 1902), under the heading *"INDECENT LANGUAGE"* reveals: *"The prevalence of this offensive habit all over the colony is unfortunately not unknown in Wanganui, but it is rarely that the offenders are brought to book and punished. Women and children have their ears constantly assailed in the streets by foul language from a lot of blackguards, who seem to think it necessary to punctuate their conversation with blasphemous and obscene words. In the busiest portion of the town, knots of idle youths congregate at all times of the day and night, to the annoyance of respectable people. The police cannot be everywhere, as there are too few for street duty, a fact the larrikin element takes every advantage of, with the result that women and children are often insulted and interfered with at night. A few convictions and salutary sentences would go a long way towards the abatement of the evil, as the offenders would find a sojourn in gaol anything but a picnic and would come out with a wholesome dread of again offending .... It would act as an effective warning and purify the air very considerably."*

To protect the tender ears of more genteel ladies, it was not uncommon for signs such as the following to be displayed prominently in public places: *"Gentlemen, while occupying this room, are respectfully requested to refrain from using profane or improper language. Ladies are in the next room."* Judging from the number of females before the courts on profanity charges it's plain that similar signs aimed at protecting the tender ears of gentlemen should also have been displayed.

Of course some occupations were known for the excessive use of bad language, as this account from the *Herald* (1 November, 1877) suggests. *"The horses were ridden by boys and these boys gave evidence of plenty of pluck and a profound knowledge of profane language. The art of swearing with some of*

112

these youths simply amounted to perfection. I never heard so much expressive language calculated to make the hair stand on end come from human lips before. To say that some of these lads swore like troopers and bullock drivers would be to do them scant justice," although that stereotype was challenged many years later when a court witness, *"exploded the cherished theory that bullock-driving cannot be accomplished without the use of sulphurous language."*

The witness, a bullock-driver himself, *"indignantly denied Mr Samuel's suggestion that he made use of foul language towards the defendant. He said he never swore, which he regarded as a very bad habit.*

'You are a bullock-driver, are you not?' queried counsel.

'Yes,' replied witness.

'And you can drive bullocks without swearing?'

'Yes.'

'So it is merely a fable that bullocks cannot be driven without swearing?'

The witness said it was. He had never found it necessary to swear at his teams, which worked well without profane encouragement." (*Herald:* 9 August, 1905).

But bullock drivers (and troopers) aside, lest an astute defence lawyer spot a loop-hole in the law regarding obscenity as it stood back then, the presiding Resident Magistrate moved swiftly on one occasion to prevent such advantage being taken. A *Herald* report (15 September, 1883) records: *"A peculiar suggestion was made by his Worship at the Court this morning, in regard to the informations laid in connection with the use of indecent language. He drew attention to the fact that at present a defendant was charged with 'unlawfully' making use of obscene language, from which some people might draw the inference that under some conditions the offence might be lawful. Such a happy delusion, however, must be dispelled, as the use of the language under any circumstances is an offence, and his Worship directed the ommission of the word 'unlawful' from all future informations."*

Find it in the classifieds!

The following are examples of early advertisements which appeared in the classified sections of the *Chronicle* and *Herald*:

"A lot of waste paper for sale. Apply office of the Chronicle."

"Wanted: A smart, active boy who can read and write. Apply at the Evening Herald."

"Wanted: A cook. Must be a good laundress. Apply sharp, Mrs Nance, Victoria Avenue."

"The person (who is known) who took the fishing rod and line from the Castlecliff Wharf on Saturday to return the same to owner at once, 14 Wicksteed Place, or trouble will follow."

"Wanted to buy: False teeth. Sound or otherwise. Top market price. Pearline & Co."

"Wanted to sell: Nearly new Edison Standard Phonograph with Cygnet Horn or would exchange a cow. Address at Chronicle."

"If my husband, Walter M'Intosh, better known as W.A. Price, Theatrical Agent, does not return or correspond, I intend to get married. Signed, Elizabeth M'Intosh."

"The Aramoho Tea Gardens & Zoo is open to the public. Admission 6d, Children 3d. Afternoon Tea 6d."

"On View and all alive: Lions, tigers, bears, kangaroos, lizards, swans, tortoises, baboons, monkeys, peacocks, jackasses, donkeys, opossums, variety of birds. Aramoho Zoo."

"King's Birthday: Sports young and old. Rifle range for ladies; 7 shots for 6d. Lovely prizes. Also shooting gallery for Gents. Aramoho Zoo."

"The brass axle cap, picked up on the No 1 Line today, may be obtained by the owner at the Opera House Stables."

"Mr Eastbury need not be afraid of his wife's debts, as she is quite able to pay them herself."

"My word, you have chopped the prices off!' So said a customer at Tingey's sale of pictures."

*"The open air baby gets on best. Leave yours out of doors most of the time, but put a North British Hot Water Bottle at his feet. Watch

him grow!"

"A stitch in time saves nine, but a bar of 'CASTLECLIFF' Brand Soap saves you several hours' scrubbing on washing day."

"One block of GILBERD & SONS Sand Soap will do as much work as two blocks of any other Sand Soap. Try it."

"Wanganui husbands simply love to hear their wives singing 'Home Sweet Home' while 'No Rubbing' Laundry Help and 'Golden Rule' Soap do the weekly washing."

"WANTED KNOWN: Servants requiring situations. Apply at once Wanganui Labour Exchange, Victoria Avenue."

"10s REWARD: The above reward will be paid to any person finding and restoring a CANARY lost from the Custom House Hotel. A Muller."

And now, lest anyone be under the misapprehension that post-Christmas sales are a relatively new sales ploy, comes the following advertisement from 1885: "WANTED KNOWN: All Christmas and New Year cards are now ½ price. Drew's Fancy Repository."

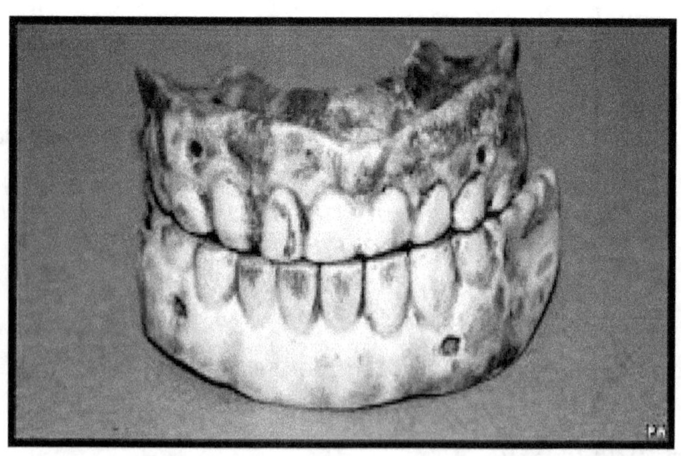

Wanted - false teeth, sound or otherwise

Fire-fighting & prevention

"Last evening about 6 o'clock," reported the *Evening Herald* (28 June, 1867) *"Mr Burnett's chimney caught fire. It was fortunately extinguished without doing any injury, but had the roof been of wood instead of iron there is little doubt but it would have caught fire. We have now had two fires within a few days, happily neither of them being serious, for which we may thank a combination of favorable circumstances. When the lean-to of the Chronicle office took fire, had there been the slightest wind, nothing could have saved the office and probably the whole block of buildings would have shared the same fate. After what has happened, will the inhabitants of our town still remain indifferent and apathetic about providing a fire engine? It used to be said in England that railway accidents would never cease until a director or bishop was killed; and it looks as if we are not to have an engine until an amount of property is destroyed by fire."*

With astonishing speed Mr John Burnett, confectioner, was the very next day hauled before the Resident Magistrate charged with neglecting to have his chimney swept. (Burnett's shop and residence was on the corner of Victoria Ave and Ridgway Street, (former site of *Anderson's For Men*). Regulations required property owners to have their chimneys cleaned every six months to lessen the risk of fire in a town comprised largely of wooden buildings. Mr Burnett was fined £2 with costs of 6s 6d.

"Major Durie requested the Press to notice this case, as he was determined to inflict the full penalty in every case brought before him."

Following an attempted arson at the *Chronicle* office the following year, articles and letters to the editor appeared in the press, warning of the main cause of fires – carelessness, after a Victoria Avenue shop had been reduced to ashes. *"Shops, stores, stables, hotels and warehouses are frequently burned down in Wanganui,"* wrote a correspondent, suggesting that the real problem was the misuse of matches which were tossed away carelessly after being used to light a cigar or cigarette. As if to prove his point a few days later, another shop in the Avenue *"suffered the narrowest possible escape from a serious conflagration owing to the reprehensible carelessness of a lover of the weed."*

Until 1866, the year the military vacated the Rutland Stockade, the town was serviced by a fire service of sorts. The stockade housed essential fire-fighting equipment – axes, leather fire buckets, a few rickety ladders, hooked poles for pulling thatch off burning buildings and a "fire engine", which was little more than a water barrel on wheels, manned by two men working a pump and another to direct the hose - a difficult job due to the intermittent nature of the water flow. A 20-foot jet of water could be obtained with this machine, with about 20 pounds of pressure. But the brigade was primarily for military use. If a fire broke out in town, permission was required from the commanding officer before the brigade was activated. The problem was that less senior officers were generally on day duty at both the Rutland and York Stockades, each approximately equal distance from the officers' mess (near the site of the former BNZ in the Bridge Block) where the senior officers would have been doing what senior officers did when off duty. By the time a messenger had located the top brass and reported back with permission to act (or not), the damage would have been done.

The first civilian fire brigade was formed when Joseph Robinson - a jeweller from England who had served as a volunteer fireman in London, Sydney, and Dunedin before settling in Wanganui, poked around the abandoned Rutland Stockade and appropriated whatever fire-fighting equipment had been left behind. But the brigade (formed in 1866) faced a challenge beyond its capabilities on Christmas Day, 1868. Its

Lieutenant, Thomas Dick "T.D." Cummins, a Sergeant in the Wanganui Cavalry Volunteers, was returning from a failed mission to winkle Titokowaru out of his fighting pa Tauranga-ika at Waitotara. Seeing an ominous pall of smoke on the horizon he hastened back home, reining in his horse at the brow of the St John's Wood hill to witness the entire stretch of Ridgway Street, from the Rutland Hotel to Rutland Hill, aflame. Just up the Avenue Holy Communion was being celebrated at Christ Church, so Fire Brigade members were quickly shunted to the front of the queue to clear them for duty. The fire had broken out just after noon and according to the *Wanganui Times*, (a bi-weekly which published from 1865-69), it had commenced in the Bowling Saloon, a building situated at the back of the Rutland Hotel.

"It then spread rapidly both up and down Ridgway Street, consuming in its upward sweep a blacksmith's workshop and the premises of Mr Harding, tailor. Here there is a vacant space, but the Odd Fellows' Hall, which is the next building, had a narrow escape, having been on fire more than once, and but for a change in the wind must certainly have perished with the others, in spite of every effort to save it. Downward again the fire first caught a store, occupied some time ago by Mr Webb, and used at the present time for storing flour (a large quantity of which, we regret to say, has been destroyed), then came the Rutland Hotel itself, one of the finest buildings in the town, which is now a smouldering mass of ruins. But the destruction did not stop here. The wind blowing obliquely across Ridgway Street, sparks were carried to the other side, and ere long the building belonging to Mr Burnett, occupied as an hospital for wounded men from the front, was found to be on fire. The first care was to get the poor men safely away, and those of them who could not walk, of course, were carried to another place of shelter. From the hospital the fire progressed up that side of the street, destroying the house and shop of Mr Robinson, watchmaker (captain of the newly-formed fire brigade) *and then the premises occupied by Mr Gower* (chemist). *The next building, used as a*

restaurant (Allen's Oyster Saloon) *was pulled down and this had the effect of arrresting the progress of the flames and saving the premises of Mr Liddell. When the spread of fire from the hospital to Victoria Avenue seemed imminent, the premises of Mr Blake* (saddler) *were also pulled down as a precautionary measure. How the fine house and* (confectionery) *shop occupied by Mr Burnett himself, which stands upon the corner site opposite the Rutland Hotel, were saved is a marvel. A number of people exerted themselves for this purpose, and something is owing to the fact that the Hotel being coated over, did not, in burning shoot up so vigorously as if it had been simply weather-boarded; something is also owing to the roof of Mr Burnett's house being zinc instead of shingles; at all events the premises remain intact, although sadly gashed and gutted. In the anxiety to save the household property and shop-goods, things were thrown out, very much knocked about and destroyed. The origin of the fire is a mystery; strange rumours, as generally happens in all such cases, are afloat, but an official enquiry will furnish us with something certain. We greatly regret that the buildings and other property destroyed were not so fully insured as they might have been, and that some of the policies are said to have expired the day previous to the fire,* (the Rutland Hotel was one). *The town narrowly escaped one of the most fearful conflagrations that ever occurred in the colony. The same may be said of Mr Burnett's large house on the corner of Victoria Avenue and Ridgway Street. It narrowly escaped, and its escape saved the entire buildings down to Taupo Quay, the Bank of New Zealand included."*

Mr Robinson, while bravely attempting to dampen down the wooden shingles on the hospital building, received word that one of his daughters was trapped inside his burning shop on the opposite side of the road. It turned out to be a false alarm, but in going to her aid he was seriously injured when a molten slug of lead from the roof struck him on the neck. The inquest referred to by the *Times* returned the verdict, *"That there is no evidence to show how the fire originated."* A Mr Dare had been implicated when evidence was given that he had *"threatened to put the Rutland Hotel out of business in three days,"* although it was accepted by the jury that the threat was the result of an argument which had got out of hand.

However, the *Herald* was of the opinion that, judging by the behaviour of some during the fire, an inquest should be held into the quality of its citizens and the effectiveness of its fire-fighting response.

"The population of Wanganui, we are afraid, requires careful weeding out before we have nothing but orderly and well disposed citizens. Previous to the war (Taranaki War), *the loafing class hardly existed in Wanganui, but since, it has sprung up like 'flies in the summer shambles.' One would have thought the Armed Constabulary would have absorbed the stray elements.......It must have filled anyone with disgust to see strong young fellows standing idly looking on at the late fire and actually refusing to assist unless they were paid. The Captain of the Fire Brigade asked a member of the class referred to, to do some slight thing and he was met with the rejoinder, *'I want 5 shillings.' During the time the goods were being taken out of the shops that were in danger, thieving was going on wholesale and a large quantity of goods is missing. In cases of fire it is the principal duty of the police to protect property and see that when a shop is being emptied none of the light-fingered gentry are present, but only those who are well-known. The police in this respect seemed to have been very remiss at the late fire."*

The *Herald* then called for the installation of underground pipes to run through all the streets. *"The fire engine was almost useless through the inadequate supply of water, which had to be brought from the river in buckets. It was with the utmost difficulty that Major Noake could get the people to form a line, but he was, after persevering for some time, successful and a small supply of water was obtained, but not one tenth of the quantity required to be of much service."*

It is interesting to note that the premises of Messrs Allen and Blake were demolished on the orders of insurance agents who must have been on the spot and acted very quickly in an effort to minimise their companies' payouts. The loss to insurance companies totalled £4,650, a considerable sum in 1868.

The following year a meeting was called to consider the establishment of a Fire Police unit. *"There was a small attendance,"* reported the *Herald, "the people evidently caring little about the matter."* (*Herald:* 29 April, 1869). Fire Brigade captain Robinson moved, *"That a Volunteer Company be formed, to be called the Wanganui Fire Police, whose duties shall be to take charge of properties at fires."* The meeting was told that at a recent hotel fire *"a great deal of property was destroyed and made away with because there was no one to look after it, and a bill of £42 had been sent to the insurance company."* (No prizes for guessing the most popular items spirited away from a hotel fire).

The Christmas Day fire was discussed and an astonishing claim was reportedly made by an insurance agent who was present. *"He found, when the fire at the Rutland occurred, that a person was in the act of throwing a piano through the window, and a man underneath holding out his arms to catch it as it fell. The same man that was going to give such a forcible illustration of Newton's law of gravity was flinging about brass candlesticks, throwing out a pier glass and acting like a bull in a china-shop."* (Readers may draw their own conclusions as to where the men in question had spent a good part of their day). The term "temporary insanity" was used to describe such behaviour.

The meeting concluded that while strong, active men were required for the Fire Brigade, elderly men would suffice for the Fire Police. Members would be sworn in as would regular police constables and be liable to the duties of such, but would not be called upon except at fires.

The *Yeoman,* another early Wanganui newspaper, reported: *"The inhabitants of the town will be glad to know, that in the case of fire occurring, the property rescued will be under the care of trustworthy persons, and that no such wholesale plunder as that from which they had suffered before, will again be attempted."* Fire Police operated throughout New Zealand, but our local force was in the main largely ineffective, due initially to the sudden death of its first captain, a Mr Taylor, but also to a general lack of support. Looting occurred at the Red Lion fire of 1874 and at another serious Avenue fire in 1875.

"Operational Support Units", which are an integral part of today's Fire Service, have their origin in the Fire Police although one hopes that now that members of the public are not permitted to take part in the rescue of property, the prevention of looting is no longer high on their priority list.

* Payment of on-the-spot recruits became an accepted practice. The *Herald* (20 June, 1871), reporting on a meeting of the Fire Brigade states: *"The question of payment of labor at fires was brought forward by Mr Secretary Lett, who proposed the following resolution as a method by which the difficulty could be arranged. 'That a number of zinc tickets stamped with the Brigade's brand be struck off .... that these tickets be given to those men who assisted at fires and to be redeemed by the treasurer on the morning succeeding.' The idea was very favorably received by the members and unanimously carried."* There are subsequent accounts of men turning up at brigade meetings to claim their rewards.

Uninsured: The Rutland - destroyed in the Christmas Day fire

A cunning plan: the "Great Eviction" plot hatched

The 14th of July, 1869 marked a big step forward for the Wanganui Volunteer Fire Brigade. That was the day its two new fire engines were commissioned. Until then the brigade was dependent on the outdated equipment described in the previous article. The *Evening Herald* sent its reporter to capture the pomp and ceremony of the occasion: *"NAMING THE FIRE ENGINES. - Members turned out today with their engines in great force, and in their gay dress presented a very picturesque appearance. After marching through the town, preceded by the Veteran Band, they halted at the Market-place, and when a cordon of the brigade had been drawn round the engines for the ladies to stand in, Mrs D.S. Durie read a congratulatory address, and concluded by breaking a bottle of wine over the large engine, naming it the 'Star of Wanganui'. Mrs W.H. Watt then read another address, and also concluded by smashing another bottle of wine over the Californian engine, naming it the *'Comet'. At the conclusion of the addresses, Mr Robinson, as captain of the Brigade, read his thanks in his usual elegant style; and with an eloquence that would have astonished Cicero, expressed the unbounded gratification he felt at the whole of the proceedings. After three cheers for the ladies the captain, in a stentorian voice, commanded his Brigade to 'fall in line' and the proceedings terminated."*

These "engines" are probably more correctly described as "manually operated water pumps". Long wooden handles, connected to a central shaft, folded out from the engine and were manned by four men on either side. An up-and-down motion on the handles drew water from tanks, wells or from the river.

But while the brigade now owned "state-of-the-Ark" appliances, it had nowhere to house them so a Mr Keen allowed them to be stored in his Rutland Hotel Stables, an arrangement which soon proved inconvenient for both parties. For Mr Keen they took up valuable space when there was an influx of horses; for the brigade it would have been difficult to easily access the engines in an emergency. So a cunning plan was concocted involving the stable owner, the Fire Brigade and the local constabulary. Step 1: Mr Keen informs Captain Robinson that he can no longer accommodate the engines. Step 2: The captain has no choice but to park them illegally on the street. Step 3: Sergeant Reid of the Wanganui Police happens along and is obliged to issue an infringement notice charging the brigade with a breach of the Constabulary Act, requiring a court appearance for the captain. Step 4: Captain Robinson duly appears before Resident Magistrate Major Nixon charged with: *"Having left a portion of the fire engine in the street, opposite the Oddfellow's Hall."* Robinson acknowledged the charge but pleaded, *"Having been turned out of the Rutland Hotel yard, we have no place to put it and have no money to rent a shed. With the exception of Mr Beaven,"* he explained, *"no other agent of any insurance company had offered the support they ought to have done."* (*Herald:* 9 April, 1870).

The RM imposed the lowest fine possible (5s with costs of 6s 6d) declaring that he had never inflicted a fine for such a charge which seemed to him so unjust and that it was a disgrace to the town of Wanganui. The subsequent publicity eventually led to the provision of the town's first fire station, which was initially little more than a shed near the site of the Royal Wanganui Opera House. This tale appeared several times in Wanganui newspapers over the years, each time told by Lieutenant Cummins (usually during firemen's get-togethers or "smoke sessions") and each time no doubt growing longer legs with each retelling.

* Some histories have mistakenly named this machine the *Meteor.* Both the *Star of Wanganui* and the *Comet* were replaced in 1903 by a steam-driven Merryweather engine, which

possessed vastly improved fire-fighting capabilites. Curiously, the following letter from the Mayor of a Town Council in Bohemia, Austria (dated 22 February, 1905) was read to a meeting of the Wanganui Borough Council: *"Sir,- As our municipality is intending to purchase for use in the Fire Brigade a motor steam fire engine, I beg you to have the kindness so to inform me on the following: The system of your motor steam fire engine, by which firm built and at what price supplied, whether it proved efficient and successful in use, especially as regards the propulsion when mounting hills and during the winter season."* After requesting further details of a technical nature, the mayor concluded: *"With expression of thanks for answering the asked questions."*

"Precisely what prompted the above enquiry all the way from Bohemia we are unable to say," pondered the *Herald* (3 May, 1905), then published an article describing the London Fire Brigade's latest acquisition – a Merryweather Fire Engine similar to the one already possessed by the Wanganui Volunteer Fire Brigade. *"Such remote places as Wanganui (New Zealand) ....have in this matter given the greatest city in the world a lead,"* said the article, which the *Herald* crowed was *"somewhat interesting"* in that it showed Wanganui was *"up-to-date in one particular at least."*

Star of Wanganui **was sister to this machine from Dunedin**

The Red Lion burns – again!

Just after midnight – May 8, 1874. The sound everyone dreaded, especially at that time of night. The fire bell ringing from Rutland Hill, culminating in a single strike. (Ward 1 - all blocks below Ridgway Street including Taylorville, across the river). The Red Lion Hotel? Gordon's Stables? The Red Lion had been lost once before to the "Great Destroyer". Then a much smaller establishment, it had been burned to the ground about ten years previously. But it was first thought that this blaze was on the town side of the river.

"At about midnight, when even the late ones were beginning to think it was time to retire and rest, the cry of fire, the hurrying to and fro of feet, and the clang of the bell caused at once intense excitement," began the *Herald's* account the next day in its typically euphuistic style. *"From the Swamp end of the town"* (at that time about from Ingestre Street to St John's Bush), *"it appeared as if some of the buildings on Taupo Quay had caught, but happily this was not the case, as it proved to be on the other side of the river and was at first confined to Gordon's stables."*

The fire had been discovered by a groom who worked at the stables. Others soon joined him and attempts were made to contain the fire with buckets of water, but it spread so quickly that those fighting it soon realised they were facing a losing battle.

"In fact it spread with such rapidity that although Mr Gordon and his men made every effort to do so, they were unable to save six of the horses standing in the stables. It was at once seen that it would be useless to attempt to stop the progress of the fire, and that the hotel as well as the stables must go; so everyone set to work with a will, to carry out everything portable. As may be imagined, there was no organization but there was something nearly as good, viz: a good hearty rush to save to Mr Ross" (Red Lion proprietor) *"as much of his property as possible. The crowd worked as only*

volunteers in such a cause can work, some of them exposing themselves to a considerable amount of danger by remaining too long in the house after it had caught fire."

But while the rescuers came in for much praise, the Wanganui Volunteer Fire Brigade did not fare so well: *"The engine and Fire Brigade had by this time made their appearance, but unfortunately had omitted to bring their hose with them, and of course were powerless to do anything until it arrived."* (Herald: 9 May, 1874).

The *Herald* admitted that had the hose arrived with the engine there would have been no possibility of saving the hotel, as the stables were full of hay and straw, the buildings were dry and a strong wind was blowing at the time.

"When the fire was at its height it was a grand sight, and must have been seen for miles around. Standing watching it, and by its aid seeing the whole of Taupo Quay distinctively, we could not help thinking what an infinitely more serious affair it would have been if one of those buildings had caught fire instead and what a number of homeless and ruined people could be made in a few short hours, and how necessary it was to have hydrants and every other appliance for the prevention of such a catastrophe."

A second report appeared in the same (9 May, 1874) edition of the *Herald* relating the aftermath of the fire and describing hundreds of people descending on the melancholy scene: *"The crumpled iron sheets of roofing, heaps of smouldering ashes, remains of saddles and harness which were incombustible, the charred calcined carcasses of 6 horses lying in different places amid the ruins, told the tale to the spectator better than words can describe it. We noticed one poor animal the last of the twenty that were rescued, who truly had gone through a fiery ordeal. The poor beast was evidently suffering intense agony, and the mercy was questionable which permitted it to linger on in pain. The nostrils were protruded and raw, the skin in many places fearfully burnt, and the tail and mane frizzled by the intense heat. When it was rescued the bedding on the floor was alight and further exertion useless, the remainder of the trembling terrified brutes had to be left to their fate and one by one succumbed. The countenances and garments of several participators in the labours and perils of the previous night shewed plainly what danger had been incurred when doing their best to assist."*

However, not all escaped serious injury: *"We regret to hear that a gentleman named Talbot who was foremost in endeavouring to save property has suffered severely through remaining in the upper story of the burning building until the floor fell beneath him and he was with difficulty rescued from his dangerous position. He is now suffering acutely and will be an invalid for a considerable time."*

The *Taranaki Herald* (13 May, 1874) noted that, *"The telegraph wires ran close by the front of the hotel and were melted by the heat; so that communication will be temporarily interrupted."*

As has been previously mentioned the Fire Police force was not an effective unit and looting again took place. One business owner, a Mr Angus Dallas whose business escaped the flames, would not allow "rescuers" anywhere near his premises, *"as he refused to allow his multifarious stock to be removed, preferring the risk of total loss by fire to that of damage by removal and deficiency by depradation."* And a correspondent signing himself *"Fireplug"* noted that *"several persons who appeared to have been there more from curiosity than to assist in quenching the flames, seemed tolerably comfortable in the liquor department."*

At that early stage the *Herald* reported that police were insisting upon a *"strict investigation"* into the cause of the fire, which was believed to be the work of an incendiary. But as well as an official enquiry, the Fire Brigade was subjected to a very public inquiry which played out on the pages of the local papers, beginning with a letter to the *Herald* editor, (16 May, 1874).

"Sir, I have been waiting for a more able correspondent to call attention to the present position of the town of Wunganui in respect to fire. Of all the exhibitions of weakness in an organised body of

men, that on Saturday morning last was the most deplorable. The moment of the greatest importance – where were they? And when they did appear what did they bring? One half their plant! Thus losing precious time before any effort could be made. I have heard of an apology of some kind being made by their Lieutenant for their failure. But surely if a body of men take this responsibility upon themselves, we may expect them to be ready for any emergency, and if they are not, let them make room for those who would have presence of mind sufficient to know what to take, and how to take it. With livery stables at their door, the whole could have been taken by a couple of horses before the engine by itself was at the scene of the fire. When they had the hose reel, where were they? All adrift! .... Now Sir, if in a town like this we trust to such a brigade, we are of all men most foolish. .... It is certain the present brigade can do nothing. I would suggest the advisability of their resigning and a new brigade being properly organised and properly drilled. ....Trusting some effort will be made in this matter, which is of great importance to everyone and that immediately, I am, &c., Q.R."

"Q.R." referred to the Lieutenant's *"apology for the brigade's failure,"* but this was hardly an apology from Lt. Cummins. No doubt piqued by the *Herald's* claim that members had *"omitted to bring their hose with them,"* he had written to the *Chronicle* several days previously (11 May, 1874) to set the matter straight: *"Sir,- Permit me through the medium of your paper to correct a wrong impression that has gained ground with the public respecting the engine having arrived at the scene of the late fire without the hose. It is generally believed that the hose was forgot and was not missed till wanted, but this is not so. The facts of the case are these.*

The Brigade does not number more than a dozen members and when the few arrived at the engine house on the alarm of fire being given they tried to take both engine and reel to the fire, but found they were not able. (The engine weighs about 25 cwt and the hose reel with 1000 feet leather hose, 10 cwt). They then proceeded with the engine intending to return for the reel. Can the Brigade, I ask, be blamed for this? Does the fault rather not lie with the public in not supporting the Brigade in point of number?"

The Lieutenant then blasted the business community. *"These merchants and shop-keepers expect the brigade to protect their property, and grumble and cast nasty insinuations at the few who turn out and do their best risking life and limb, and get nothing but hard words and abuse for it...........We have a good plant, engine, hose, buckets, everything we require but men to work them. If we cannot get them there will be one alternative; break up the brigade and sell the engine, and then what? Let the town burn?"*

"Q.R.'s" reference to *"livery stables at their door"* indicates the means by which the fire engines were transported to a fire. An advertisement which appeared in the local press reads: *"FIRE BRIGADE. Wanted the public to know that a reward of £2 will be paid to any person who shall have two Harnessed Horses at the Engine House on the alarm of Fire being given."* (Larger centres may have had access to sufficient land to keep horses, but Wanganui certainly did not).

So how were the engines moved when horses were not available? A reply to *"Q.R.'s"* letter (*Herald:* 19 May, 1875) written by *"Old Fireman"* gives the answer: *" The following is the plant and the very lowest numbers required to haul it to a fire:- 'Star' engine: 6 men. 'New Zealand' engine: 4 men. 'Comet' engine: 2 men. Hose reel: 2 men. Ladder carriage: 4 men. Total: 18 men. It would not be too much to say that the above numbers ought to be doubled, especially considering that many of our streets are hilly, rough and sandy; and that there ought to be some half dozen extra men available as lamp bearers, messengers &c. The brigade should then consist of at least forty men .... Abusing the few men who have stuck it through good report and evil report won't make it better. Let Q.R do his share to put things on a better footing. This will best be done, first by a friendly talk, and then by a certain amount of work. Except Q.R. is willing to go in for the latter, he will not be welcomed by any."*

But leaving the matter in no doubt, a second letter from

130

Lieutenant Cummins which had appeared the previous day in the *Chronicle* (18 May, 1874) read: *"Sir, - A correspondent signing himself 'Q.R.' has addressed a letter to the Evening Herald, which requires correction to disabuse the minds of the public on several points with the Fire Brigade. The first portion of the letter, referring to the Fire Brigade having arrived at the late fire with only half the plant, I shall pass over as that has already been satisfactorily explained and I think the writer should have made himself acquainted with the facts before rushing into print. The writer says, 'with livery stables at their door ....' Is he aware that there are but two stables in town where the necessary gear for harnessing horses to the engine is to be had, and that niether [sic] of these is close to the engine station? There is a standing reward of £2 offered by the Brigade for the first pair of horses harnessed at the station on the alarm of fire, but on this occasion none arrived till some time after the alarm was given. Further on in the letter 'Q.R.' says, 'When the hose did arrive, where were they? Why, all adrift!' He concludes by suggesting the advisability of the Brigade tendering their resignation and a new brigade being properly organised and drilled. Now if Mr 'Q.R' will come to the meeting tonight at the engine house, and bring as many of his friends with him as he can to join the Brigade, the officers and members will, I have no doubt, be glad to allow him to carry his suggestion into effect. For my part my resignation is always ready when I feel it is in the interest of the Brigade to tender it. I am,&c., THE LIEUTENANT."*

Needless to say nobody with the initials "Q.R." or going by that *nom de plume* is on record as attending the meeting. And the strategy of brigade officers - and indeed whole brigades - threatening to resign *en masse* was a tactic used on more than one occasion by volunteer fire brigades throughout the country at a time when they were under-manned, under-funded and often vilified by the press and public.

The *Herald* (13 May, 1874) could not resist an opportunity to stir the pot regarding a sector of the business community that had long been seen as extracting inflated premiums for underinsured properties: *"The Insurance Companies of Wanganui, it is cruelly said of them, believe in a fire now and then as a good advertisement. Of course there is no ground for such a belief, though it may be popularly entertained – yet we cannot say that the companies have not given encouragement to the slander by their apparent indifference over the late fire at Campbelltown. People ask why were Insurance Companies not represented at the Inquest. We regret we cannot suggest even an excuse for the Companies."*

And when a critic suggested the public should not escape censure for its indifference and lack of support, the *Herald* replied sarcastically, *"It is futile to blame the 'public' for anything; this indefinite body admits no responsibility, and listens with a deaf ear to all reproach."*

But with all the criticism, grandstanding, explanations and denials the *Chronicle* called for better preparations to be put in place to combat such conflagrations, pointing out that in such seemingly favourable circumstances (the hotel was isolated and easily approached from all sides), the Fire Brigade was powerless to save it. *"But supposing the flames had first appeared in one of the stores on Taupo Quay, with the same wind blowing, what could have saved a large area of the business part of town from ruin? ....Neither carelessness nor incendiarism can be absolutely prevented, and a drunken man smoking his pipe, or a revengeful spirit nursing a wrong, may at any time cause a conflagration. As we have repeatedly pointed out, however, precaution can be taken which will reduce the risk to a minimum and if the evil arrives, will keep it within the narrowest possible bounds. Inspection of premises, a rigid night watch, the roofing of houses with non-combustible material and a well-appointed and thoroughly drilled fire brigade, would all be useful means towards this end."* (*Chronicle:* 11 May, 1874).

Two days after the fire (11 May), the *Herald* published an update on the condition of the injured man: *"We regret to hear that Mr Talbot is still suffering severely from the effects of the fiery ordeal through which he passed on Friday night. His eyes are*

132

seriously injured and his hands require to be treated for the severe burning which has temporarily disabled him. We hope soon to hear that his suffering has been relieved and that he is in a fair way to recovery."

Several notices appeared in the *Herald* after the fire. One from the Red Lion proprietor reads: *"THE FIRE. The undersigned begs to tender his sincere thanks to Captain Robinson, the Brigade, and the Public in general for the assistance rendered during the late fire at Campbelltown. GEORGE ROSS May 9, 1874."* Another was from a rather hopeful Mr G. Grahame Orbell, who offered a £1 reward for the return of a *"Gentleman's Gold Bloodstone Ring"* which he had lost at the fire.

For want of a horse ....

"Fiddler Bill" suspected of arson

Public meetings and inquiries were often held in hotels in colonial times. In the very early days there was no other option, but when public halls became available the custom persisted due to one obvious reason in particular that need not be stated here. It was no different for the inquest into the Red Lion/Gordon's Stables fire and so it was that a 17-man jury met at the Steam Packet Hotel before Mr C.H. Borlase Esq., (coroner). The following accounts come from both the *Herald* and the *Chronicle*.

The first witness, Harry Stonell (groom), stated that he was in the employ of Mr Gordon on the night of the fire. He was harnessing horses shortly before midnight with another groom. As he was leading a horse to its stall he saw a glimmer of light through the cracks in the timber wall and told his companion that there was someone in the loft with a light. He climbed a ladder to the loft to discover the straw was on fire, then ran to the water buckets which he used to try to douse the fire. When questioned about the state of the building's roof he described it as being *"in thorough repair and everywhere secure .... The only ventilation in the stables is at the back, where there is about half a board deficient. The place is always open up to the time of going to bed, except when it is raining."* A second groom, Thomas Websey, gave similar evidence but told the jury he saw a man coming round the corner of the hotel.

"He stopped when he saw me. He was rubbing his hands. His name is Bill Ellis, better known as 'Billy the Fiddler'. I could see the man quite plain. I am sure it was Ellis. He did not come to assist us at the stables. I saw him no more. Ellis was in Gordon's employ before I went there. I took his place. I took particular notice of him and pointed him out to Harry saying, 'There is Fiddler Bill. It is an unusal [sic] thing to see Ellis about so late'."

The first witness was called back and confirmed Websey's

testimony, adding that his mate had said, *"Look how unconcerned he is."* He told the jury that Ellis had been employed and discharged several times by Mr Gordon and that it was two weeks since he was last discharged.

A third witness, roadworker William Burrows, said he ran to the fire as soon as he saw flames bursting through the stable's roof. *"I met Fiddler Bill at a distance of perhaps 20 yards from the Red Lion. He was coming towards the Red Lion towards the Bridge at a brisk pace. I said, 'Halloo Bill, what's up.' I turned round and watched him go on to the Bridge."*

Sergeant Reid of the Wanganui Police then testified that he also saw Ellis: *"When I saw Ellis he had a smile on his face and was rubbing his hands. He looked as if evil disposed. Bill is not on very good terms with Mr Gordon. His presence there at that hour of the night seemed very suspicious. The fire had just burst through the building. Ellis was the first person I saw and I spoke to him because I had known him for several years."* He also testified that he had spoken to the toll-keeper, who informed him that he had retired to bed at about 20 minutes to 12, after which anyone might have crossed over without his being aware of it.

Then stable owner Mr Gordon was questioned. He confirmed the earlier evidence given by his grooms and stated that Ellis was in his employ about ten days before the fire. *"I did not see him about the place during the day of the fire. I discharged him because he was drunk. I always clothed and looked after him when in my employ. He has never shown any animosity towards me, or has he to my knowledge any reason for so doing."* He added that Ellis was wanting to be re-employed at his stables. He thought the straw may have been set on fire from outside the building as there were two gaps for ventilation. *"Any person standing on the bank could have ignited the straw."*

Harry Stonell was then re-examined and testified that he had seen Ellis once up in the loft after Mr Gordon had turned him away. *"He is a very good groom and Gordon had always taken him in. He was discharged about a fortnight previous to the fire.*

Wisby and I were leading a horse out when we saw Ellis run." Another stable owner, James Smiley, stated that he was in bed at his home on Rutland Hill when he heard the fire bell. Ellis was in his employ at the time and he knocked on his door. *"There is a side gate leading to the road. Ellis could have got through that gate at any time. Ellis answered me immediately after I knocked. He appeared to be half asleep. I told him Gordon's Stables were on fire and he said, 'What? Where?' I saw him about fifteen minutes after at the fire."*

Another groom said Ellis *"never said anything about Mr Gordon while he was in Mr Smiley's employ,"* and that he was always sober at the stables and that he didn't see Ellis until the next morning.

George Ross, Red Lion proprietor, stated that he had seen Ellis at the time of the fire and although Ellis had never made any threats towards either himself or Mr Gordon, he had once complained to police that he (Ross) was a bully.

The jury retired and after summing up all the witness statements returned the following verdict: *"The jury believe the said fire was caused by an act of incendiarism, but no evidence of the origin of the said fire doth appear to the said jury."*

William Ellis *aka* Fiddler Bill, Billy the Fiddler, Slusher Bill, Slushy Bill and Squasher Bill first came to the attention of the authorities in 1870 and appeared before the courts on numerous occasions over the following decade and a half. Charges were always of a similar nature – drunkenness, disorderly behaviour, threatening behaviour and vagrancy. On one occasion, several months after the Red Lion fire, Ellis was charged with lunacy after seeking refuge at the local police station because of fears for his own life. *"I'm frightened to go out,"* he complained to an officer. *"People are threatening to murder me."*

In September of 1874 further evidence against Ellis was considered at a second inquest into the cause of the Red Lion/Gordon's Stables fire. A Mr Talbot (draper), possibly the same man seriously injured in the fire, testified that he was quite positive that the prisoner was the man he had seen running away. Besides one of the grooms adding to his previous testimony that he had threatened to *"wring Ellis's nose off"* the evidence was much the same as that produced at the inquest. The *Chronicle* considered that the new evidence was weaker than that put forward at the original enquiry, while the *Herald* stated that it *"regrets the actions of those who came into the court with stale and exploded evidence on which to found the most serious criminal charge."*

Several witnesses who had previously been sure of their evidence were now not so certain and did not want to see Ellis *"get into it,"* as a result of their testimony. The jury decided there was insufficient evidence to establish a case and the accused was discharged.

Stable owner Mr Smiley, whose evidence largely exonerated Ellis in the first inquest, soon afterwards turned him over to the police after finding him unlawfully on his premises, (sleeping off a hangover). The final newspaper reference to Ellis was in January 1884 when he was charged with trespass, having being found sleeping in a first-class carriage at the Wanganui Railway Station.

Of course a hotel, especially one meeting the needs of thirsty colonials, did not stay out of business for long, as the *Herald* (13 May, 1874) documents: *"A temporary building is now being erected on the ground lately occupied by the Red Lion Hotel which will have to serve the purposes of a 'pub' until the new hotel is built, which we are informed will be put up with all possible despatch. Mr Gordon has taken the stables at the rear of Atkinson's Hotel, but in addition to these he intends shortly erecting large and roomy stabling somewhere near the old site. We hope he will have better luck with these and will soon recover his losses."*

Then the 20 May, 1874 edition of the *Herald* reported: *"We have seen the design of a new hotel and stables, about to be erected by Messrs Henderson and Farrah on the site of the buildings destroyed by fire at Campbelltown. The design of the hotel has been drawn by Mr Donald Ross, and appears to be one of the most complete and convenient models of a hotel we have yet seen. The front elevation is most handsome and imposing, while the sides are attractive and pretty. The internal conveniences appear perfection, every part being subordinated to convenience and comfort. The stables have been designed by Mr Farrah, and are a great advance on anything we have seen in the province. The new Red Lion will be an ornament to the town."*

This building served the community for 60 years before being demolished to make way for the fine building we have today – the fourth Red Lion Hotel.

Risen from the ashes but facing a new threat - Wanganui's 3rd Red Lion Hotel

The "Great Destroyer" strikes

"A fire broke out about four o'clock this morning in an upstairs room of part of a building occupied by Mr Thomas Anslow, draper, the other part being occupied by Mr James Bain, baker and confectioner. By the time it was discovered it had taken a firm hold, and it became evident that the building could not be saved." (Herald, 25 March, 1875).

The *Herald* reported that a light northerly was blowing at the time, but fortunately not strong enough to drive the flames before it, otherwise the ensuing destruction would have been much greater. The usual attempt to rescue stock from the shops was immediately mounted but, *"by this time the flames broke out through the window, and then spread over the whole building with appalling rapidity."*

The Fire Brigade arrived on the scene promptly, but was hampered by an inability to access for long the water contained in tanks and wells at the rear of buildings. The *Chronicle* was critical of the brigade for having sent the smaller *Comet* engine to the river and not down the narrow access ways behind at-risk buildings, which it was designed to do, *"those in charge not seeming to understand how to set about their work."* So it seems the threats made by brigade members in the aftermath of the Red Lion fire the previous year had been carried out, at least in part. *"One after another of the engines arrived on the scene in charge of amateurs, the fire brigade having been practically disbanded some weeks ago, in consequence of not receiving anything like adequate support."*

The brigade was further hampered by a low tide, making access to the river difficult, but eventually a hose was run up the Avenue only to find it *"would not reach more than half way to the scene of the wreck. The No 2 engine (Star of Wanganui) was then connected with the first and water pumped into it; but as the the plug had been removed the water escaped as fast as it was supplied, nor was the fact discovered until a considerable time was wasted, the escape of water being attributed to some defect in the hose. More time was lost in endeavouring to ascertain the whereabouts of the plug, which was at last found and fixed and the engine opened play on the drapery and other goods piled on the roadside."*

The Post & Telegraph building came under serious threat and was saved only by the heroic efforts of Post Office employees, some of whom had climbed onto the roof to put out hot spots. *"One of the operators, with commendable forethought, armed himself with blankets off his own bed, and protected the walls of the office therewith."* A telegraph operator fired off a quick message to Wellington, alerting head office of what was happening in Wanganui. The *Herald* attributed the saving of the building partly to its iron roof and partly to the nature of its paintwork, *"the coat of paint on the walls being heavily mixed with sand also resisted the heat to a greater extent than it would otherwise have done."*

The *Chronicle* had praise for rescuers: *"Large numbers of willing hands were working with energy and zeal – some in retarding the work of destruction, others in assisting to remove to a place of safety the stock and furniture of shops and dwelling-houses in the immediate vicinity. Seldom have we seen so large a body of workmen acting with such coolness and decision under circumstances of excitement as was manifested by those who were employed in the removal of the stock of endangered houses,"* although a doctor operating from one of the doomed buildings was not so fortunate, according to the *Herald: "Those who made efforts to carry out some of the bottles took too many, and the result was generally that they would drop them and thus break them. Dr Samuels has lost a very valuable collection of a varied kind which is not likely to be replaced."*

Suspicion fell on Mr Anslow, the draper in whose building the fire began when he admitted that a kerosene lantern had fallen on to a mattress. Incriminating evidence was given by witnesses at the fire and he faced intense interrogation regarding his assets, liabilities and insurance cover. However, the following report appeared in the *Herald* (7 April, 1875): *"The charge of arson against Thomas Anslow was dismissed this morning and no one, judging from the evidence produced against him, will disagree with the decision. There were circumstances which no doubt looked peculiar .... Of course everything depends on evidence and not on suspicion. Anslow will not have and does not deserve much sympathy ...... Admittedly he was the cause of the fire and if there was not arson, there seemed to have been great carelessness and apparent indifference as to results. The impression will remain that if the kerosene lamp did fall, a little exertion would have put it out, and that no exertion was used."*

What the enquiry did not know was that Thomas Anslow was behind an equally disastrous fire in suspiciously similar circumstances six years previously – in Westport on 4 December, 1869. On this occasion an overhead kerosene lamp had fallen onto two cases of kerosene which he had stored beneath it and on his own admission one of the cases had been leaking for some time, saturating the floor around it. *"The jury found that the cause of the fire was the explosion of a kerosene lamp and that it was purely accidental."* (*Westport Times*, 14 December).

Following the Wanganui fire, the *Herald* had this to say concerning the rebuild: *"We are glad to notice that those who suffered through the recent fire were not long in making a fresh start, of course, in temporary premises. Mr D.M. Hogg (butcher) was the first, having erected a tent on an open piece of ground adjoining his former premises almost as soon as the last of the shop tumbled to the ground. Since then he has erected a small shop on the site of the former which will do as a make-shift until another building can be put up. Mr John Anderson (cabinet maker) will carry on a temporary business on the premises adjoining Mr Borlase's office. He has already called for tenders for the erection of two new shops......... Mr Loftus (shoe-maker) has found temporary premises in Ridgway Street. Mr Bain (baker/confectioner) will open today, Monday, in his old business place in Campbelltown and will, we believe, proceed with a new building as soon as he can. Mr Barr (draper) has found new quarters in the shop at the corner of the Avenue and Ridgway Street, known as McNiven's. Mr Testar (tobacconist) has put up a small shop on the old site, while Dr Samuels is in the meantime making use of his private residence, to which he had fortunately removed a short time before the fire. All are doing their best under the circumstances and we have no doubt that in a short time the gap will present a very busy scene and eventually look better than it did before the conflagration."* (Herald, 29 March, 1875).

Early Wanganui Volunteer Fire Brigade members

How to extinguish a chimney fire

"Mr J.W. Robinson met with a nasty accident about eleven o'clock this (Monday) morning," recorded the *Evening Herald* (6 October, 1876). *"A chimney in the Roman Catholic Presbytery had taken fire and Mr Robinson ran over from his hotel with a loaded pistol in his hand which he intended firing up the burning chimney. On reaching the back entrance to the presbytery the pistol exploded and his left hand covering the muzzle was badly shattered. Mr Robinson fainted and was carried over to his hotel, where he was attended to by Drs Tripe, Marshall and Earle. The sufferer was immediately placed under chloroform and two of his fingers were amputated. The pistol was loaded with a blank cartridge."*

It may be thought that Captain Robinson, whose hirsute facial enhancements made him a dead ringer for the famed Buffalo Bill Cody, was merely attempting to emulate his look-alike's stirring deeds, but no. We are advised by the 1822 edition of the *Family Cyclopaedia: A Manual of Useful & Necessary Knowledge in Domestic Economy*, that *"firing a loaded gun up the chimney has sometimes dislodged the burning soot."* Unfortunately Robinson's injuries forced him to relinquish his position as captain of the Wanganui Volunteer Fire Brigade, although he took on the role of the town's Fire Inspector. He died aged 57 in 1884 after a long illness. An estimated 600 people attended his funeral, indicating the respect with which he was held by the community. His coffin, upon which rested his fireman's helmet and axe, was transported by a gun carriage drawn by ten firemen. The procession included the Garrison Band and members of several lodges and community organisations, with the fire brigade providing a guard of honour. A *Chronicle* obituary (25 January, 1884) states: *"He will be best known in Wanganui as the founder of the Fire Brigade of which he was captain for twelve years and in which he yielded undoubted public service, he took a prominent part in establishing a municipality in Wanganui, and was one of the first Borough Councillors."*

Robinson served his jeweller's apprenticeship in London and spent some of his early years in France. After exiting the jewellery business he became the proprietor of the Victoria Hotel, but retired due to the ill-health which eventually claimed his life. His obituary also states: *"He was incapacitated by an injury to the right hand from engaging in any continuous occupation,"* which sounds like the Victorian equivalent of Occupational Over-use Syndrome. Was this injury, along with his illness and the injury caused by the gunshot wound, the reason for this curious statement which also appeared in his obituary? *"He leaves behind him a widow and a large family, all of them utterly unprovided for,"* although the writer expressed confidence that the generous sympathy of his many friends would be continued to his bereaved family.

A flag pole, newly installed on the fire station's tower, performed its first function by flying a Union Jack at half mast on the day of his funeral.

****

Thomas Dick (TD) Cummins was the other larger-than-life character in the Wanganui Volunteer Fire Brigade. Born in 1846 at Port Macquarrie, New South Wales, he came to New Zealand in 1859. He was a pioneer of the flax-dressing industry and for a time was engaged in soap manufacturing. He rose to the rank of Troop Sergeant-Major during the Taranaki Wars and was a crack shot with the rifle, winning the Carbine Championship of the Colony in 1872. Another of his great shots was bagging the formidable Kereopa in the backside during the previously-mentioned unsuccessful move against Titokowaru, although his colleagues surely would have played down his prowess on that occasion with the observation that that particular part of Kereopa's anatomy was of such proportions that he could not have missed.

Cummins was the first New Zealand firefighter to be awarded the Gold Star which recognised 25 years' service, receiving it in 1891. He rose to the rank of captain in the W.V.F.B. in 1877, following the resignation of Joseph Robinson. He became the fifth president of the United Fire Brigades Association and was the first president of the United Fire Brigades Accident Assurance Society. In 1916, after 47 years' service, he was elected an honorary member of the W.V.F.B. He also served on a commission which investigated the 1918 Foster's Hotel Fire, an event which led to the establishment of a professional fire-fighting force in Wanganui.

Cummins operated a grocery business on the corner of Ridgway Street and Wicksteed Place (now Drews Avenue) where Cohen's Business Centre now stands, although he was burnt out twice - on one occasion the damage limited due to a quick response from a *Chronicle* staff member, (*Chronicle:* 4 July, 1903). But although he bore a passing resemblance to Arkwright of "Open All Hours", Cummins was not your stereo-typical white-aproned pencil-behind-the-ears grocer. As well as his military service and contribution to the fire brigade he was a Wanganui Borough Councillor, returning officer for the Electoral District of Wanganui in 1905, a judge for the 1908 Billy Webb/Dick Tresidder World Rowing Championship on the Wanganui River and overall was one of the most popular townsmen of his time.

He was writing reports for the Wanganui River Trust until the time of his death in 1920 and one of the trust's vessels was named the *"TDC"* in his honour. Following his death, tributes from the following organisations were published in the newspaper: The Wanganui Fire Brigade, Wanganui Harbour Board, Waitotara County Council, Wanganui River Trust, Wanganui Schools' Committee, Wanganui Chamber of Commerce, Wanganui Caledonian Society, Alexandra Cavalry Old Members' Association and the Agricultural Association.

He was also a past master of the Tongariro Lodge.

Joseph W. Robinson

Thomas Dick Cummins

Jumping Sheet? What's a jumping sheet?

The *"Life Safety Net"* or *"jumping sheet"* has long been the butt of firemen's jokes. Now obsolete due to advances in fire rescue techniques, its invention is attributed to Thomas Browder, an American who patented the device in 1887. However jumping sheets were in use in Wanganui nine years earlier according to the *Wanganui Herald*. On 8 July, 1878 it advised its readers that the fire brigade was canvassing the town for subscriptions towards the purchase of necessary items of equipment.

"We understand also that the brigade contemplate the purchase, as soon as funds will allow, of an affair termed a 'jumping blanket' which has often been found instrumental as a means of saving life, or at any rate, injury. This consists of a large canvas sheet, bound round with rope, by which it can be supported at some distance from the ground, and into which persons can jump from upper story windows without fear of injury."

Three months later the *Herald* announced that the item had duly arrived and on 14 November it reported on the first tryout: *"A Fire Brigade practice was held last evening at which the new Jumping Sheet was tested with the most satisfactory results. Two members of the brigade jumped from the ridging of the Rutland Hotel, a considerable height, into the sheet suspended above the payment* [sic].*"*

Soon afterwards it was incorporated into the brigade's annual competitions and *"was brought into use to rescue a fireman who had accidentally (?) been left in the bank, and also two who had been sent to the top of the Rutland parapet."* Unfortunately a training session a year later did not go so well. Brigade members had been keen for another workout with the sheet, so the captain asked for volunteers only, but with the proviso that only lightweights step forward. Four men were duly selected. They mounted the parapet of the Empire Hotel while the sheet, held by 25 men, was made ready below.

"The signal being given to the man on top, (Mr Aldridge) he jumped off, but not jumping far enough, fell close to the edge of the sheet. The strain thus came upon the men on that side only and the sheet went down. Aldridge must have kept his legs stiff, for he jarred his spine and suffered great pain. He was carried into the hotel and the Brigade surgeon was sent for....... This morning Aldridge was much better, being able to use his legs all right, but feeling very stiff and sore."

The *Herald* considered the jump to be ill-judged and that the men holding the sheet could not be blamed. Aldridge would have been better to have fallen in the middle of the sheet, it advised, *"where the strain would have been equally divided and satisfactorily met."* But even though a man on the ground was also injured the *Herald* thought that the sheet should be persevered with. *"We have heard it said that the practice is an unnecessary one, involving a risk that should not be taken. We cannot subscribe to that view, for the risk is not greater than that incurred by footballers or even cricketers."* (There is no indication that the *Herald* sought the opinion of footballers and cricketers as to whether they would rather play their sport, or trust that Newton's laws of gravity could be circumvented by a bunch of nervous volunteers grasping a flimsy canvas sheet).

And a letter to the editor pointed out that it was one thing to take part in a voluntary exercise, but asked what would happen in a real-life situation when someone overcome by smoke or *"hopelessly tight"* had to be evacuated by means of a jumping sheet. Improvements were made over the years, including the painting of a bull's-eye in the centre, aimed at concentrating the mind in an emergency situation. Jumping sheets had mixed results internationally over the years – sometimes saving lives, but sometimes causing death or injury to both jumpers and firemen. New recruits would be unlikely to find instructions on the use of jumping sheets in today's training manuals.

"Go on, jump! You can trust us."

Firefighters' competitions an old tradition

The North Island Firefighter Combat Challenge due to be held at Peat Park next Saturday is the latest in a long history of firefighting competitions. Its billing as the ultimate in sporting challenges could equally apply to 19th century events, but with competitors of those days having to contend with primitive equipment – at least by today's standards.

In 1896 the United Fire Brigades' Demonstration & Competition was held in Christchurch, with the local team given a rousing send-off by the *Wanganui Herald*, which declared: *"We hope our boys will assiduously practise and we have not the slightest doubt they will give good account of themselves."*

Members of the public were traditionally canvassed to help raise funds for the competitions and this usually occurred during the brigade's annual New Year's Eve torchlight procession, *"the Brigade starting from the station at 11 o'clock with their decorated reels and ladder carriage, and parading the streets until midnight, when they retire to their supper room to enjoy some refreshments."*

The competition itself comprised twelve events including the *"Manual Engine Competition"*, *"Hose Reel Flat Competition"*, *"Hose & Ladder Competition"*, the *"Fireman's Race"* (250 yards in full uniform) and the curiously titled *"Coupling Practice for Two Men,"* (for which an alternative name will likely be used should it be included in this month's contest). Also listed was the *"Hose & Hydrant Competition for Two Men"* which, being new to New Zealand, the *Herald* thought would create considerable interest.

"The conditions are that the men are to run 10 yards to bicycles, mount and ride 100 yards; dismount and pick up 50 ft wet canvas hose, hydrant and branch; mount and ride half a mile to the plug; dismount, fix hydrant, connect and run out hose, fix hose and, with water, strike disc 10 ft from ground. Men to be dressed in full

working uniform and may use own bicycles or those provided by the committee."

But it was the invention of a Wanganui man which sparked considerable interest prior to the competitions being held. Under the heading *"MR HARWOOD'S CLEVER INVENTION FOR TIMEKEEPING,"* the *Chronicle* (3 March, 1896) reported that *"an official trial of the electrical time-keeping apparatus invented by Mr P.G. Harwood of Wanganui, for use in Fire Brigade competitions, was held on the local Brigade's new practice ground last evening."*

The accuracy of the contrivance was tested against the conventional method of two men holding stop-watches. A team from the Brigade then held a 150 yards "hose and hydrant" practice. *"The result was a triumph for the invention, which was dubbed by all present as perfect."*

Judging from the *Chronicle's* description it was an impressive looking apparatus mounted on a 2-foot by 1-foot polished wooden base and powered by an electro-magnetic system. The *Chronicle* described the workings of the apparatus in great detail, but summarised the action as follows: *"The team being on the mark, the starter pushes over the lever. At the same instant the gong sounds and the watch starts and keeps going until both discs are blown back* (as in Hose & Hydrant competition), *when it instantly stops. The time is then taken and registered against the team, the watch put back to zero by pressing a knob, the starting lever pushed over and the discs replaced. It is then ready for the next team as soon as they like to come up to the mark."*

The device was said to accurately record times to the smallest fraction of a second, *"a feat that is practically impossible with the ordinary stopwatch."*

Mr Harwood had been working on the time-piece since 1887, when Mr Cummins had asked him whether he could devise such an instrument. But due to work commitments, *"he was unable until last year to bring the idea to a practical issue."* The *Chronicle* stated that it would be more than probable that the invention would be used at the upcoming Christchurch competitions and concluded by describing it as *"beautifully finished, both as regards the wood and the metal work, and is a credit not only to Mr Harwood's inventive genius but to his practical skill."*

In April of the same year a Grand Fete was held to raise funds for the furnishing of the new hospital and local firemen were only too happy to show off their newly-honed skills. A firemen's competition and firemen's races were held, along with a *"baby rescue"* competition. The public were assured that the brigade would present *"four of the most exciting, interesting and amusing items on the programme."*

"On yer bike!"

Rodents' rights ratified

An Australian man is likely to face animal cruelty charges after his recent decapitation of a live rat by biting off its head, while two Gisborne men were recently convicted of wilful ill-treatment of a goat – an animal often deemed to be a pest in New Zealand. By bringing the full force of the law against perpetrators of such crimes, we may consider ourselves more enlightened than previous generations when it comes to the treatment and welfare of animals – pests or not. Not so, according to an article in the 23 August 1882 edition of the *Wanganui Chronicle*.

A Mrs Margaret Smith, *"wife of a well-known storekeeper at Otaki,"* had the previous week appeared in the Otaki Police Court. The charge? Cruelty to a rat. Mrs Smith had caught the rodent in a trap, but as it was still alive was faced with the problem of how to despatch it. Her solution? Douse it with kerosene and set it alight. Her counsel argued that burning alive was *"quite as legitimate a means of destroying an animal as drowning it."* JPs Hadfield and Kebbell disagreed, convicting Mrs Smith and fining her £1 plus costs. By coincidence or otherwise, the New Zealand SPCA was established in the same year as Mrs Smith's innovative approach to pest control. And was it coincidence that saw a sudden drop in the number of animal cruelty cases in our district in 1883, just one year after the SPCA's inauguration? Although a local branch was not established for some time, Wanganui's Crime Report for 1882 listed 19 cases of animal cruelty. In 1883 there were just 6. In 1903 the organisation led the charge to ban the wearing of birds' feathers in ladies' hats. The 2 December edition of the *Wanganui Herald* drew attention to *"the increasing cruelty caused by fashion, especially in regard to birds."* SPCA officer Mr Atkinson stated that the practice of ornamenting hats with feathers had been discouraged lately in England, but he believed that the prevalence of the custom in New Zealand was due to exporters *"sending out here the feathers for which no demand exists in England, resulting in good, kind Christian people thoughtlessly offending in the matter."* The *Herald* pondered as to whether or not the society would *"put their inspector to the task of dealing with these offenders."*

Even those in high places were not immune to charges of animal cruelty, as Premier Sir William Fox would have discovered had he perused the *Wanganui Herald* (6 January, 1872). The paper accused him of *"deplorably un-Ministerial cruelty to animals,"* the alleged offence having taken place at the Marton-Rangitikei races. Sir William, well-known for his stand on teetotalism, had apparently been *"riding his hobby horse to death, by protesting against liquors being sold on the race course, notwithstanding that the Justices had given their permission!"*

Many cases of animal cruelty are documented in our early newspapers, with a large number resulting in court appearance for the offenders, indicating that when brought to their notice, the authorities generally viewed such cases seriously. But one thing is certain - over 130 years since the introduction of the SPCA in New Zealand, its officers are unlikely to ever work themselves out of a job.

Even rats have rights

Ladies' hatpins – more than just a fashion statement

"No person or passenger shall in any (tram)*car wear an unprotected hatpin so as to cause risk of injury to any other person or passenger."* (Borough of Wanganui By-Law No.1, Part XXV, {Sub-clause 878}, 1918).

Formerly used to hold veils or wimples in place, the humble hatpin suddenly leapt up the popularity stakes as a fashion accessory when ladies' bonnets, traditionally held in place with a chin-tie, went out of style. A new innovation was required to securely fasten the newly sprouted forests of head-gear which fashion now demanded, resulting in a surprising number of hatpin variations registered at patent offices worldwide.

Hatpins first appeared in Wanganui in the mid-1890s, the New Zealand Clothing Company in Victoria Avenue advertising them *"in all the latest and most fashionable shapes."* However, an unforeseen outcome of the introduction of this sartorial necessity was an alarming rise in the number of reported injuries and even deaths as these lethal weapons were unleashed upon an unwary public. A tramcar passenger in Belgium was blinded by one and awarded £400 compensation, borne equally by the tramcar company and the fashion-conscious wearer. Oregon lawmakers limited the length of hatpins to nine inches, classifying anything longer as *"an offensive weapon"*. Also in America a Mrs Gateman was applauded as *"New York's bravest woman"* when (albeit weighing in at over 12 stone), she fended off a burglar with a hatpin before despatching him out of her 6th storey apartment window to his death on the pavement below.

Unfortunately a Mrs Douglas, also armed with a hatpin, died after being attacked, although not without inflicting severe injuries to her attacker – a raging bull!

Injuries closer to home began making headlines. When the

Chronicle (29 April, 1911) reported that a Dunedin tram conductor had been blinded by a hatpin, the suggestion was made that a penny charge be made with the purchase of each hatpin as an insurance against such accidents. Some bizarre cases occurred. A lady alighting from a tram was killed instantly when she slipped and fell, driving a hatpin through her brain, while another suffered severe burns when struck by lightning, *"through the medium of a large hatpin."* The instrument of many a murder perpetrated by the "fairer sex" was a hatpin. Several suicides were attributed to its use and some accidental hatpin-inflicted injuries led to death by blood poisoning.

Increasing numbers of authorities around the world began enacting legislation limiting the length of hatpins. In Sydney (1912) over 100 women were fined 5s each plus costs for wearing protruding hatpins but many rebelled, no doubt maintaining their rights to the use of a newfound weapon of defence. It was even reported that some of those charged opted to go to gaol and if necessary begin hunger strikes rather than *"submit to iniquitous and unnecessary legislation."* Authorities were said to be facing *"a situation similar to that growing out of the suffragette demonstrations in England."* In Chicago the chief of police, frustrated by the reluctance of officers to enforce hatpin regulations, planned to avail himself of the offer of young female supporters of the regulations who had volunteered their services. *"I will call my new squad the Beauty Force,"* he declared, *"and I shall have enough help to suppress all illegal hatpins."* (*Herald*: 24 August, 1912).

It wasn't until June the following year that the problem was addressed locally. Under the heading *"The Hatpin Menace"* the *Chronicle* (18 June, 1913) reported that the secretary of the Wanganui Tramways Union had approached the Borough Council requesting that unprotected hatpins be prohibited on tramcars. *"As some of the conductors have had very narrow escapes,"* he wrote, *"we think it only fair that something should be*

156

done before a serious accident happens."

An obvious solution was to attach a protective device to the business end of the weapon and this gave rise to a further round of patent applications. These refinements also became fashion statements for the more well-to-do, and although cheaper versions were available *"for a reasonable cost at any draper's"*, many women of a lower social standing had to make do with a cork or small potato. And although men were usually on the receiving end of these fiendish devices, some of the "sterner sex" actually found them quite useful – as pipe cleaners or for piercing cigars.

Interestingly, Sub-clause 878 was only expunged from our by-laws about 20 years ago in a purge of obsolete regulations, but with the re-emergence of trams on our city streets and the fickleness of fashion which ebbs and flows like the tide, perhaps it should have remained.

(Those of a similar age to the author and older will recall forking out a hard-earned 1/9d for admisson to the cinema, only to have our vision 90% obstructed by a securely pinned hat which would remain in place for the entire duration of the "flicks"). Many years earlier the *Herald* (2 March, 1898) had spoken out about a similar situation: *"The male portion of the audience attending the Oddfellows' Hall during the present season of the Pollard Opera Co will take it as a distinct favor – not to say obligation – if lady patronesses will dispossess themselves of their bonnets or hats (especially the latter) during the time the play is in progress. Last evening, in the forest of headgear, it was almost impossible for the sterner sex to view anything going on on the stage. No doubt the ladies only require the hint to abate the inconvenience complained of."*

Apparently not, as only a few years later, this appeared in the same journal: *"An editor, who has contracted the habit of occasionally attending church, has this to say. 'Ladies should take off their hats in church. No preacher can inspire a man who is looking into a lopsided aggregation of dead birds, stuffed weasels, chameleon skins, ribbon, beads, jets, sticks, straw flowers, corn tassel and thistle down. It makes a sinner feel lost in the wilderness."*

The hatpin – a useful defensive weapon

Tentative tintinnabulatory timing trials trashed

With two of our churches turning 150 this year (2016), it's appropriate to talk church bells. A newspaper correspondent, calling himself *"Blue Bells"* (*Herald:* 24 February, 1874), suggested that Wanganui's various churches integrate their calls to worship, thereby creating *"the formation of a peal of bells, composed of the tintinnabulating instruments belonging to our various places of worship."*

The editor was doubtful, opining, *"We fear the idea is not capable of practical development. Discord would be the prevailing element of such an amalgamation."* He likened the likely diversity of tones to what horror-story writer Edgar Allan Poe must have had in mind for his celebrated composition *"The Bells,"* which begins with the melodic tinkling of sleigh bells, draws the listener into the tales their terror told and concludes with the *"moaning and the groaning of the bells"*.

"We have the deep toned fire-bell of the Scotch Church, the 'tinkling gun-barrel' of the Putiki Church, the shrill bullock bell of the Church of England and the vigorous clear alarm like that of the Catholic Church," the editor wrote. He noted the absence of Methodist bells, but excused the Weslyans on the grounds that they probably imagined that we are *"belled"* too much.

"On a still Sunday evening the fierce contests between the rival Churches in this respect, is the more audible and does not add to the harmony of the scene. But concentrated as a peal, we doubt if any improvement would be perceptible – the tones are not sufficiently mellow to harmonize. When the Weslyans are supplied, perhaps the effect may be more pleasing."

But a somewhat better tintinnabulatory outcome was achieved one day in the main street, according to the *Herald* (6 August, 1891). *"One often hears of the effect of music on animals. A case in point occurred yesterday in the Avenue, where a fractious horse was being wheedled for a long time, but with no effect until a bystander went into the Rutland Hotel and brought out the dinner-gong, which he proceeded to strike. At the first tintinnabulation the animal pricked up his ears, at the second, he stopped his gyratory movements, and the third was sufficient to put him in the humour necessary to resume his journey, much to the edification of those present and the relief of the owner."*

Synchronising Sunday's symphony

Gobblede-what?

There are some superb words in the English language, many of them wonderfully onomatopoetic. A previously unknown one, (or more correctly a derivative of an existing word brought to new life by means of a cleverly placed suffix) and which leapt from the pages of our local newspaper recently, was the little gem - *"gobbledegook-ness"*. While perhaps not onomatopoeia in its purest form, (unless it imitates a turkey's gobble) the word nevertheless conveys meaning by its sound, so we must congratulate Whanganui & Partners for not confining the term exclusively to economic development deliberations but – by way of the medium of the *Wanganui Chronicle* – for allowing its release into the public domain.

There is another word worth noting which was once loved by reporters and editors alike and scattered prolifically throughout our early newspapers, (or blab-sheets as cynical Victorians liked to dub them). The term is now rarely used and while it also may not be strictly onomatopoeic, to presume to feel it necessary to define its meaning to anyone enchanted by hearing it for the first time would be to question their intelligence. The meaning is obvious and will surely be apparent the instant you hear it. So what, you may ask, is this sublime word? It is - *"euphonious"*. Repeat after me: *"eu-phon-i-ous"*. Say it once more but slower this time, allowing its individual syllables to flow through the airways as if through the caressing valves of its brass instrument namesake, thus delighting your admiring audience. So that we may better appreciate this now superannuated literary treasure, here are a few examples from our local papers.

"The two new steamers for Mr Hatrick's fleet are the Wairua and the Waiora, both pretty and euphonious names."

"A practical joker, whose ruse backfired, remembered a number of euphonious words he had once heard a shearer use. He used these up

rapidly and wished his inventive genius had been equal to using a few more."

"Wakefield Park is to be the new and more euphonious name for the Duppa-street Recreational Ground."

"Residents of Poverty Bay have long been dissatisfied with the name of their district. There is now an organised movement afoot to have it altered to one more euphonious and less depreciative."

"Expenditure on hospital matters is assuming large proportions in Wanganui. New additions are to be made to the Plague Hospital, which by the way is to be given a more euphonious title."

And surprisingly – in recent years – Whanganui's "h" campaigners failed to uncover Mayor Hatrick's argument for the insertion of that contentious letter when in 1902 he proposed our name be revised to celebrate the coronation of Edward VII. *"Wanganui is not the name of our town,"* he argued. *"Neither is it so euphonious as its proper Maori name."*

But like many words it may also – by its context – convey a negative connotation as in the following.

"There is nothing more difficult than to get an original name, and at the same time euphonious. What a frightful name Foxton is."

"Mr Bull is quite unknown to fame, except as having conferred his own not euphonious name on a certain township of the district."

"I don't know how Mr Cross felt on reading the tirade of abuse hurled at his devoted head, where such elegant and euphonious terms as 'windbag', 'sheer ignorance' and 'wilful misrepresentation' are used."

"Although this new veterinary medicine for the treatment of horses has the very euphonious name 'Neulasthenippouskelesterizo', we recommend offering a prize of a dozen bottles to the trainer who succeeds in pronouncing the word and two dozen bottles to one who achieves the tremendous feat of writing it."

Of course those clever wordsmiths of a bygone age also knew how to phrase an article in such a manner as to insult or amuse according to one's perspective, as in this sly dig. *"Our cousins across the Tasman are reported as desiring a more euphonious name for New South Wales. They are now presented with a fortuitous opportunity with the impending arrival of the Duke of Edinburgh, and may see it named Alfredland."*

Then there was the lawyer who was defending a man on trial for murdering his wife. *"Seeking some euphonious and innocent phrase with which to describe his client's crime, he finally said, 'He winnowed her into paradise with a fence rail.'"*

And to prove the truth of the old *"there's nothing new under the sun"* proverb, here's an idea from 1876. When the subject of re-christening our land came up a correspondent suggested the name New Zealand be abolished by an Act of Parliament and the epithet *"Loan Land"* be substituted. His reason? *"It is both euphonious and suggestive."*

Wairua – a pretty and euphonious name

Euphonious name changes

The Minister for Land Information (Maurice Williamson) has responded to calls to bestow more inspiring names on our geographically-correct, but homely-sounding North and South Islands. Henceforth they may also be known as Te Ika-a-Maui and Te Waipounamu, with the likelihood of a joint name for the country itself in the near future.

Those leading the cause may believe they are on the cutting edge of 21st century thinking – or perhaps they've just been reading the *Evening Herald,* in particular the 23 October, 1869 edition which, under the heading *"A NAME FOR THE COLONY"*, proposed the following: *"Now that the country is progressing so fast, it is certainly time for the Government to devise some handy, euphonious and appropriate names for at least the islands which are its great division. New Zealand itself is not a very happy or expressive term, but it is quite monstrous that the islands should be only known still as North, Middle and South. Indeed the middle one is so often, and more properly, called the southern, for there are two great islands – the third, sometimes called Stewart's, bearing no more proportion to the others than the Isle of Man does to Great Britain and Ireland. This clumsy and confusing nomenclature ought to be amended."*

At least (unless one happens to be Irish), North, Middle and South were preferable to those foisted upon us when New Zealand was separated as a colony from New South Wales in 1840. They were then given as New Ulster, New Munster and New Leinster.

And the "h" debate, which generated so much heat and a little bit of light a few years ago is hardly new news either. A report in the *Herald* (3 December, 1876) reads: *"We have received the first number of the Church Chronicle publication for the diocese of Wellington and have much pleasure in welcoming our contemporary into the ranks of journalism. ....We may remark that it would have been better if the Maori element had been sufficiently suppressed and not to have spelt Wanganui, 'Whanganui'."*

On 17 May, 1882 a contributor grumbled at a journalistic contemporary: *"The Southern Cross spells Wanganui 'Whanganui' and persists in doing so in spite of every teacher. What I have to say is this. If it is good for the natives to learn English, it must be good for the Cross. Let it put its native lingo aside then, drop its pedantic, vile 'h' and place itself in the family of English-speaking peoples. The 'h' is hopelessly gone and cannot be restored."*

However the mood for change was in the wind and the mayor was all for inserting the 'h'. But no, we're not referring to Annette Main. It's 1902 and the mayor is Alexander Hatrick. In early August the *Feilding Star* congratulated itself with this statement: *"We are pleased to notice that the Wanganui Borough Council proposes to adopt a suggestion we made some years ago to the effect that the original Maori mode of spelling the name of the town (Whanganui) be reverted to."*

Sure enough, at the 12 August, 1902 council meeting, Mr Hatrick suggested that to mark the Coronation of His Majesty King Edward VII, an application be made *"to have the name of our town spelt correctly viz., by reinstating the letter 'h', making it 'Whanganui', in accordance with its original native name and meaning. Said the mayor, Wanganui is not the name of our town, neither is it so euphonious as its proper Maori name and had, he understood, really no meaning. Many old residents always wrote the name of our town 'Whanganui'; in fact, quite objected to the way in which it is now spelt and pronounced. The way in which some people pronounced Wanganui was, to the feelings of those who admired the pretty, soft Maori language, quite too dreadful. Further,"* he noted, *"in all correspondence and deeds connected with the Native Department, the name of the town was spelt correctly."*

He added that several other places in the colony had applied to have the spelling of their towns officially corrected in accordance with Maori pronunciation and that in order to allow time for *"consideration and controversy"* he gave notice that at the next meeting he would propose to do likewise.

A week later the *Herald* reported that the Wanganui Supply & Agency Co evidently favoured the mayor's suggestion, noting that a large sign in the process of being painted featured the name Whanganui *"blazoned forth."*

Then came a correspondent's letter calling attention to the fact that in the publication *Te Koromako*, *"which professes to give the correct orthography of Maori names,"* several mistakes had occurred. *"There is the name Wanganui,"* he pointed out, *"whereas all Maori scholars know there is no such place in the North Island, but a town and a district named Whanganui."*

Letter writers debated the matter as keenly as they did a century later, with many of the same arguments for and against and there was considerable debate over the appellation's various interpretations. One believed that to change a name which had been in place for over fifty years would cause confusion and lead to name changes of *"every person and place."*

Another wrote: *"Some years ago I was in a place spelled by the ignorant English, 'Jubbelpor'. Now they have become more intelligent by the assistance of Britishers who are not English, and the name is spelt properly, 'Jabalpur'. The ignorant English do the same here in New Zealand and this place is called 'Wanganui', whereas its proper name is 'Whanganui'. Although the mispelt name is recorded tentatively by New Zealand officials, it is only a matter of time until the correct name will be recognised, vis., 'Whanganui'."* (It should be noted, of course, that experiencing difficulties with another cultures' spelling and pronunciation is not confined only to the "ignorant English" as our rather intolerant correspondent seems to imply).

However the Wanganui Chamber of Commerce of the day had a contrary opinion. Mr Lloyd Jones argued that it was most disadvantageous to alter the name of a person or place, particularly as Wanganui had been known as such for over fifty years. He maintained the town would lose its identity and that it would take many years to accustom the outside world that Wanganui and Whanganui were the same. Another problem would be confusion over mail deliveries, as the New Zealand Postal Guide contained the names of thirteen places commencing with the prefix 'Whanga', and of those several had the affix 'nui'. Four members voted for the status quo, with two favouring the 'h'.

So when the next meeting of the town leaders was convened, Mayor Hatrick faced a largely unsympathetic council, having support only from Councillors Manson and Griffiths, but opposition from Liffiton, Bell, Perrett, Calman, Bridge, May and Horsley. The principal arguments against the proposal were that it would cause confusion and inconvenience, with no advantage to be gained. Moreover, it was argued, the name of the town had been altered from Petre to Wanganui at the express wish of the earliest settlers and their wish should be respected. It was also questionable whether it was correct to insert the 'h' anyway, with Cr Bell stating it was his understanding that "Whanga" was purely a North Cape pronunciation and few, if any, natives in this district spelled or pronounced the name with the 'h' inserted, (indicating that the proponents of the change back then also sought a change in pronunciation which would have aligned it with all the dreadful variations so favoured by newsreaders and weather presenters of today).

So the matter lay on the table, never to be considered again. (Insert *Tui* punchline here). But was the name Wanganui *"never officially gazetted"*, as was asserted by Land Information Minister Maurice Williamson when in 2009 he officially declared either spelling to be acceptable? The following is a report from the 1902 "h" debate and is reproduced in full, bearing in mind that the name change referred to was a reverting back to the original "Wanganui", from the much detested "Petre".

"That there was a doubt 50 years ago about the correct way of spelling the name of our town is evident by the wording of the Act authorising the changing of the name (from Petre to Wanganui). *It will be noticed from the following that the name of the town was spelled without the 'h', though the letter was inserted in the name of the river:-* <u>*'An Act to change the name of the town of 'Petre' to the name of Wanganui: Session 1, No 11 – 'Assented to 26th January, 1854.*</u> *Whereas the town situated on the River Wanganui in the Province of Wellington now known by the name of 'Petre' was formerly called by the name of 'Wanganui' and whereas the inhabitants of the said town are desirous that the former name thereof should be restored. Be it therefore enacted by the Superintendent of the Province of Wellington with the advice and consent of the Provincial Council thereof as follows: (1) That the said town on the river Whanganui aforesaid now called and known by the name of 'Petre' shall from and after the passing of this Act be called or styled by the name of 'Wanganui', be referred to in all official proclamations, notices or otherwise. (2) All proclamations and notices now in force and all grants and conveyances respectively refrring* [sic] *to or affecting the said town by the name of 'Petre' or any part thereof shall continue to refer to and affect the aforesaid town or any part thereof in like manner to all intents and purposes as if the name 'Wanganui' had been written or printed therein respectively instead of the name 'Petre'."* (Herald: 2 September, 1902).

Distaste of the name "Petre" was so ingrained that it was a wonder officials had pushed ahead with it in the first place. Petre has its origins in the British aristocracy. The Honourable Henry William Petre, son of Lord Petre, returned to England from its furthest colony in 1842 to *"be led to the Hymenial Altar"*, marrying Helen Walmesly. The press lauded the youthful bridegroom as *"one of the founders of New Zealand, and to which settlement he will shortly return,"* although the newspaper account of the wedding, titled *"Marriage in High*

168

Life," tactfully omitted a detailed description of the young man who was said to be *"immensely tall and thin and looks like a set of fire irons hung badly together."* It seems the name of the unfortunately-assembled fellow was as appealing to our early inhabitants as was his physical appearance. Dissatisfaction was expressed as far back as 1843, as a letter to the editor of the *New Zealand Colonist & Port Nicholson Advertiser* (7 February) reveals. Beginning with a rehashed Shakespearean quotation, *"The rose by any other name might smell as sweet"*, the writer, using the *nom de plume "A Colonist"* begins: *"Ever since the formation of British Colonies, the vanity of individuals has been most conspiciously marked in the changing of Native names of places, however beautiful, for their own, though ever so unharmonious and grating. It only gains from mankind the sneer of contempt."*

The writer made an exception in the cases of famous people who had earned the privilege of having a place named after them, then continues: *"But when we hear the names of places being attempted to be changed to please some* stripling, *merely because there is the vain hope of some mercenary end to be gained by it, every one who has the least spark* of *independence remaining, ought, most decidedly, to set his face against such nonsense and oppose it with all his might. Happily our Colony is in its infancy, and now is the time to put a stop to it."*

After ridiculing the recently bestowed name of Hutt over its former native name, *"A Colonist"* continues his diatribe. *"It is rumoured that the fine-sounding name of Wanganui is about to be* tried on *to be altered (and who could conceive it?) to that of* Petre!!! - *Splendid!"*

He then asserted that on the same basis it would not be unreasonable to call the emerging township of Manawatu by the delightful name of Snooks, *"if ever any English gentleman of such a name came out to New Zealand and promised to accomplish great things there,"* although it could be argued that Snooks is preferable to Palmy.

As for renaming our town Petre, the writer called on the departed spirits of the natives of Wanganui to rise up and condemn it, and for every landowner to eschew it.

"Who have been more played upon (and abused to boot, with the unjust epithet of grumblers)," he raged, *"than the purchasers of land at Wanganui? And are they to be pestered in this way, by having such an absurd name foisted upon the place of their earthly sojourn? Hoping that the Goddess of Vanity may never have an altar in New Zealand."*

By way of a footnote the editor of the *New Zealand Colonist* agreed with *"the impropriety of altering many of the native names of places for others of far less significance and harmony,"* but took the liberty of omitting some of the correspondent's remarks, *"considering them of too personal a nature."*

A second Wanganui correspondent, *"Criso"*, whose letter appeared in the 14 March edition of the same journal, commended *"A Colonist"* for his opinions and also criticised the New Zealand Company for foisting the name Petre on the settlers, but noting it would be of very slow adoption and that if it ever came into general use, *"an accent must crown the final vowel, for the sake of euphonizing the inapposite appellative,"* which probably means that if the town's inhabitants were forced to have the wretched name dumped upon them, then he considered the incorrect pronunciation (Pe-tree) sounded better.

Criso, while making it plain he had nothing personal against Lord Petre, questioned what he had done for the human race in general, or for Wanganui settlers in particular, to entitle him to such distinction on the map of New Zealand. He then pointed out that apart from *"a barely swarded hill in the vicinity of your town* (Wellington), *and a fern-clad knob in the centre of ours* (Wanganui)," that James Cook, so famous in this country, *"had not a clod of soil perpetuating his memory."* He proposed therefore that if an English patronymic was the fashion of the day, would not Cook's-town or Cookston be more grateful and appropriate for the town of Wanganui?

(Criso puts to bed the debate as to whether our Cooks Gardens were named after the great navigator, or from the appropriation of the area by the York Stockade cook to grow his vegetables. His letter predates the stockade by several years, as does another to the same paper (16 May, 1843, written by "K"), which also identifies the area as Cook's Gardens, thus confirming they were named after Captain Cook).

While Criso considered the new name of Petre would be of *"very slow adoption"*, some were (reluctantly) trying to get used to it. They just wanted to know how to pronounce it! The letter of a third correspondent appeared in the *New Zealand Colonist* on 14 April, 1843 and, contrary to the custom of the day, is concise enough to be reproduced in full.

"Sir,- Be good enough to satisfy the Wanganui people as to the proper pronunciation of the name of the town on the banks of the river Wanganui. Some who have breathed the atmosphere west of Bloomsbury tell us that at Almacks it is pronounced Pe-ter; *others who pride themselves on a musical ear, tell us that euphony demands* Pe-tree, *and that it would be excruciation to say else. Wishing to be correct, I asked that man of letters, the Postmaster; but Irish as he is, he says, "which you please, my dear!" My own opinion is, that it is a most inappropriate and petty name, and entitled to general disclaim. It tells us nothing; we cannot attach an idea to it; and the sooner it falls into desuetude, either by common consent, or application to authority, the better. PERCUNCTOR."*

The editor's reply, in the quaint style of the day, was as follows: *"We cannot pretend to decide the question raised by our correspondent; but we believe that the word is pronounced* Pe-ter.*"* That settled, the problem remained of getting rid of it and reverting to the name Wanganui. In May, 1844 thirty-five prominent citizens including Gilfillan, Churton, Watt and Taylor (Rev) presented a petition to the authorities requesting a name change. *"The name Petre is not appropriate, either in sound or sense,"* they wrote, *"and is likely to be productive of confusion and mistake,"* although it took ten years for the change to be finalised. (It was another five years before "Petre" disappeared as a postmark. That's how long it took for the Post Office's stamp to wear out before a miserly government would replace it). The Petre influence has not been entirely erased from our identity. Whanganui's coat of arms, presented to the city in 1955, contains two silver shells which denote a pilgrimage and were taken from the Petre family's coat of arms.The name has also been adopted by a local commercial enterprise and a couple of community organisations.

Even lesser places came under scrutiny, with early settler Henry Churton writing to the government suggesting that the name Aramoho, as given to the railway junction, was inappropriate. Aramoho, he claimed, was the name of a place further upriver. *"The native name of the place is Kaikokopu and Mr Churton proposed that it should be shortened to Kokopu. A reply has been received from Wellington to the effect that it was not intended to make any change, 'the present name being suitable, known throughout the district and not yet complained of by anyone.'* (*Herald*: 26 May, 1880). The *Herald* thought the reply curious, as Churton's letter had in fact addressed a specific complaint. *"We think Mr Churton is right. The native names, wherever they exist, ought to remain attached to places. They are more euphonious and more suitable than the imported – especially should they be given to the places with which they have been associated in the native mind. A native never thinks of Aramoho as the railway junction and he no doubt greatly wonders at the ignorance of the Pakeha."*

And so, fellow W(h)anganuians, no matter what our opinions on the naming of our islands, the 'h', the pronunciation of Petre, (which is occasionally disputed to this day), the location of Aramoho - or conversely, the correction of place names such as Atene (Athens) and Koriniti (Corinth) to their orthodox spelling and pronunciation? - perhaps we could at least unite in bringing back into general usage that beautifully onomatopoetic word which is quoted several times in the above (and previous) articles and which increasingly defines our community spirit. The word "euphonious." It's just so – well, euphonious.

His Majesty King Edward VII – named in a failed bid to insert the "h" in Wanganui

A railroad through the middle of the town?

Tramways Wanganui Trust wants to establish a tramline route around the lower part of the Central Business District, but how would residents feel about a railway line running down St Hill Street? That's what the government was planning when considering routes connecting branch lines to the main trunk. This was after a previous plan to run lines along the river-bank from Aramoho was rejected due to excessive cost.

In anticipation of a proposed visit to Wanganui by Premier Sir Julius Vogel, the *Herald* (1 March, 1876) ran this editorial: *"We believe it is intended to make strong representations to Government on the subject of bringing the railway down St. Hill Street, a line which would undoubtedly interfere with traffic to a considerable extent and prevent progress to that part of town. But the most inconvenient part of the proposal is that the traffic from the wharfs would be seriously impeded and rendered dangerous. This traffic will continue to increase, and in view of the future, a better route may easily be selected. The line which seems to possess the greatest recommendations, since it has been determined that the river bank line is too expensive to construct, is that by way of Churton Street, on the bank of the creek known by the same name. Mr Edward Churton has conclusively proved, that by a slight deviation, a great injury to the property of the Industrial School Estate might be avoided. If this line were adopted, the railway would go through the least available part of the Estate for building purposes....... The station would be in the place now proposed, but the trains would cross at Churton's Bridge and run up the foreshore into the station. We hope to see this deviation from present plans take place, the reasons for it appearing quite conclusive. The future traffic and growth of the town ought to be a primary element in forming lines for railways."*

Local opposition along the lines of the *Herald's* views was voiced to Premier Vogel when he attended a meeting of the

Wanganui Municipal Council in March 1876. But the St Hill Street option championed by the premier was seen by the government as the cheapest and Sir Julius pointed out that the council's preferred option along the beach (Taupo Quay) would involve the expense of land reclamation, which the government would not meet.

"Sir Julius Vogel said that they could not do more than contribute the railways," reported the *Herald* (16 March, 1876), *"but natural works would have to be done locally. Reclamations seem to be a most profitable work in the colony and I should advise the Corporation to consider whether it was worth their while to undertake the reclamation of the Foreshore themselves."*

However, objections to the government plans were many. They included the cost of purchasing land along St Hill Street, shifting the massive sand hill at Cooks Gardens which at the time stood in its path (along with ongoing protection works), compensation for damage to properties, fire hazards with so many nearby wooden buildings, cutting through numerous busy intersections (Ingestre/Guyton/Ridgway Streets and Taupo Quay) thus inconveniencing and endangering residents, to say nothing of the difficulty of negotiating carriages around a sharp angle to access the station which would, in any case, have to be built at the beach upon reclaimed land! All this, argued the councillors, would more than negate any savings the government was hoping to make. And, as the *Herald* had previously noted, a St Hill Street line would have to cut through the Industrial School Estate (now Collegiate), which was then sited at the foot of St John's Bush.

"Sir Julius having promised to bring the matter before the Minister for Public Works, the discussion dropt," reported the *Herald.*

But the government seemed intent on sticking to its position, prompting a letter from Mayor Watt stating: *"The Borough Council of Wanganui join with me in regretting that the Engineer does not see his way clear to comply with our views with regard to changing the route of the railway from St Hill Street."* The letter also asked for estimates of cost excesses over the government's preferred route. The reply from Vogel informed the council that the Churton route would cost £4,400 more than St Hill Street. Cr Farrah, who had originally favoured the river-bank route (estimated excess over St Hill Street - £79,000), moved that a petition be presented to the government asking that the proposed St Hill Street line be diverted to Churton Street, as the extra cost would be justified.

The petition was duly drawn up and presented, restating the objections previously voiced. *"By adopting the route known as the 'Churton Street Route' these perils, difficulties and dangers would be totally avoided, inasmuch that as Churton Street is situated at the extreme end of the town the railway crossings would therefore be nearly avoided, the danger from fire almost nil, and the damage to private property very trifling."*

The petition also declared that due to *"their intimate knowledge of both routes"* the petitioners estimated that compensation costs for the St Hill Street route would be double that of Churton.

The *Herald* lamented, *"It must be confessed that in the matter of railway construction, no district in the Colony has been treated with greater indifference than Wanganui."*

However, good sense finally prevailed and we have the persistence of our former councillors to thank that a railway doesn't run through the middle of our town.

Government's St Hill Street plans derailed

Women's (in)equality - & seriously politically incorrect statements

Today's woman may feel there is still a long way to go to achieve equal rights with men, but judging by the following selection of newspaper articles (when women were variously referred to as the weaker, fairer, gentler and sometimes the unrepresented sex) the gap has closed considerably, with perhaps the unscrewing of tight container lids one of the few remaining barriers to full equality.

"Although in the race for life everybody is willing to concede the place of honour to the ladies (especially in the Leap Year), their capacity to row a serious boating struggle seems a matter of doubt. A member of the Regatta Committee suggested there should be added to the programme a 'ladies' race' and it is painful to record that the suggestion was received with general derision. The proposer withdrew the idea and the opinion of the meeting was that a ladies' race was a fit subject for the Sports Committee, who would probably dovetail it in between a duck hunt and a greasy pole contest." (Chronicle: 24 January, 1884).

"Some of the women here would like to have a law similar to one that obtains in the United States. At Brooklyn two wives sued publicans for selling intoxicating liquor to their husbands, and receiving respectively £500 and £100. What a haul some Colonial wives would make. In Brooklyn a good drinking husband must be almost as good as a gold mine." (Herald: 28 January, 1884).

"Is a revolt impending in Methodism? A strike of the unrepresented sex would certainly be an appalling calamity, for how could there be any bazaars or tea meetings?" (Chronicle: 18 November, 1895).

"The employment of females in the Post & Telegraph offices appears to have affected a great saving, as they do the work for less money, and thus enable offices to be opened, where otherwise none could be maintained." (Herald: 19 June, 1874).

"May Wanganui never possess a 'Young Ladies' Practising Society' – at least not one like that in Sanson where 30 ladies have banded themselves together to devote an hour a day to practising the piano, under penalty of fines for neglect. A 'Young Ladies' Practising Society' to help their mothers and learn to cook would be more useful, not half so noisy, and likely to lead to better results in the matrimonial market than piano thumping!" (Herald: 3 December, 1886).

"The Scientific Review praises the invention of a new glove for ladies, which contains a purse in the palms. Good gracious! Don't these scientific writers know that women never keep money in hand?"

"There are three ways of sending a message," declared Mrs Harrison Leo. "It may be sent by telegraph, by telephone or by tell-a-woman, with the latter method the most effective."

"A statistician calculates that every man, on an average, speaks 52 volumes of octavo pages per annum, and that every woman yearly brings out 520 volumes of the same size in talk."

"Racing women become not womanly and yet they do not become rightly manly, for a manly man is a splendid thing, but a manly woman is a terror."

"Dunedin Superintendent of Gardens & Reserves, David Tannock, addressing the Wanganui community, urged mothers to supervise their children's play. 'Far better than gossiping over the back fence or gadding about town in the afternoon.'"

"By the groom, to the minister of religion officiating at his wedding when his bride baulked at agreeing to obey. 'Keep going, Reverend. It don't matter. I can make her.'"

"District Court judge to woman defendant. 'There is only one difference between a barmaid and a prostitute. One works standing up and the other makes her living lying down."

Women employees - a great saving for P&T

Early health care

Letters often appear in our newspapers from patients who are appreciative of the care they have received while in hospital. Consider then the conditions endured at the Colonial Hospital which once stood on the River Bank (now Somme Parade), near St George's gate. Built by Thomas Higgie for £383 from timber floated downriver from Kaiwhaiki, the hospital was opened early in 1851 for out-patients and admitted its first in-patient, a Maori teacher at Richard Taylor's mission station at Putiki, later that year.

But it was soon in a sorry state of repair as a report commissioned in 1867 by the Superintendent of Wellington revealed. Dodgy foundations, rotten shingles (particularly in the "Dead House"), decaying spouting, crumbling brickwork and disfunctional chimneys were just a few of the problems listed. Patients were said to be in danger of injury from plaster falling from the ceiling, caused by leaky roofs. The grounds were also in a poor state, with boundary fences and hedges requiring attention and gates needing to be rehung. Repairs were estimated at £445, more than the cost of the original building.

Nothing seems to have changed much four years later according to the *Herald* (30 August, 1871). *"The circumstances call for further reference to that weather-beaten, leaky, cold and dreary tenement, the hospital. In every ward the visitor may have a shower bath, as the rain is beating through the roof, with the wind whistling through hundreds of little crevices on the pallid faces of the patients. One poor fellow, who braved the hardships of the Crimea is on his death-bed, in a consumption which must carry him away in four or five days at the most, and the pangs of his fatal malady are aggravated in this Christian community by exposure that would ruin the constitution of a man in the vigour of perfect health. Could room not be made for the hospital patients at the Rutland Stockade?*

Can nothing be done to remedy the present state of things? ....Would it not be possible to obtain a small grant to at least repair the roof of this building for the sick? Is there no one to have any pity?"

Additions to the hospital were set to start four years later, but the *Chronicle* (4 September, 1875) had serious reservations about the design. It considered that a *"very serious blunder"* had been made and called for a re-think by the Building Committee. *"A side wing is to be added, forming a T at the west end of the present building, and the only mode of ingress to, and egress from, the new ward will be through that in which patients are at present accommodated. This arrangement will naturally give rise to cause for very serious complaint. The patients in the ward at present forming part of the western end of the original building will be liable to repeated disturbances .... which may possibly be attended with serious consequences as concerning physical effects, especially in the case of persons in a critical stage of disease ....Should a death occur in the ward about to be constructed, the corpse must be carried through the present ward and ....the shock caused by the prominent display of the surroundings of death would probably exercise a highly injurious and probably fatal tendency."*

But there was another serious deficiency in the proposed plans, according to the *Chronicle*. *"In a gaol are usually found some of the worst types of humanity, and in too many cases the same rule applies to an hospital. With this extra facility for effecting egress at will, the evil-disposed class of patients, when attaining a state of convalescence, could, if they felt so disposed, visit the public house after hours, or to absent themselves for other improper purposes, and generally adopt habits of irregularity, the obtaining of which would be attended with very prejudicial consequences."* (The *Chronicle* suggested that a wing at each end connected by a verandah would be the best solution).

The *Chronicle's* fears proved true on several occasions, including an incident of *"very unseemly behaviour"* not long afterwards. *"It would seem that some of the patients had been absent and had returned in a state of intoxication. This was especially the case with one of the female inmates, whose conduct and language were of the most violent and disgraceful character .... Her paroxysms of semi-drunken violence were so ungovernable that she had to be tied to her bed. The whole neighbourhood was alarmed by her maniacal shriekings and the obscene and disgusting epithets addressed by her to all in the building could have been heard distinctly some distance outside. Those of the male patients who were the worse for liquor, were not uproarious, and retired quietly to their beds."* (Chronicle: 31 August, 1876).

The hospital was approaching 25 years old at the time of the extensions, so what was it like ten years later? A government inspector's report gives some insight, first describing the general layout of the building which comprised seven wards accommodating 26 beds and providing care for surgical and fever patients. Gas provided the lighting, but no provison was made for heating during winter.

"The rooms have a somewhat bare and poverty stricken appearance," wrote the inspector. *"The walls and ceilings are very dirty and do not appear to have been whitewashed for many years. Straw palliasses are provided, while the mattresses and pillows appear to be filled with a coarse kind of flax. Some of the beds are very loose and hollow in the middle."*

Sanitary arrangements failed to impress the inspector, who described them as *"very defective"*. There was just one water closet, bandages and poultices were thrown into an old well situated close to the male ward and kitchen scraps and rubbish were thrown into a nearby hollow in the ground. The fee for enduring such care was 21s per week. Patients who could not afford it would work off their costs when they were judged to be well enough.

But there was at least one grateful patient, *"a gentle old Wanganui identity"* who went by the name of *"Old Fox"*. In his declining years he was found lying in a helpless state in a miserable old tumble-down *"rookery"* in St Hill Street. Some good Samaritans came to his rescue and had the dying man conveyed to the hospital where he was washed, put to bed and given some wine.

"Oh, how thankful people should be," he exclaimed, *"that such a nice comfortable place has been prepared when sickness or old age overtakes them."*

The inspector's report must have stirred the authorities into action, for improvements were made immediately, although judging from a *Chronicle* story (7 August, 1883), they seem to have been largely cosmetic.

*"ORNAMENTING THE HOSPITAL: Anyone interested in the Hospital, and every ratepayer certainly ought to be interested, will be gratified at the pleasant and cheerful appearance which the building now presents inside and out, thanks mainly to the hearty exertions and personal time and trouble expended over the matter by the Mayor (Gilbert Carson) and the Hospital Committee. Yesterday the various wards were hung with a number of carefully selected and interesting framed pictures ...... very suitable to the institution. They include prints of domestic and historical subjects, animal life and Scotch lake and mountain scenery, and their appearance on the walls of the male and female wards cannot but materially aid the convalescence of the patients. The various alterations inside the building are practically complete and the workmen are busily engaged in forming and fencing off a roomy concrete yard outside the kitchen. Mr Adcock, the Steward, has planted some spring flowers in the little garden plots right and left of the front entrance, and the approach of spring time is already visible in the trees and shrubs of the pleasant enclosure in which the Hospital stands. Mr James Laird has kindly promised some flowering shrubs and plants to adorn the centre pathway and the garden just within the main gates, and there is every prospect that the Wanganui Hospital will speedily be ornamental without, as well as useful within. It should be added that amongst the pictures which now hang on the walls are a complete set of beautifully coloured copies of *Raifaelle's cartoons,*

which were presented some time ago by an ex-patient, and have just been framed."

But the occasional spruce-up was not sufficient to keep the institution viable. In desperate need of the palliative care it so often struggled to provide its patients, the Colonial Hospital eventually succumbed to its many ills and was replaced by a new up-to-date hospital in Heads Road.

*These had been donated the previous year by a grateful Mr James Phillips *"as a small expression of gratitude for the kindness and unremitting attention bestowed on him by the doctor, custodian and attendants while he was an inpatient."* (Chronicle: 14 December, 1882). The *Chronicle* declared at the time: *"When they are properly hung in conspicious places in the wards, these brightly coloured representations of memorable Scripture incidents will gladden the heart of many a sufferer."*

Colonial Hospital

184

Health news

"The hospital returns for the month of February showed that 39 patients had been treated, 15 admitted and 18 discharged and that 22 remained under treatment on the last day of the month. The 'grog' bill showed the consumption of 70oz of whiskey and 6oz of wine for the same period."

"Miss Hope, the Matron of the Hospital, wishes us to publicly acknowledge four vases, presented to the inmates of the institution by Mrs Gregor McGregor. Gifts of this kind are very acceptable as they help to give the interior of the building a homely appearance, and when this is known we have no doubt the ladies will respond heartily with their assistance in so laudable an object."

"The Matron of the Hospital, Miss Hope, will be glad at all times to receive old linen for surgical purposes."

"We have been requested by the Hospital Authorities to acknowledge an acceptable donation of veal from, 'A Friend'."

"We are asked by the Hospital Authorities to acknowledge, with thanks, a donation of one case of Lane's Emulsion from Mr. G.W. Hean, Chemist, Victoria Avenue."

"We are requested by the Charitable Aid authorities to acknowledge a box of biscuits donated to the Jubilee Home by Mr F. de L. Robin and also a parcel of tobacco from Mr John Duncan."

"The Hospital Authorities desire to acknowledge the following donations: One case of fruit from Mr John Duncan; butter, fruit and flowers from a friend; jam from Mrs Siddle; magazines from Mrs Empsom; fruit from Mrs Duncan; Christmas cards from Mrs Basil Taylor and a lot of flowers from a number of friends."

"Mr Fred Hall of Wicksteed Place met with a nasty accident last week. A chair on which he was standing when hanging up some beef gave way beneath his weight and his hand catching upon a meathook, the ball of his thumb was fearfully lacerated. He remained hanging in this manner until one of his employees caught him in his arms and held him up, thus giving him an opportunity to jerk his hand clear. The wound, which was an ugly tear, but did not bleed

externally, was dressed by Dr Earle, and the sufferer is progressing as favorably as could be expected."

"A new story is being told of the fashionable malady, 'appendicitis'. A man was struck by a tramcar and was removed to hospital in an insensible condition. After a cursory examination a surgeon said, 'We had better operate at once for appendicitis.' The patient was stripped in order that he might be prepared for the ordeal, and this legend was found tattooed on his chest, 'In case of accident, do not operate for appendicitis. It has been removed twice already.' Then they concluded that he was only suffering from shock."

"The many friends of Mr G.S. Robertson of Upokongaro will learn with regret that he met with a serious accident while running to catch the train at Turakina yesterday morning. Upon his arrival he was met by Dr Earle, who found that his left ankle was badly sprained."

A welcome gift for hospital patients

A firebug strikes – Colonial Hospital burns

"Perish all microbes!" yelled the firebug, as he fled the burning building. Behind him flames licked around the insides of the Colonial Hospital. Crowds had gathered as they always do whenever there is a good conflagration. The Volunteer Fire Brigade was on hand, but only stood and watched as flames burst through the roof, destroying the upstairs staff living quarters and signalling the end of the institution that had served the town of Wanganui for nearly half a century – all to the accompaniment of the ecstatic cheers of an excited crowd!

Onlookers were estimated at around 4,000 and had been eagerly awaiting the second big pyrotechnic display of the day, which was Wanganui's way of celebrating the diamond jubilee and *"record reign of the noblest Queen that has ever occupied the throne of Britain,"* (*Herald:* 23 June, 1897). The hospital was by this time redundant and local authorities had been looking for ways to declare their loyalty to Queen Victoria, *"whose name will be carved high on the scroll of fame, and whose beneficent reign has never been equalled."*

According to the *Herald*, celebration plans initially called for a *"modest turn out of school children."* However Tom Cummins (former fire brigade captain) *"with his usual energy, set the ball rolling by suggesting and arranging for a pyrotechnic display,"* extending the celebrations from a modest Sunday afternoon event through to the following Wednesday. Suggestions had been thrown about in the columns of the local papers until, *"ultimately the assistance of the Volunteers, Fire Brigade, Maoris, athletic bodies, friendly societies, trades, etc., were enlisted and the proposed procession grew to great proportions."* The usual *"large and influential committee"* was set up and the big event advertised far and wide, with the result that a great influx of visitors converged on Wanganui for the occasion.

"Never before in the history of this town has it been so crowded as

at present, Wanganui just now being taxed to its utmost to find sleeping accommodation for the crowds of visitors who have come to witness the jubilee celebration. One thing is certain, however, and that is that our business people are quite equal to supplying all that every man, woman and child may require before they turn their steps homeward." (*Chronicle*: 22 June, 1897).

"During the early part of last week the population of the town gradually swelled, the late trains on Saturday bringing large numbers here from both north and south......... It is computed that fully 15,000 persons witnessed the procession in the morning, while if anything a larger number were present at the Racecourse at the pyrotechnic display," (which was a foretaste of the Monday night event described above).

The *Chronicle's* reporter asked a party of Wellington visitors why they had deserted the *"Empire City"* when they could have attended their own celebrations. *"We came to Wanganui because we had heard that it was the only place where the record reign is being properly celebrated,"* was their reply.

Meanwhile preparations for the grand parade were well in hand. Participants were reminded to be ready to march when the signal was given at 11.00am, while *"Mr Gilmour and his staff were putting the finishing touches to the beautiful triple arch in the Avenue, the Gas Company's staff were effecting the transformation of the Watt Memorial Fountain and erecting the arches at the Town Bridge; and the business people with few exceptions vieing* [sic] *with each other in the artistic and appropriate decoration of their respactive* [sic] *premises."* (*Chronicle*: 22 June, 1897). The Post Office and the NZ Insurance Company attracted special praise.

"It may be mentioned that ....the supply of Chinese lanterns and flags from every available source has been exhausted, that every stitch of bunting will be in evidence and that an unprecedented display of national colours will be shown."

Around 30 community groups and bands assembled at Market Square for the parade which marched along Taupo

Quay, up Cemetery Road for a tree planting ceremony, along Guyton Street to Victoria Avenue, then down Ridgway Street back to Market Square where the children sang the National Anthem.

Barrels of tar were placed in prominent positions on *"Durie's Hill, St John's Hill, Cook's Gardens and Queen's Park, the most effective spot being chosen in each case."* Residents who had built their own bonfires were reminded to coordinate their lightings at *"9.30 o'clock"*.

The idea of torching the hospital had not been unanimous, with those opposing the idea saying the timber should have been salvaged. *"Some people had expressed the opinion that it was a wicked waste of good timber to burn the old building down,"* but Alexander Higgie (son of the original builder Thomas Higgie), who had the honour of destroying his father's building, declared, *"They had acted on the advice of the medical staff of the Hospital Board and solely in the interests of the public health of Wanganui. The old walls were permeated with the germs of disease, and he thought that the best possible thing that could be done was to fire it."*

Mattresses impregnated with tar and other flammable materials were strewn about and stuffed under stairwells and at 7.30pm the Wanganui Fire Brigade, led by the Garrison Band, marched from the St Hill Street Fire Station to the scene of the big event. After declaring *"Perish all microbes that have ever accumulated in this institution,"* Mr Higgie applied the torch.

"Had such an occurrence happened many years ago it would have involved the person who perpetrated such an act in having to suffer the extreme penalty of the law," said the *Herald*, adding that the sentence of death would have been passed on the offender.

"It has now done its duty," proclaimed Mr Higgie of the condemned hospital. *"It has to give place to a new building – a splendid up to date institution, fitted with all the latest conveniences that man could derive – equal to anything in the colony."*

"As the flames quickly asserted their authority and increased in volume the surrounding locality was brilliantly illuminated, the faces of the assembled crowd, the trees, and all the objects animate and inanimate being distinctly visible and forming a striking scene." (*Chronicle:* 22 June, 1897).

And the band played on! Meanwhile the fire brigade ensured that nearby buildings were protected and an hour after the fire began, nothing was left standing but the chimneys. *"We are pleased to hear today that very little damage has resulted to the fine trees of nearly half a century's growth on the site,"* recorded the *Herald.*

The jubilee celebrations were summed up by Mayor James Stevenson: *"Words fail us in describing the very great pleasure we feel at the undoubted success of the demonstrations in Wanganui."*

Hospital torched in honour of Her Majesty

Truth in advertising

If businesses of yesteryear were required to adhere to the requirements of the Advertising Standards Authority, it's doubtful that many of their offerings would have made it into print. Others should have been left to the professionals to write, while those purporting to demonstrate the author's poetical aspirations should not have been written at all. Here is a selection of advertisements, ranging from the quaint to the downright dreadful, that appeared in our early newspapers.

"We are asked, 'If these New Century Soft Rubber Hair Curlers are so good, how is it that you have to advertise them?' If we didn't advertise them, people might think we had run out."

"'SWEEP' HANDBAGS! Why, the big range of ladies' handbags at sacrifice prices. They're simply flowing out at slaughter prices. Your chance is now at Young & Collins Ltd. Monster Sacrifice."

"A NEW HEAD ON YOU: If your head aches, try Stearne's Headache cure. Your head will soon feel like a new one. It's the same head, but the ache is gone."

"That poor, bedridden invalid wife, sister, mother or daughter can be made the picture of health by American Co's Hop Bitters, costing but a trifle. Will you let them suffer?"

"We are at a loss to know why people should allow themselves to be imposed upon by imitations of Wolfe's Schnapps."

"During a severe attack of Rheumatic Gout, I tried RHEUMO. All pains left me in twenty minutes after the first dose and by the following morning all swelling had disappeared. Hearing that a friend of mine was suffering from Rheumatic Gout, I went up to his place with a bottle of RHEUMO and the result was, as in my case, a

cure. I can honestly recommend RHEUMO to sufferers from Rheumatic Gout, as a cure is a certainty."

"The poor consumptive, pale and ill,
Had caught a sudden violent chill.
Distressing coughs had made him weak,
While hectic flushes tinged his cheek;
But what at last has made him strong,
When after suffering so long,
He now can damp and cold endure,
Why, Wm. E. Wood's Great Peppermint Cure."

"ROUGH ON PILES! Why suffer piles? Immediate relief and complete cure guaranteed. Ask for 'Rough on Piles'. Sure cure for itchy, protruding, bleeding or any form of piles."

"ROUGH ON CATARRH! Corrects offensive odours at once. Complete cure of worst chronic cases; also unequalled as gargle for diptheria, sore throat, foul breath."

"ROUGH ON ITCH! Cures skin tumours, eruptions, ringworm tetter, salt rheums, frosted feet, chilblains, itch, ivy poison, barber's itch."

"ROUGH ON RATS: Clears out rats, mice, roaches, flies, ants, bed-bugs, beetles, insects, skunks, jack-rabbits, sparrows, gophers and chemists and druggists." (Subsequent advertisements were amended to read, "At chemists and druggists").

"Disinfectants are good in their way. They neutralise contagion and dissipate noxious odours that invade the atmosphere. But they cannot destroy miasma, nor can they render the human frame proof against their mephitic influences. To guard against these requires internal remedies. Something that will have a repellent tendency and will so operate on the frame as to render it impervious, as it were, to those poisonous exhalations. The best internal disinfectant is

Udolpho Wolfe's Schiedam Aromatic Schnapps."

"SHARKS & SUBSTITUTIONS: The world is full of trade sharks and pirates. When any chemist or ignoramus tries to persuade you that some deleterious rubbish is 'just as good as Valaze', don't let yourself be fooled. There is none so good as the best! The best is unquestionably Valaze. (Jars 4/- and 7/- post free)."

"While in Topeka last March, E.T. Barber, a prominent newspaper man of La Cygne, Kan., was taken with cholera morbus very severely. The night clerk at the hotel where he was stopping happened to have a bottle of Chamberlain's Colic, Cholera and Diarrhoea Remedy and gave him three doses which relieved him, and he thinks saved his life. Every family should keep this remedy in their home at all times. No one can tell how soon it may be needed. It costs but a trifle and may be the means of saving much suffering and perhaps the life of some member of the family. For sale by R.M. Gatenby."

"PROSECUTE THE SWINDLERS! If when you call for American Hop Bitters, the vendor hands out anything but American Hop Bitters, refuse it and shun that vendor as you would a viper, and if he has taken your money for anything else, indict him for the fraud and sue him for damages for the swindle and we will pay you liberally for the conviction."

"To all who are suffering from the horrors and indiscretion of youth, nervous weakness, early decay, loss of manhood etc., I will send a recipe that will cure you, FREE OF CHARGE. This great remedy was discovered by a missionary in South America. Send a self-addressed envelope and 6d to prepay postage to the Reverend Joseph Inman, Station D, New York City, USA."

"WICKED FOR CLERGYMEN: I believe it to be all wrong and even wicked for clergymen or other public men to be led into giving testimonials to quack doctors or vile stuffs called medicines, but

when a really meritorious article is made up of common valuable remedies known to all, and that all physicians use and trust in daily, we should freely commend it. I therefore cheerfully and heartily commend Hop Bitters for the good they have done me and my friends, firmly believing they have no equal for family use. I will not be without them. Rev. ---"

"Oh what a shabby hat! If you are a man with a spark of respect, throw it over the bridge and get a new one for 1s at Nicholls & Co's Giant Sale."

"From early May to late September,
These are the chilly months, remember?
When coughs and colds do most prevail,
And weakened health begins to fail.
And all humanity's coughing and sneezing,
And bronchial tubes are stuffed and wheezing.
It's time to get that mixture pure -
W.E. Wood's Great Peppermint Cure!"

"A rumour has been current during the past few days that a large amount of floating capital has been withdrawn from the town. We hasten to contradict this. Not an extra penny has, to our knowledge, so disappeared. It has simply been diverted into another channel, having been paid into Nicholls & Co's banking account, the natural result of their Giant Sale!"

"A SCOLDING WOMAN! The barbarities of the ducking stool for the cure of scolding women, though abolished by law, are now often-times practised by a kind of social barbarity none the less reprehensible. Women scold only when they are ill. Instead of blaming them we should prescribe American Hop Bitters. The entire system will undergo a genial and pleasant change. The nerves will be quieted and accrbity of word and thought will give place to amiability and affection. Healthy women do not scold or fret!"

"His cough did well nigh drive him mad,
It made him thin, before so fat.
He'd act that strange, he felt so bad,
That someone said he'd got a rat;
He had more sense than people thought,
That's why his health is now secure,
He'd eighteen pence and with it bought
A bottle of Woods' Peppermint Cure."

"How many people are in their graves today who would have been alive and well if they knew the virtues of Wolfe's Schnapps?"

"For good workmanship and quick despatch in scissors and umbrellas, go to the world renowned of both Hemispheres, Tim Bethel, Taupo Quay, who sells everything but customers."

"Skill in the workshop: To do good work the mechanic must have good health. If long hours of confinement in close rooms have enfeebled his hands or dimmed his sight let him at once and before some organic trouble appears, take plenty of Dr Soule's Hop Bitters. His system will be rejuvenated, his nerves strengthened, his sight become clear and the whole constitution be built up to a higher working condition."

"THE EARTH SYSTEM:- Is now in full operation. Estimates for all kinds of the latest in proved principles of Earth Closets.
Skeleton Frontpool: To fix to any old closet. £1 5s.
Side-pull seat complete: £2 10s.
Double do do: £4 10s.
Self Action: £3.

Estimates for alteration of old closets or building new ones, at very moderate charges. Robert Palmer, from Moule's Patent Earth Closet Manufactory, London. Ridgway Street, next door to Mr T. Reid's Store."

"The people of this country have spoken. They demand by their patronage of Canadian Healing Oil that they believe it to be an article of genuine merit, adapted to the cure of Rheumatism, as well as relieves the pain of fractures and dislocations, external injuries, corns, bunions, piles and other maladies."

"In this colony, where climatic changes occur so often, a gentle stimulant like Wolfe's Schnappes is needed."

"IS MARRIAGE A FAILURE? Well, just cast your eyes down the Avenue. Perambulators coming up three abreast, and some with two passengers in each of them and every one of them is wearing a pair of Hannah & Co's 1s Boots or Shoes. The eldest girl is driving one of the 'prams', decked out in a pair of Hannah & Co's 2s 6d Kid Elastic Sides. Then, here comes 'Ma' with a pair of Hannah & Co's 3s 6d Kid Shoes on, and there is 'Pa' and the son following in the rear, one with a pair of Hannah & Co's brand new 5s 6d Bluchers and the other wearing a pair of Hannah & Co's 7s 6d School Boots. In fact, there is the whole family rigged out in Hannah & Co's Boots for a pound. So you see, if a married man spends his money judiciously, as in the above case, he need not make marriage a failure, but a decided success, and that is the humble opinion of Hannah & Co, Victoria Avenue, Wanganui."

"TO MEN ONLY: When all things were made, none were made better than Tobacco; to be a lone man's companion, a bachelor's friend, a hungry man's food and a sad man's cordial, a wakeful man's sleep, a chilly man's fire; there is no herb like it under the canopy of Heaven. So says everybody who buys their smokes at Crichton's, nearly opposite Chevannes Hotel, Avenue, Wanganui."

"Nine men out of ten now-a-days are worshippers at the shrine of the Goddess nicotine. The question is being eternally raised that smoking is injurious, and undoubtedly it is if inferior tobaccos are smoked. Every man can, without injury to himself, indulge in a pipe of the 'soothing weed' if he only sticks to such excellent articles as

the 'Queen Aromatic Tobacco' or Cameron's 'New Venus,' which brands are now becoming such firm favorites with smokers.-ADVT."

A cure for all complaints

First white child born in Wanganui

According to early Wanganui surveyor Henry C. Field (who gave his name to Fields Track and whose house on Somme Parade still stands) the first white child born in Wanganui was to Richard and Johanna Matthews, early missionaries to Wanganui. Field wrote to the *Herald* (26 May, 1906) in response to a claim made at a reunion of Wanganui Cavalry Corps veterans a couple of days previously in which a Mr Anthony Nathan was toasted as being the first white child born in Wanganui. Mr Field pointed out that Anthony Nathan may have been the first white child born to New Zealand Company settlers who arrived here in 1841, but that the Matthews had arrived much earlier and had two or three children born to them before other settlers arrived. The following is the text of Mr Field's letter.

"TO THE EDITOR. Sir,- In last evening's paper I saw a paragraph stating that Mr Anthony Nathan was the first white child born in Wanganui. This is a mistake. He was the first child born to the New Zealand Company's settlers, but a lay Evengelist of the Church Missionary Society, named Matthews, came here with his wife in 1836 or 1837, and started a mission station just where the Moutoa monument now stands, and they had two or three children born to them before the settlers arrived, the oldest of such being a girl. When the Matthews family left here in 1843 or 1844, they journeyed to Hokianga in a whaleboat, travelling by day, and camping on the beach at night. I had occasion many years ago to inquire into this subject, and my principal informant was Mr A. Nathan's mother, who had known the family well, and who spoke very highly of the courage of Mrs Matthews in coming to a place where she could have none but Maori assistance in her confinements. - I am, etc., H.C. Field. Aramoho. May 25, 1906."

Liquor trade employees live dangerously

Temperance movements were in full swing in the early days of the colony and much was said both for and against the demon drink. The following article (showing that the emergence of the ubiquitous statistician is no recent phenomenon), appeared in the *Chronicle* on 2 August, 1886. Under the title *"LONGEVITY OF THE PROFESSIONS"* it compared the death rates of males according to their respective occupations, setting them against a standard average annual mortality rate of 1,000 deaths per 64,641 males, probably the estimated white male population in the colony at that time. Published by the National Temperance League Depot using figures supplied by the Registrar General, it found that those in the liquor industry were at serious risk of a premature demise, while ministers of religion could generally look forward to a long retirement.

"Clergy and ministers	*556*
Farmers and graziers	*631*
Labourers in agricultural counties	*701*
Carpenters and joiners	*820*
Coalminers	*891*
Masons and bricklayers	*969*
Plumbers, painters and glaziers	*1202*
Brewers	*1361*
Innkeepers, publicans and beer-dealers	*1521*
Public-house and hotel servants	*2205*

"Temperance workers will do well to widely distribute this telling and effective plea," opined the *Chronicle*, *"if for no other reason than that it contains the following sentence from the Registrar-General's own pen: 'The mortality of men who are directly concerned in the liquor trade is appalling; and that this terrible mortality is attributable to drink might be safely assumed* a priori,

but the figures render it incontestable."
<u>Slogans of the Temperance Movement:</u>
   "Temperance leads to health, wealth, happiness and long life."
   "'Tis here we pledge perpetual hate, to all that can intoxicate."
   "Touch not, taste not, handle not the unclean thing."
   "We serve the tyrant Alcohol no more."
   "Prevention is better than cure."
   "To the cause of Temperance, £10; to King Alcohol, not one penny."
   "Lips that touch liquor must never touch mine."

Sure to drive any man to drink

Young people & parental responsibility

The moral standards of Victorians and Edwardians were exceedingly high. Young ladies waited until their wedding night before surrendering their virginity and their husbands, who perhaps may have sown a few wild oats in their youth, remained faithful to their wives once married. Children obeyed their parents and had respect for the law, while the local bobby whistled a jolly tune as he strolled his regular beat, gazing up wonderingly at the unusually large number of winged creatures of the porcine variety which somehow succeeded in defying the laws of gravity.

If, Dear Reader, your image of morality in the "old days" is anything like that above, then consider the following article titled *"Juvenile Depravity"*, which appeared in the 27 June, 1903 edition of the *Herald*.

"The prevalence of juvenile depravity, with all its hideous accompaniments, is one of the saddest phases of colonial life, and one of the most perplexing problems of the day. The most serious part of it is that it appears to be greatly on the increase, and this notwithstanding the disquisitions from the press, the pulpit and the Bench. Wherever juvenile immorality prevails to any extent it must have the effect of sapping the very foundations of national life; and judging from the conditions existing in the colonies, the future prospects of the race are anything but promising.

The appalling state of affairs in Victoria ...... is sufficient to make every true colonial citizen stand aghast. His Honour's experience forced him to the opinion that the class of young people growing up there was little better than savages, so far as sexual relations were concerned: the girls had neither virtue nor modesty, and the boys neither honour nor honesty, and apparently feared the laws of neither God nor man .... not only juvenile depravity but impurity in every class of society – from the street-walkers to those occupying the highest positions in the colony. New Zealand, unfortunately, is not free from the blighting curse. Only a few days ago at Wellington the Chief Justice had occasion to refer to juvenile crime, and at the Christchurch Supreme Court last month the presiding judge animadverted in a similar strain; indeed, scarcely a Supreme Court session passes without some reference from the Bench to juvenile depravity. None but those who are wilfully blind to the happenings in our towns and cities can but be convinced of the existence of a large amount of vice, and the Salvation Army Rescue Homes and similar institutions in the colony, which contain but a small percentage of the fallen, testify to the existence of an alarming extent of immorality and vice amongst young New Zealanders.

The lack of parental control and the indifference of others who have charge of young people are in a large measure responsible for this distressing state of affairs. Sir Robert Stout, who has always taken a deep interest in the improvement of our social conditions, felt so strongly on the subject that he suggested parents ought to be sent to prison, as well as their children, when the latter are not kept under proper control. It may be useless moralising about juvenile depravity, for until there is a very material alteration in the constitution of society generally the evil will go on largely unchecked, but it is outrageous that parents should exercise no sort of control over their children. Those who study the physical and moral welfare of their offspring keep a strict eye on their movements and associations, but too many parents permit their children to go when they like, where they like and how they like, with the result that they are preparing a rod not only for their own backs, but for that of the whole community .... Some years ago the Premier introduced 'The Young Person's Protection Act' into Parliament, but it had to be dropped owing to the strong opposition it encountered. Its main provision enacted that if a constable found a girl loitering in the streets or in out-of-the-way places after 10 o'clock at night, without a satisfactory explanation, he could take her to the nearest Justice of the Peace, or clergyman, or house of some married person of good repute in order to find out where the parents were, and then take her home .... Provision was also made empowering the police to arrest boys who frequented gambling dens or places of ill-repute. Parliament considered the Bill put too strong a weapon into the hands of the police, hence it was thrown out.

Juvenile depravity still goes on unchecked and parents continue to show an indifference and callousness in regards to the upbringing of their children. In such cases it seems incumbent on the State to step in ...... even though it may be in the direction of the curtailment of personal liberty, for this is no trivial affair. It affects not only the present, but future generations, and by checking the corruption in its initial stages we may prevent terrible wrong being done to posterity."

Juvenile delinquency - a perplexing problem of the day

Technological innovation

Some astonishing scientific and technological advances were made during Victorian times, a period when the pursuit of scientific knowledge became a profession in its own right. While many inventions in their original form may seem quaint and outdated by today's standards, they were groundbreaking in their time and laid the foundations for many of the modern devices and innovations we enjoy today. When Queen Victoria ascended the throne, who would have believed it would be possible to talk to someone hundreds of miles away, that music could be recorded and played back to enthralled listeners. That the newly invented steam engine would transform the world and revolutionise transport. New ideas and discoveries were coming thick and fast to a bewildered but excited populace and looking back on newspaper reports of the time it is hard to tell which were true, false, crazy, hopefully optimistic, steam punk or (unless published on April 1st) just downright fraudulent. Judge (or Google) for yourself:

COMMUNICATION REVOLUTION: *"The first message from Wanganui by electric telegraph will probably be sent on Monday (31 October, 1869) as by that time communication will be established with Wellington."*

A CAPTIVATING IDEA: *"A new device has been invented for telephone stations. It is so constructed that a person wishing to use it enters a box and on depositing a coin in the fare box a clock indexes his entrance and he is permitted to occupy the box for five minutes. At the expiration of that time he must leave the box, or, if he remains he must pay a second fare. Should he decline paying the fare he is bolted within and the machine telephones the fact to the central office. Then he must remain until released by a messenger from said office."*

AND NOW – THE TELEGASTOGRAPH:"The Saturday Review

once declared that the greatest benefactor of the human race would be he who could enable men to drink an unlimited quantity of wine without their getting drunk. Such a man has been found. Dr Bell invented the telephone, but its wonders pale before the Telegastograph. This is an electrical machine by which the palate can be tickled and pleased by any flavour and for any length of time without fear of any indigestion or of inebriety. By putting soup or fish or wine into a receptacle connected with a powerful battery, the taste of the daintiest viands can be conveyed along a telegraph wire for miles and to an unlimited number of bous vivants. *They have only to put the wire in their mouths and they seemed to be eating and drinking. They may get drunk or overfed, but the moment the contact is broken off the evil effects pass off and nothing remains but 'a delightful exhileration'. The inventor, however, keeps the* modus operandi *a perfect secret and wishes to perfect his discovery before he discloses it to the world."*

(N)ICE: "Our enterprising townsman, Mr B. Strachan, has just imported one of Fry's refrigerators, and is at the present time turning out blocks of ice in sufficient quantity to supply all the hotels and private houses in Wanganui. This is a luxury that ought to be highly appreciated here, and we feel sure the demand will be equal to Mr Strachan's anticipation."

IN CAMERA: "The camera promises to become as indispensable in business affairs as the typewriter. It is now being used in the reproduction of documents, statistical tables and other papers whose duplication by hand would be laborious and expensive. In a very brief period the camera reproduces these things with absolute correctness and with much labour saved."

TRUNK-ATED LIFE BOAT: "This life saving invention is of very considerable dimensions – six cubic feet per individual – weight about seventy pounds. It can be used to carry clothes for ordinary travelling purposes, and in case of emergency, can be instantly converted into a lifeboat, of which it has all the essential features, and it has been shown to possess an extraordinary degree of safety. Two occupants can keep themselves dry in the roughest sea and carry with them provisions for a month. The trunk occupies only half the space per individual of that of boats; and the inventor – Mr G.G. Grade – believes it is destined in a great measure to take their places as a means of saving life."

MURDER WEAPON: "The Melbourne Telegraph is informed that by the outgoing mail Dr L.L. Smith and Captain Fitzgerald, a retired military officer, have forwarded to the Imperial Government plans and drawings of a weapon they have invented, termed the 'annihilator', which is said to be capable of firing a million bullets in fifteen seconds. Armed with such weapons, our artillery alone, without police or volunteers, might possibly be a sufficient defence for the Colony, and the public will no doubt desire to know why the patent for such a murderous weapon was not eagerly seized upon by the Government."

TORPEDO PROOF: "Hudson Maxim announces an invention which, when placed around a ship, causes torpedoes to explode harmlessly. It is applicable cheaply to existing ships."

REMEDY FOR SEA SICKNESS: "We understand that Mr Bessemer's plan for obviating sea sickness, by means of an oscillating chamber, supported on bearings similar to those of a compass, will shortly be put to a practical test. A chamber of this description is now in course of construction."

CONFERENCE CALLING: "Yesterday while two gentlemen were conversing through the medium of the telephone, two others were also heard employed in like manner. One of the former pair, recognising the voice of one of the latter, immediately commenced an animated conversation with him, to the amusement of the other two. It appears therefore to be possible for four persons at different terminations to talk to one another, although not directly connected to the Telephone Exchange."

CONVENIENT: "The Borough Council is evidently determined that the Opera House shall be up-to-date. Last evening it was decided to have the building connected by telephone; an innovation which will no doubt add to the convenience of the building."

NOT SO CONVENIENT: "We are requested to state that tickets for the Opera House cannot be booked by telephone. This rule will be strictly adhered to at the box office."

Strictly NO telephone bookings!

The New Zealand death

A press report from 1912 records that there were 1737 deaths from drowning in New Zealand over the previous ten years – an average of over 170 each year (out of a population a fraction of what it is today), prompting the Royal Life Saving Society to stress the importance of teaching school children how to swim and how to save lives. At the society's AGM it was proposed that a deputation approach the Minister for Education to urge that swimming and lifesaving be made compulsory subjects in State schools. The move was well overdue as newspapers for decades had chronicled the sad and seemingly never-ending lists of people who had met their deaths by drowning. In the early days of the colony, partly due to the scarcity of bridges in New Zealand, it was inevitable that many settlers' lives would be lost while fording dangerous rivers, especially considering the heavy clothing worn and particularly the totally unsuitable and voluminous garb of the women. Even today drowning rates are unacceptably high, with twice the number of drownings per head of population than that of Australia. So high was the mortality rate in colonial days that drowning was known as "the New Zealand Death" (sometimes the New Zealand Disease). A cursory search of the Papers Past website throws up hundreds of articles entitled *"Drowning", "Bathing Fatality," "Drowned While Bathing," "Boat Capsize," "Body Recovered"* etc. The first European missionary to die in New Zealand lost his life by drowning. He was the Reverend John Mason, who came to Wanganui around 1840 with his wife but was swept away one day while crossing the swollen Turakina River mouth. His body was recovered and buried at Putiki near to the church he had established six months previously. Reports of Mason's demise appeared several weeks later in both the *Nelson Examiner* and the *New Zealand Colonist & Port*

Nicholson Advertiser which described heroic, but futile, efforts by Rev. Octavious Hadfield to rescue his companion. The party had been forced, due to shifting sands, to cross at a point where there was deep water. Rev. Mason, *"wishing if possible to avoid getting wet, knelt on his saddle, and when in the middle of the stream unfortunately lost his balance and fell into the water."* (It was later found that the horse he was riding had a bad habit of violently throwing back its head when stressed, possibly knocking Mason unconscious). Rev. Hadfield had already reached the shore, but when he realised what had happened he dismounted and swam to his friend's assistance, supporting him in the water for a time. *"After a long and fruitless endeavour to regain the shore, and finding his own strength failing, Mr Hadfield was compelled to relinquish his hold and leave his friend to a watery grave. His body was found the next day washed on shore at some distance."*

The danger faced by early settlers is again shown in an article which appeared in the 1 August, 1883 edition of the *Herald,* under the heading *"Narrow Escape."* Doctor Hooper of Marton was on his way to the home of Major Willis to see a patient but to save time, decided to cross the Tutaenui River at a particularly dangerous spot. *"It certainly proved to be so, for the horse got out of its depth, turned over, and getting free from its rider, left him struggling in about 14 feet of water. Swimming was out of the question, as the weather being stormy, the doctor was dressed in long, tight boots, a mackintosh and a heavy wrapper twice folded around his neck. After sinking several times, to use the doctor's own words, he thought 'all was over', when the force of the fresh carried him down to a bend in the river where the water shallowed, and he was enabled after strenuous exertion to reach the bank."*

Dr Hooper finally reached the Willis homestead, where for a time the carer became the patient, receiving *"the greatest kindness and attention,"* and suffering no long term effects from what was nearly an untimely end.

But why did New Zealanders continue to succumb to the New Zealand death as the colony developed, river crossings were built and transport improved? A look at the attitudes concerning bathing protocols and what was considered appropriate bathing apparel may uncover some contributing factors.

In 1886 three young lads were apprehended early one morning for bathing in the Wanganui River without trunks. A sympathetic *Chronicle* correspondent thought the police must have been hard up for something to do, *"straining at a gnat and swallowing a camel,"* to be ferreting out cases of indecent exposure when no-one was around, when they could arrest any number of men between 10.00am and midday on Sunday, *"when there are more females travelling up and down the river bank than at any other time of the week."* (Perhaps the ladies were interested in much more than a Sunday constitutional).

But as the letter writer pointed out, *"It is not in the act of bathing that we are guilty of exposure, but in dressing and undressing."* He advocated the provision of suitable dressing sheds placed at intervals along the river bank to replace the ones below Market Square which in his opinion were not fit for use, filthy and a disgrace to the town.

Another correspondent called the editor's attention to the practice of some to bath in the river on Sundays, *"just at the time that those who live down the river are passing to church."* The editor sympathised replying: *"This is a most indelicate proceeding and is without excuse, as during the summer months it is quite within the range of possibility to finish ablutions before half past ten o'clock."*

A letter to the *Chronicle* in the summer of 1889 implored male bathers at Castlecliff to take the trouble to move up the beach before undressing. *"Today,"* wrote an upset local, *"a resident deliberately undressed a few yards away from the ladies' bathing shed and not content with that, swam along in front of the bathers."*

210

Our Taranaki neighbours also agonised over the matter as evidenced by a letter to the *Taranaki Herald* in 1894: *"Sir.- Some years ago the Borough Council approved of the following division of the day for bathing purposes – males, up to 9 o'clock in the morning and after 4 o'clock in the afternoon, and the intervening hours between 9am and 4pm for females. As the hours allotted to ladies are less convenient than those allotted to men, it is hoped that the police authorities will take care that the ladies are not molested or inconvenienced.......... I would add that a person has no more right to bathe within view of a street or public place without a suitable bathing costume, than he has to take a walk in the streets without decent covering. I am, Ex-Councillor."*

The provision of "bathing machines" was once discussed by our local authorities. These contrivances, popular in England and Europe, were mobile bathing sheds which enabled a modest lady to be wheeled in and out of the surf (fully togged up in great swathes of suitable swim-wear, of course) or perhaps not, in a manner that shielded her from public view. Water would fill the machine when it was pushed into the brine and drain out when it was wheeled back to the shore. The *Herald* (1 February, 1886) suggested their provision would be a great asset for our popular Castlecliff seaside resort and a good business opportunity for some local entrepreneur.

"There is a chance for some enterprising man to make a good thing out of the love of sea bathing, so widely held by those who visit the Heads during the present warm weather. A few bathing machines would pay well during the summer months, and the enterprising person who starts one or two will soon reap a golden harvest from the letting of them."

Several reports of bathing machines being constructed were published over the years but nothing much seems to have come of the idea. The council itself considered it, but the practicalities (requiring the presence of brawny men or horses to wheel them in and out of the surf), soon saw councillors calling for the next item on the agenda.

Public attitudes appear to have been evolving, however, for in 1914 the *Chronicle* cites the experience of our cousins across the Tasman regarding indications of change with an article titled, *"Should Men and Women Bathe Together?"* With summer at its height the Australian papers were fiercely discussing the vexed question of mixed bathing, drawing on the wisdom of Lord Mayors, Archbishops, Canons, the Commissioner of Police, a lady doctor, ambassadors from various consulates and – the famous surf champion Mr "Snowy" Baker. The majority were in favour, *"within reasonable limits."* The Lord Mayor of Melbourne was of the opinion that, *"the sea is quite big enough for both men and women to swim in, provided bathers do not overstep the boundaries of moderation."* His Sydney counterpart endorsed the practice of surf bathing but *"condemned the too lax oversight of certain beaches where indiscriminate bathing is indulged in."*

The Lord Mayors' fears of boundaries being overstepped were well-founded, according to a story reported in the New Zealand press at about the same time, when a saucy young Auckland miss announced her intention of going for a swim and asked: *"Could someone hold up a handkerchief for me while I get changed?"*

In 1891 a proposal to build public baths at Market Place surfaced in the local press, the plan being to pump water from the Wanganui River by steam power. The total cost of the project was expected to be approximately £800. Eventually the Central Baths were built further upriver at about the site of the former hospital. But an article in the 8 March, 1915 edition of the *Chronicle,* while its wording may these days be considered seriously politically incorrect, indicated the continuing shift in public attitudes.

"Mixed bathing at Marton has hitherto been tabooed, but in future the sexes are to have the pleasure of each others company in the water twice a week. A meeting of the Committee of the Marton Swimming Club was held last night when the whole question was

thoroughly gone in to. Pros and cons were discussed and it seemed to be the general opinion that the ladies would never learn to swim properly without the assistance of the stronger sex."

The outcome? Mixed bathing was permitted on Wednesdays and Saturdays between 2.00pm and 4, public decency was preserved and hopefully the drowning rate, at least among the "weaker sex" would be reduced.

The other change that improved a struggling bather's chances of survival in an aquatic emergency was the switch - albeit very gradual - to more suitable swimsuits (although our aforementioned Archbishops, Lord Mayors, lady doctor and famous surf champion {perhaps} would be aghast at what can be seen on our beaches today). An article in the local press in 1915 advised female sea-bathers first of all to take with them their own bathing costumes, thus avoiding the cost of hire.

"Serge, galatea, alpaca, well-shrunk flannel and stout cottons are the fabric for bathing dresses," advised the writer, who suggested the one-piece was preferable. (The modern reader, however, should not for a moment imagine there was anything like the option of the skimpy two-pieces which are so common today, the existence of which would surely not have entered the mind of your average well-bred Victorian or Edwardian young lady).

"Dark blue serge, trimmed with white braid, always look well for a bathing dress," continued our fashion writer. *"Black serge is also very suitable for water wear, and striped red or white or blue and white galateas mingle well with darker costumes, white alpaca and flannel materials are really very pretty. The two-piece tunic bathing dress may be cut round, square or pointed at the neck and finished with a sailor collar, or simply bordered with braid."*

The article concluded with advice on further trimmings, buttons and button-holes and advice on knickers constructed of the same materials. Children's bathing suits were smaller versions of the above. Men were required to wear neck-to-knee bathing suits (another of our bylaws which has only recently been rescinded) with extra trunks or a built-in "modesty skirt" so as not to offend. (No net or flesh-coloured fabrics allowed for men or women).

And so modern transport, bridges over rivers, shrugging off our inhibitions and eventually shedding voluminous bathing costumes have all played their part in reducing the horrendous toll of "the New Zealand Death".

But it's still far too high!

Bathing machines protected a lady's modesty

More colonial capers

"Jurymen need not be under any alarming apprehensions as to an enforced abstinence when fulfilling their responsible duties in this position. In future they are not to be debarred of their accustomed libation, but, at the expense of the Sheriff, the necessary stimulants are to be handed round, to comfort the weary and thirsty arbitrators and assist them in their vigilant, discreet and impartial deliberations."

"Not far from our office, last night, might have been heard some choice colloquial phrases which issued from an individual who gave free reign to a very abusive tongue, the epithets used being of a choice description. We hear that the matter will form the subject of enquiry before the R.M. Court."

"On Monday morning Edward MacCartney, aged 18 years, was taken from his work and lodged in the civil gaol by order of the Officer commanding the Militia in this district. This morning at 11 o'clock MacCartney was taken from the gaol to the militia office where he was sentenced by Lt. Colonel Gorton to four days' imprisonment and to have his hair cropped close."

"The gaol is invested with more terror for the impecunious and shiftless than ever. The dietary scale is altered and tea is not found on the bill of fare, so that herein is an additional inducement for people to endeavour to pay their way. The commissariat for the hard labor men is on a more liberal scale than prevailed formerly, but then it must be remembered that those who do not work are not permitted to eat, except dry bread; cold water being the beverage."

"The booming of great guns last night had the effect of raising Wanganui from its slumbers and sending some of the female portion of the inhabitants to the stockade and the male to the Militia Office, and in such haste that several arrived without their rifles."

"Last night, about 11 o'clock, the residents near St John's Bush were much alarmed at hearing a party of mounted men coming down the hill shouting and yelling. Not unnaturally, considering the intelligence received yesterday, and being awoke from sleep, the

inhabitants thought that Tito Kowaru had arrived at last and while one rushed to warn the soldiers, others made themselves as safe as possible. Ludicrous as this may seem, we can hardly condemn too strongly the perpetrators of this cruel practical joke and would be glad to see the culprits punished. It might have happened that some of the families of the settlers were ill, and in such a case the consequences might have been fatal."

"BREAD FALLEN: Not in price though; that feature maintains its apparently permanent standard. But on Saturday, as a bread cart was proceeding along Ridgway Street, the doors flew open and the staff of life was scattered broadcast on the roadway. Finally the conveyance was stopped and the loaves collected by the assistance of some passer-by and returned to the cart."

"The Otago Guardian considers the New Zealand Times to be most degraded and despicable."

"Some persons made extensive preparations in anticipation of the projected cutting off of the water supply. One gentleman in particular caused every utensil, from the filter to the bath, to be filled; but an earthquake disturbed all his calculations. A tidal wave was caused in the bath which did considerable damage to the ceiling of the room underneath."

"The Greytown paper declines any longer to chronicle buggy accidents, because doing so casts a reflection on the sobriety of the drivers."

"Australian and Tasmanian opossums are henceforth to be deemed game in the colony."

"A lady used some 'Rough On Rats' in place of spice for a pudding. The pudding was bitter and could not be eaten – was given to the pig – pig died – lady did not, but was very ill for a time."

"A woman who took proceedings against her husband on account of domestic troubles, made some pointed remarks at the Magistrate's Court yesterday. She said money was no good without love and expressed the opinion that the war was a good place for bad husbands. She finally said she had made one blunder in her life – getting married!"

"We are requested to mention that at Mr Ballance's meeting

tonight the dress circle will be especially reserved for ladies. Gentlemen who accompany ladies will be admitted to the circle with them, but on the understanding that should their seats be required to accommodate ladies, they will take the back of the gallery."

"We are glad to learn that Sylvester Vincent, who was fined £50 for being concerned in the late distillery case, has had his fine remitted in accordance with the recommendation of the Resident Magistrate."

"The new Railway Station on Taupo Quay is rapidly approaching completion and the Department should (under ordinary circumstances) be in a position to open it in about a month's time. Useful and fairly commodious as the building will be, and great improvement as it is over the old station, the general effect is disappointing and some people will even consider it paltry and unworthy of the town. One thing is certain – a glance at the plans of the new station, and then on the station itself, will convince everybody of the difference between a thing on paper and the reality. One thing is urgently needed – a verandah over the platform, and it is surprising that the architect of the Public Works Department should have neglected such an obviously useful portion of the Railway Station."

"A correspondent, who is evidently a recent arrival, writes to us pointing out the inconvenience caused by there being no clock at our railway station. He says that besides its principal use, railway clocks are generally used to verify watches by, and that those coming here from towns possessing stations that are not clockless, when finding themselves near our terminus repair thither for the purpose mentioned, only to be disappointed. We hope soon to see our station possessed of a good clock conspiciously placed."

"We are informed that a shark 14 feet long was seen between the Railway Bridge and Aramoho on Saturday evening."

"The News Letter states that there is something wrong in the mail service between Masterton and Wanganui. It cannot pretend to say where the fault lies, but asserts that two letters, posted at different times, took eight days to reach Wanganui."

"We have heard the wish several times expressed by the habitues

that the town library and reading room possessed arrangements for quenching the natural physical thirst of visitors as well as their thirst for knowledge. In similar institutions in other towns there is generally a large filter and several glasses placed in some convenient position where those who need may help themselves to a drink of water. If our local institute were similarly provided it would no doubt be largely availed of and might prevent a visit to the adjacent taverns. The water would help down the dry reading to be found in the building, to say nothing of its effect on the dust accumulated in the throats of visitors while getting there."

"A reward of £10 is offered by the Government for information that will lead to the conviction of the person who dropped lighted matches into the Post Office receiving box at Mr Ball's store, corner of Bell Street and River Bank Road on or about the 11th April last."

"When the good folks of the Church of England went yesterday to church, they found staring them in the face a hideous board having the gratifying announcement that poisoned wheat was laid on the premises. We find on enquiry that this cheerful kind of food was intended, not for the congregation, nor for rats and rabbits, but for a neighbour's chickens who make sad inroads into the churchyard. Those unlucky roosters will have either to avoid the premises or take a scientific analyst around with their next excursion into ecclesiastical territory."

"There were two marriages yesterday and we would not mind if there were two every day of every week in the year. There would then be fewer grumpy croaking bachelors and disconsolate maidens, trade would be brisk and the schools multiplied."

"English housekeepers are complaining because their servants are leaving them to go to the colonies. They say that England offers no matrimonial opportunities. Evidently the woman who considers marriage as an end worth striving for is not yet extinct."

"Letters are lying at this office (Chronicle) addressed to 'C', 'H.T.', 'Willing', 'E.A.', 'Romeo', 'Rooms' and 'O'.

"Lionel Brandon was charged with allowing a vehicle to stand in Ridgway Street unattended and without a chain tied to the wheel. Defendant was fined 10s."

218

"*Yesterday a monkey escaped on the racecourse and an animated chase ensued, in the course of which poor Jacko suffered considerable damage.*"

"*Some mean person is in the habit of removing copies of the Chronicle from houses in the Avenue. We give him warning this morning that should detection ensue, proceedings will be taken against him in the Police Court.*"

"*Either owing to a want of gumption on the part of the compositors or our own 'bad copy' – or perhaps both combined – two or three extraordinary blunders occurred in yesterday's leading article, which completely spoiled the sense.*"

"*At a regatta the other day the whaleboat that was comfortably expected to be first only came in a bad third, though her crew was most decidedly the best of those competing. Subsequent to the race the mystery was explained. Some ingenious gentleman had nailed a kerosene tin to the bottom of the boat.*"

"*Peebles, the great spiritualistic preacher and insufferable humbug, is on his way to New Zealand.*"

"*When the colony was being ransacked for a hangman to despatch Woodgate, two worthies, residents of Wanganui, proffered their services and enquired the probable rate of remuneration for the services required to be rendered. We were not before aware that we possessed talent of such a high order in our community.*"

"*William Gatley, the hangman, is about to have the knot tied, which is to unite him in marriage.*"

"*At the Auckland Police Court last week a good deal of amusement was caused by a constable producing a sixpenny toy revolver which he had drawn on a recent occasion to intimidate a man who was inciting a prisoner to resist.*"

<u>On the death of Queen Victoria:</u> "*On Wednesday last a Stratford businessman draped the front of his shop with crape. During the night some miscreant stole the drapings. This is the meanest theft we have heard of for some time.*"

"*Amongst the different business places in town draped in mourning, the decoration in purple and black at the Economic are particularly noticeable for the artistic manner of arrangement and the general effect produced."*

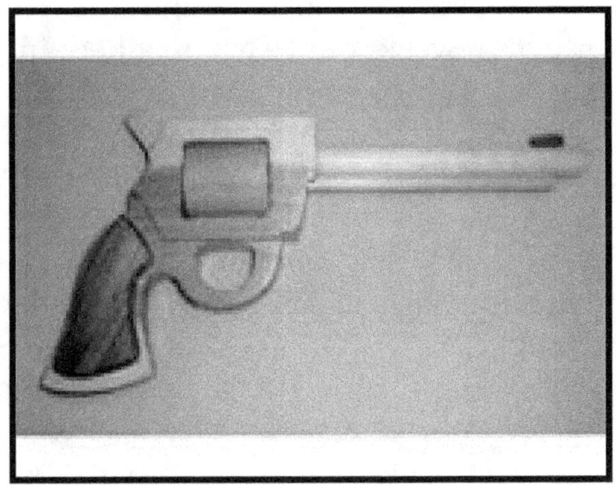

Police issue revolver - circa 1902

220

Eschew obfuscation

The reader will by now have realised that many journalistic writers of yesteryear appear to have written their commentaries in such an obfuscated manner that they would have trumped any tactful physician's attempt at trying to explain a patient's fatal prognosis, without revealing he was unlikely to see the week out. This resulted in newspaper readers of the day being conditioned to having their news couched in such round-about terms that seem absurdly quaint to the reader of today. Perhaps the reason lies partly in the fact that access to news was not as easy as it is today and a plethora of logorrhoea was a useful way of filling up the pages. The following article appeared in the 29 July, 1876 edition of the *Chronicle*.

"NOCTURNAL PROWLERS: Wanganui appears to be infested with a few free-booters, whose particular weakness is – firewood. Long and loud have been the complaints to which we have listened from all quarters, respecting the infringements of the rights of property in this particular, and dire have been the threats used that the guilty ones should yet have their reward in this life. But so far, the unfortunate sufferers have been compelled to grin and bear it, and the thieves, full of the confidence which is begotten of success, have now turned to higher game and have inaugurated a wholesale business in connection with the coal and firewood yards. Messrs Cross Bros. of Wilson Street have suffered so considerably from the depredation of these midnight robbers, that they are determined to use every possible means for their detection and punishment, a result in which it is to be hoped they will be successful, as it will conduce materially to the benefit of others similarly circumstanced."

A journalist of today would simply write: *"Thieves have been stealing firewood from private properties and commercial yards around Wanganui, with Cross Brothers in Wilson Street particularly hard hit. Police are investigating."*

Another example comes from the *Chronicle's* court reporter: "*This disease* (kleptomania) *seems, however, to be infectious and yesterday a candidate for jail honours presented himself as a representative of the perpetrators of this class of depradation.*"

And this, the opening sentence reporting two funerals: "*Yesterday there were two mournful ceremonies conducted with the giving of dust to dust and ashes to ashes,*" while the melodic capabilities of some entertainers were described as follows: "*The vocal powers of several were called into requisition, till midnight put an end to the social gathering.*"

An article calling for a more efficient system of collecting hand-me-downs for distressed families was worded thus: "*The intentions of the ladies are of a most laudable nature and we trust to see their expectation of beneficial results accruing most abundantly realised.*"

And this report of an accident which occurred during an eclipse of the moon: "*A local MD ran foul of a lamp post during the darkness which ensued, the crimson current staining his patriarchal beard.*"

The *Herald* editor had some advice for photographer W.J. Harding. On being shown Harding's new pictures of the courthouse and Post Office, he suggests eliminating moving figures from the images: "*We do not know that this is Mr Harding's fault, as from the kind of camera he uses, time is essential to produce the impression; and time is fatal to fidelity when it is sufficiently prolonged to make the personal subject feel at all irksome.*"

The following is the correction of a previous day's story, in which Fireman Cummins had been commended for "*effecting the connection with Ridgway Street on the occasion of the late fire.*" The *Chronicle* pointed out that it was in fact Lieut. Turnbull and Fireman Shaw who, "*acting on their own responsibility, accomplished successfully that somewhat difficult undertaking. Afterwards, Fireman Cummins by his judicious manipulation of the branch, assisted materially to quench the flames, and to his instrumentality in a great measure may the subjugation of the conflagration be attributed."*

The *Chronicle* documented the sale of a local business in the following manner: *"Mr Villers of Ridgway Street, having determined upon a lengthened visit to the Old Country, has disposed of his old established tobacconist business to Mr T.W. Ferry, in whose hands it should lose none of its extensive connections which has gathered round it during the presidency of its erstwhile popular proprietor."*

This also from the *Chronicle*: *"Mr Clapcott's lecture tonight* (on insurance) *will, we feel sure, be numerously attended, as the interesting nature of the subject to be handled, and the well-known ability of the lecturer will, combined, secure the attainment of the former consummation."*

But when it comes to truly dedicated obfuscation, this little gem from the *Chronicle*, entitled *"POLICEMAN X"* must surely rank above all others: *"A new addition to our local force was very solicitous in his enquiries which, on Friday, he addressed to several residents, as to had they been to the fire. He was loud in his reflection upon the unskilled hand by which the tintinnabulator was manipulated. Our friend is almost oppressively communicative."* (Which probably means that a newly appointed, loud-mouthed police officer was highly critical of the way the fire bell was rung).

The laughing policeman and other constabulary tales

"It is said, 'A policeman's life is not a happy one,' but this is not true with respect to the constable who upholds the majesty of the law in the thriving little township of Marton. He really appears to be one of the happiest men in the place. On a rainy day he comes forth with an umbrella, he is quite familiar with the small boys and calls them by their names, pats them on the head with paternal tenderness. It is said he even lifts his hat to his lady friends and talks to strangers with a familiarity which is quite novel. Indeed he is the happiest fellow out."

"The Marton policeman sets down the number of thieves in that township as four. How such a small place can possibly support four thieves is a mystery."

"A constable has arrived to take Spry's place. His name is Warren and he has been for some time in the force in London. This, however, is no guarantee of efficiency, as we have seen policemen in the colony who have been years in the force in large towns in England, and yet their intelligence was of no more exalted order than would scarcely qualify them for the position of the driver of an ass in a pug mill. We understand that Constable Warren's credentials are satisfactory, as he has the credit of being an active, intelligent and efficient officer."

"At the Police Court yesterday William Keys was charged with not keeping a light over certain material exposed for sale in the Avenue. Constable Browne gave evidence that no light was burning from 12.30 to 5am when he went off duty. (Fined 10s. Costs 5s)."

"The police should interfere to stop the reprehensible practice of boys wearing masks in the streets. There are some timid people who are liable to be much frightened at such unseemly sights."

"It is a pity a law cannot be passed to empower the police to spank every youngster who is seen with a cigar in his mouth."

"Joseph Ryan, a boy about 12 years of age, for damaging a fence was fined 40s with 1s damages and 9s costs. In default of payment 7 days imprisonment. His Worship said he was sorry he could not order the boy to be flogged, as that would be a more suitable

punishment."

"*One of our local 'bobbies' must have had his wits tried, equally with his patience, the other day, whilst endeavouring to take an intoxicated new arrival of the weaker sex (we use the word in an accommodating sense only) to the lock-up, there to have her very questionable ideas concerning the malformation of our side-walks corrected. He assayed to take her the orthodox way, but finding that she did not know the road, and was just as unwilling to be shown, a wheelbarrow was obtained to facilitate her removal. Her legal guardian had not proceeded but a few steps, when the occupant was suddenly precipitated on the ground, through the boards of the vehicle yielding to the vast weight of sin. The barrow mended, our indefatigable officer of justice again started; but alas! His hopes were again frustrated by the wheel leaving its proper position and also succumbing. But he was not to be beaten, so, with the courage of desperation, seizing in his manly arms the unhappy woman, he landed her high and dry in the dock, there to remain for 48 hours.*"

St John's Hill – a nursery for ciminals?

We don't normally regard St Johns Hill as being a hotbed of illegal activity, but at least one hilltop resident thought differently. His letter to the editor appeared in the 7 December, 1907 edition of the *Herald*.

"*Sir,- I trust the mild agitation for police protection for St John's district will have your further assistance. It is badly needed. Foul language, drunkenness and larrikinism are appallingly prevalent and only require the presence of a strong, tactful officer for their suppression. Other and more serious offences are being committed, and evidence will be communicated to the department direct, when certain proof has been obtained. Motor racing is a matter of daily or, I should say, hourly occurrence, and such minor offences as riding bikes or horses on footpaths are scarcely worth mentioning. I have a great respect for the members of the local police force and in no way reflect on their efficiency, but they cannot be in two places at once, and their efforts for the preservation of law and order in the town area are likely to be sadly hampered by the lawless state of the upper end of Wanganui which may easily become a nursery for criminals, and a safe retreat for the conier, (swindler) burglar or illicit distiller, three professions which are admirably catered for by the absence of any residential constable. Thanking you in anticipation, I am, etc., UPPER END."*

Is this what appalled UPPER END about Wanganui's high society?

9/11 – a dark day for Wanganui

September 11 will forever be remembered for the 2001 terrorist attack on the World Trade Centre in New York, but in 1877 it was a day which brought shock and deep sorrow to the township of Wanganui.

This year (2017), 9/11 marks the 140th anniversary of the sinking of the *Avalanche* in the English Channel after a collision with the Nova Scotian vessel the *Forest*. From the two vessels more than 100 passengers and crew lost their lives, including 21 who were returning to, or had connections with, Wanganui.

Such a loss to the community, comparing per head of population then and now, would be roughly equivalent to an Airbus A380, carrying mostly Whanganui passengers, going down with few survivors.

News began filtering home soon after the collision and it was not long before the extent of the tragedy became clear. The *Wanganui Herald* (14 September), reported that all passengers on board the *Avalanche* had perished, although three crewmen had been saved: *"We would that we could hold out any hope, but the facts are against the possibility."*

The next day's *Chronicle* brought a further mournful message. *"It has been suggested, as showing public feeling in the matter of the Avalanche disaster, that so soon as it is known to what extent Wanganui suffers in the general bereavement, that the town go into mourning by putting up the shutters of the shops, hoisting flags half-mast and that the bell of St Paul's be tolled at intervals. Today will be a gloomy one for Wanganui."*

The writer of a separate article in the same edition could not refrain from the euphuistic style typical of the day by recording: *"The Avalanche, a well-appointed passenger ship, has met with her doom – been stricken down beneath the hungry waves, ere her voyage was well commenced – and of her human freight of ninety-nine souls, but three remain to tell the story of her destruction. Stricken relatives of the lost will scarce yet have realised the full measure of their grief, or felt that intensity of crushing sorrow which gradually steals o'er the heart and expels every vestige of earthly light and gladness from the soul. There will have been many a sleepless couch last night; aye, and many a tear-stained pillow. Those who parted in hopeful anticipation of a speedy reunion are now separated until the sea gives up its dead. Parents are mourning the loss of idolised children; brothers and sisters will see their loved ones no more; widowed hearts refuse consolation, and the cry of the bereaved goes up to heaven. Wanganui, it is much to be feared, has been a special sufferer, and universal sympathy will be with the afflicted, upon whose sorrow none may intrude, and whose poignant griefs are beyond human consolation. The passengers were principally returning colonists; but we must remain in suspense, which to some will be prolonged agony, awaiting the receipt of the full passenger list."*

The writer offered a slim cause for hope by reminding readers of cases where fortuitous changes of travel plans had resulted in lives spared, but concluded, *"We do not wish to unduly buoy up the expectations of anxious friends and relatives, to whom authentic intelligence may confirm the worst and change their hope to despair."*

Although there were one or two happy endings it was good counsel, in light of what later became clear. Saturday evening, usually a busy night in town, was more crowded than usual. Anxious groups discussed the tragedy and awaited further news which was eventually telegraphed from Wellington, prompting the *Herald* to issue an "extra", confirming the fears of all. Monday's papers carried fuller accounts of the disaster in columns edged in black and naming many of the victims, eight of whom came from one family, six from another and four from a third.

"Suspense is now no more and we have before us in harrowing detail the mournful intelligence ..... Wanganui has suffered a

bereavement, in the foundering of the Avalanche, compared to which all previous social calamities fall into insignificance." (*Chronicle:* 17 September).

Epitaphs were installed on family graves in the Heads Road Cemetery, but the most significant local memorial was established in the name of Margaret Watt, daughter of Mayor William H. Watt, albeit many years later. The Margaret Watt Orphans' Home was opened in 1931, later becoming the Margaret Watt Children's Home. Changing government requirements eventually rendered it unable to operate under the original stipulations of Watt's will and the building is now a private dwelling. However, the Margaret Watt Children's Trust Inc continues to award scholarships and make grants, enabling children to enhance their educational and career opportunities.

A second memorial stands just a short distance from the central city. Originally installed outside St Paul's Church in Victoria Avenue, it was transferred to its present site at St Paul's in Guyton Street when the new church was consecrated in 1913. Not only does it immortalise Margaret Watt, but also Annie Taylor, who was a fellow passenger. Annie was the daughter of Watt's business partner T.B. Taylor, who himself is memorialised having also been drowned several years earlier.

A third memorial is the central triptych window in St Mary's Church at Upokongaro which was installed in 1879 in memory of Archibald Montgomerie, who lost his life in the Avalanche disaster. Another permanent reminder is the Avalanche Memorial Church which stands at Portland, England. Consecrated in 1879, it honours both the victims and local fishermen who rescued the few survivors.

The Avalanche

Stop me if you've heard this one

Adult humour in colonial times, at least that considered suitable for polite company, appears to have been about on a par with that foisted by eager children on to their grandparents, or at best the (alleged) jokes that are found inside Christmas crackers. Here is a selection of the very best Victorian and Edwardian adult humour, presented by our local newspapers to their subscribers - although any reader who skips this chapter will be forgiven.

Q: Why should a conceited person not patronise the skating rink?
A: Because it will make him more bump-*tious!*

Q: Why is Wanganui the most religious and apostolic town in New Zealand?
A: Because it has St John's Hotel, drink is served by Parsons, groceries provided by Stephen's(son), clothing by Peter and Paul, hardware by Abel (A. Bell), boots by Hannah and the peace is kept by James.

Q: Why do the swallows build in my chimney?
A: Because they have a tendency to my-grate *(migrate).*

Q: Why are a gentleman's love letters liable to go astray?
A: Because they are generally Miss-directed.

Q: Why is the letter "g" like a peacock?
A: Because it is nothing without its tail ("g" with no tail is a nought. Geddit?)

Q: Can anything that is baleful be a blessing?
A: Yes. A bale of cotton.

Q: *What marine excresence can be likened to a man who lives idly on his friends?*
A: *A sponge.*

Q: *Why is a field of turnips like a tailor's bill?*
A: *Because it's hoed (owed) a long while before it gets spade (gets paid).*

Q: *Why does a man with his sweetheart on a wet day look brighter than on any other occasion?*
A: *Because he has all the appearance of a rainbow (rain beau).*

When a young gentleman kisses a young lady, she very naturally says, "Oh Dick, the idea!" And he, also naturally, replies, "No love, not the eye dear, but the cheek *dear!"*

No matter how excellent the streets of Paris are, those who travel in them are sure to rue *it.*

****

And so, dear reader, because by now you will be rolling about helpless with laughter, I shall conclude this riotous little interlude with what was judged to be one of the best ever puns made by (American poet) Phoebe Cary and served up by the *Herald.*

Q: *Why was Robinson Crusoe's man like a rooster?*
A: *Because he scratched for himself and Crusoe (crew so).*

Local inventor wins international awards

Wanganui hasn't been short of inventors over the years, with all sorts of useful devices originating from the River City. Thomas Ellis, of Primrose Farm, Goat Valley, may not be a household name today, but he was a prolific inventor in his time. His most notable achievement appears to have been his "Patent Improved Cross-Acting Butter Churn", which was a marked improvement on previous churns and which won him recognition on both sides of the Tasman.

The *Herald* (25 June, 1879) reported that Mr Ellis was sending to the Sydney Exhibition a churn of his own invention and manufacture, claiming that it was superior to anything then in use. *"The churn will make from 5 to 45 pounds of butter, and produce ten per cent more butter of better quality than any other, as all the milk is taken out. There is less wear and tear than with other churns, great cleanliness, moderate cost, and a child can do the work. Mrs Ellis has had one of these machines in use for several years and it is now as good as ever. A model may be seen at the Bank of New Zealand."*

Several days later the *Herald* expanded on its original report, going into great detail as to how Mr Ellis's innovation worked and listing its various internal parts including a screw propeller which had *"the same action on the cream as the screw propeller has in the water .... in these colonies an effective churn is a desideratum, and we trust that the verdict of the Judges of the Exhibition will be of such a nature as will warrant Mr Ellis making arrangements for the manufacture of his churn."* The judges considered the churn, *"Very well made and designed"* and awarded its maker a *"Second degree award of merit."* Mr Ellis was well placed in the Sydney Exhibition two years later and in 1885 the *Evening Post* noted that his churn produced 6% more butter that any other and that its unique internal cross-action made it self-cleaning. *"The machine is constructed of native wood (kauri) and is so adapted that any part can be replaced when required."* Manufactured by Wanganui sash and door company York & Cornfoot, it sold for £4 and was available at all local ironmongers and from various agencies around the country.

Mr Ellis also patented a candle extinguisher. The *Chronicle* (30 November, 1889) described it as a clever piece of mechanism. *"The extinguisher is placed on a candle, and when a certain amount has been burnt down, by the aid of a spring, it puts the light out. It can be adjusted so as to allow the candle to burn for any time, and although sleep may have overtaken the occupants of the room, the extinguisher will do its duty and put the lights out of its own accord."*

The *Herald* also noted that Mr Ellis had figured in other types of exhibitions before with some credit. *"We were shown by him a bronze medal from the London Exhibition of 1862, the article for which the medal was awarded being a lady's cotton-stand, made of New Zealand woods."*

The Thomas Ellis patent improved cross-acting butter churn

Ejamakashun standids

Who says education standards are slipping? Judging by this schoolboy essay written in 1918, they have always been questionable: *"A cow. I have got one already name called Daisy; every morning when I stand up she is ready for to be milked. She is kind to her family and to us always. When she wants milk for her family she jumps the fence and we don't get some that day. Next day we milk her to the factory. She is a red cow amd test 4.6 with white spots and long horne and tail and a brindle calf name called Monica and is for sail for two pound when she don't want enny more milk. Keeping a lot of cows is called derrying and if we keep too many we have to pay inkum tax."*

The above, however, is not all that remarkable if the following story which appeared in the *Chronicle* (30 May, 1883) is an example of teaching at the time. It referred to *"the extraordinary way in which some of the school teachers in the district impart tuition to the youthful mind."* School inspector Mr Foulis was giving a report to the Education Board about a Feilding teacher. *"He said that when visiting an important school in the Manawatu he saw the female teacher add up 246 and 606 on the blackboard, by commencing the addition at the left-hand figures instead of the right. The result was that the surprising total of 8,412 was offered to the scholars as the correct solution. The same ingenious mistress (who is the holder of a government certificate) also multiplied figures by starting at the left hand, the result, as in the case of the simple addition, being so startling to the horrified inspector that he felt it his duty to inform the board how the State school system was being administered in the district."*

When her novel form of arithmetic was questioned by Mr Foulis, the teacher replied that she had never noticed there were mistakes and that it was the plan taught to her in the South Island.

"That is evidently the locality in which talents such as hers would

be more profitably employed," opined the *Chronicle*.

A charge of incompetency was brought against the teacher by Inspector Foulis. After sending a delegation to the school in question the Education Board concluded that such a damaging charge should not have been made without further investigation. *"We understand that the committee, after investigating the circumstances on the spot, are fully satisfied with Mrs Brown's general ability as a teacher, but consider that her method of teaching arithmetic is rather calculated to perplex and confuse young children."* (*Chronicle:* 28 July, 1883).

Mr Foulis's own competency came into question when he applied to the Education Board for an increase in salary, referring to his *"honorous"* duties. *"Weakness in spelling is a serious fault in a schoolmaster,"* decreed the *Chronicle*, although a correspondent wrote to the paper in Mr Foulis's defence. The inspector also managed to get himself offside with a number of teachers, although the Board chairman ruled that, *"With regard to certain little grievances which some of the teachers thought they had against the Inspector, he believed these would all be dissipated when the teachers and Mr Foulis became better acquainted,"* noting that no specific charge had been made. A board member observed that *"the charges were mainly made by those who were hardly qualified to pass an opinion upon the merits of his work."* Another member declared, *"There was one thing about which there could be no mistake and that was that the Inspector's whole heart and soul was in his work."* Another said that one of the most specific charges brought against him was *"that the gentleman was a Scotchman and the children could not understand him, but they should not heed such frivolous complaints as these."*

Later that year the *Chronicle* (11 August, 1883) reported on a special meeting of the Education Board, *"to consider irregularities attending the scholarships examination, and if necessary, to appoint fresh examiners and hold a fresh examination. We understand that the parents of some of the candidates have raised objections to the form and nature of several of the questions."* (Hmmm, sound familiar)?

****

Still on the education theme, here are a few anecdotes which open a window into the highs and lows of teaching, although nothing of which precedes or follows should be seen as a definitive treatise on the standard of colonial education in New Zealand.

"It is much to be regretted that education should be at such a very low ebb in this town. This remark is called forth by the fact that out of about twenty boys who have been working at our office, we have not been able to find one sufficiently educated to be able to read correctly or write legibly." (Herald).

"THE TRUANT INSPECTOR: Mr Henry Wagstaff, the newly appointed Truant Inspector, began his duties on the 1st of May, and seems to be going to work in the highways and byways of Wanganui very energetically. In the performance of his duties he finds it necessary to perform a house to house visitation, and, as he possesses what the ladies call 'an insinuating way with him,' and, in his thirst for information has no objection to kiss the baby and make himself generally agreeable, he should have a good harvest of truants to report to the School Committee."

"The inspector considered that a boy, eight years of age, who had been at school for two years and could not pass the first standard, an 'unsatisfactory pupil'. There were about 300 of these. He further stated that 1500 children had not passed any standard at all."

"Mr Toomath said the board ought to see for itself from Miss Vernon's conversation that she would not prove a suitable schoolmistress. Her Irish brogue was against her. Mr Lee said he had spoken to several school mistresses about employing Miss Vernon in their schools and he was met with the same objection. Besides, parents would object to having their children taught by a person whose pronunciation was so peculiar."

"I find," wrote a school inspector, *"that only a few of the children know that the British Isles, so often shown them on the*

map, were the places from which, generally speaking, their father and mother came from. Of Queen Victoria, knowledge was very indefinite. Of the Prince of Wales, in whose honour they had lately kept holiday, the knowledge was still less. Wishing to ascertain whether they understood what his future rank would be, I asked what he would be when Queen Victoria died. The only reply I got was from a little girl, 'Please Sir – an orphan.' Most could tell me that the coming holidays were given on account of Christmas Day, but to the question, 'What do we celebrate on Christmas Day?' the only answer was, 'The races!'"

"The parents are criminally careless with their children and are solely or wholly to blame. Impertinent rudeness they call smartness and allow their rude, ill-bred offspring to grow into bad habits until it is too late. We want a few schoolmasters of the good oldfashioned type and a plentiful supply of 'tawses' and last, but not least, less petty-fogging interference with the teachers by bumptious, ignorant school committees. These and a good, heavy reformatory special rate would make parents less absurdly tolerant of their children's caprices – caprices that too frequently end in crime."

"The master of an important school 'outback' is living with his wife in a habitation 12 feet by 12 feet in extent, there being two rooms 6 feet by 6 feet. 'It's better than a tent,' remarked the teacher. Is it any wonder that there is a dearth of competent teachers for the backblock schools?"

"Mr J.K.Law took up the cudgels on behalf of teachers, who, he said, were often kicked and maligned, but who were not such bad fellows."

"Notwithstanding that some of the pupils of Mosston School have to be located in a tent during the year, the school children have been remarkably free from colds and infectious diseases. The prevention of the spread of epidemics is probably due to the amount of disinfectant used. All the water which is used for slate cleaning purposes contains a quantity of Jayes' Fluid."

"A novel method of choosing a teacher has been reported. Recently the Board of Education submitted the names of three teachers for a country school. The committee thereupon solemnly decided to shake

the names in a hat and draw for the winner. This was done, and the matter so far settled, the successful candidate has since declined the honour, so no doubt the process will be repeated with the two remaining names."

"The following letter from Miss Evans was read at the Education Board meeting. 'I, being assistant teacher at the Central School, desire to call your attention and that of the rest of the board members, to the great difficulty in carrying on my work effectively without having the power to use the strap. I should not wish to use it to any great extent, but I should be able to do much better work if the children know I could inflict punishment upon them for disobedience, idleness and continual carelessness." (Mr Dempsey, the master, replied that Miss Evans' request had his approval).

"Things are evidently looking up; teachers are beginning to exercise more confidence in the stability of their position, and some of them have even been so rash as to add to the demands hitherto made upon their limited incomes. The Wairarapa Standard informs us that application was made to the Board at its recent meeting on behalf of no less than three masters who desired the whole of Easter week as a holiday, as they intended taking unto themselves wives. The Board readily consented and wished them joy."

A schoolmaster disciplines his pupil's parents

Buy local

Campaigns encouraging shoppers to "buy local" emerge from time to time. Online shopping, the close proximity of Palmerston North and the mobility of the modern customer all put pressure on struggling Whanganui retailers, but out-of-town purchasing by penny-wise customers was a problem for local shopkeepers before any of these factors took their toll, with householders in colonial times often ordering supplies from as far away as Auckland and Wellington.

The *Chronicle* thought it knew the reasons for this and was quick to lay the blame squarely upon the shoulders of the retailers themselves, particularly those who supplied the basics. In an article dated 4 December, 1895 entitled, *"A FLUTTER AMONG THE GROCERS"*, the editor was of the opinion that the grocers of the town had been doing very well for themselves.

"By mutual agreement they determined to refrain from competition, and from publishing or issuing price lists, and agreed among themselves as to the price the public should be required to pay for their goods. This plan operated splendidly for the grocers for a long time, and if they have not done well on it, it is their own fault. A mistake they made was that in fixing their prices, they fixed them a little too high. Indeed we have often heard it said that Wanganui, notwithstanding its port, is one of the dearest places to live in New Zealand."

The outcome, according to the *Chronicle*, was that the town began to lose its share of legitimate trade, *"first in ones and twos, then in dozens and scores."* It claimed that customers were more than just tempted by lower prices in the main centres – they were driven away from local suppliers by the high prices here, resulting in hundreds of pounds a month being lost to the local economy.

"But if we ask the storekeepers they at once begin to pour out the

vials of their wrath upon the people who do not support their own town. If we ask the people who are sending away their orders why they do not support the town in which they live, their answer is that they feel no call to pay, out of their limited earnings, unnecessarily high prices merely to enable a handful of storekeepers to make larger profits .... It is the business of all, by mutual help, to try to rise together. Grinding is a sin – whether it be the grinding of the working people by a combination to charge high prices, or the grinding of the business people by a combination to force them to sell at ruinous prices. It appears to be generally admitted that the 'war on prices' that has now set in must, if continued, result in some of our storekeepers going to the wall. Is that a thing to be desired? Does anybody want it?"

The *Chronicle's* assertions were in response to a *Herald* article (2 December) which had criticised the Government Employees Cash Purchase Association for its push to force retailers to provide goods at heavily discounted prices to its members. It challenged them to put their hands into their own pockets and set up their own co-operative supply store.

"That would be at least better than tempting some impecunious trader or traders to undersell their neighbours ..... If everyone followed the practice sought to be inaugurated here by these selfish hankerers after cheap supplies, a very large number of people would be driven out of business, and the labour market unduly congested, with the natural result that wages would suffer."

The *Herald* suggested that those who were behind the scheme might one day find that the Government would be forced into getting its work done for the lowest price possible, inferring that the result would be the laying off of many Government workers. *"How would this suit the members of these associations of Government employees?"*

The inevitable letter to the editor (*Herald*: 4 December) followed. It was from Horsley & Co (grocers) who were responding to the *Chronicle's* accusations: *"Sir,- We noticed with considerable surprise the editorial in your contemporary of this morning's issue, and think the writer must either have had his imagination fired at the lecture by Mark Twain last evening, or gleaned his information in a very careless manner. As regards ourselves or our predecessor, we emphatically assert that we have never entered into an agreement with the Wanganui or any other grocers to refrain from publishing and issuing price lists, and fixing the price the public should pay; and it is information to us to know that such an arrangement existed. Further, with respect to the scores that have been driven away to Wellington for their goods, it may be information to the writer of that article to know that months ago we offered to take the price list published by Wardell Bros. and supply the goods in Wanganui delivered to the purchaser's residence at those prices, provided they ordered in quantities of £5 worth and paid their money down; and this we can prove by the evidence of those we canvassed. The tone of the whole article is to lay the storekeepers of Wanganui under the imputation of having entered into an agreement to plunder the general public, which we on our part calmly and deliberately affirm to be false."*

The writer then offered to open the company's books for perusal by representatives of both newspapers and concluded with a dig at its accuser. *"Had we any desire to retaliate, we could easily prove that we can get our bill heads etc., printed outside the district at a reduction of 40% below that charged by the Wanganui Chronicle Coy."*

The secretary of the Trades Council in Wellington weighed into the dispute with a letter to the *Herald* (4 December) in which he complained that the mushrooming membership of the Government Employees Cash Purchase Association was already having a serious effect on his members, by having to reduce their employees' wages and losing customers. *"If the Government employees mentioned in connection with this matter were driven by necessity to this unfair method of dealing there might be some excuse for them, but as they are men whose rate of wages is based on a fair method of comfort, and who are further in the enjoyment of continuous employment, we think there is no possible defence of their action."* He reiterated the *Herald's* suggestion of the association setting up its own co-operative, *"instead of as at present inducing cut throat competition amongst the tradesmen of the city."*

In the same 4 December edition, the *Herald* challenged the *Chronicle's* assertion that Wanganui grocers had *"worked in a ring"* to keep prices up. *"If this were correct these traders should all be in affluent circumstances, but it is no secret that most of them have all they can do to meet their engagements .... If the present 'war on prices' continues and the members of the Cash Purchase Association are to get their supplies cheaper than the rest of the community, what chance have these struggling traders of paying their way?"*

Referring to the letter from the trade union secretary, the *Herald* reminded association members employed at the Aramoho Railway Workshops of the *"strong efforts that had to be made by the late Hon. John Ballance, this journal, and the storekeepers of Wanganui to prevent those workshops from being closed and the staff and machinery removed to Wellington, where the late Railway Commissioners asserted the work could be more cheaply done by a much reduced staff."*

The *Herald* appears to have had the last word on the matter in two articles which appeared on 5 December. Because the content of the first seems to accurately reflect feelings expressed so often today, the article is reproduced here in full. *"THE CURSE OF CHEAPNESS. An inevitable result of the demand for cheapness – be that demand for groceries, boots, drapery and clothing, furniture, or any other commodity – is sweating. When powerful organisations are banded together to obtain the best articles at the lowest possible prices, without regard to the principle of 'live and let live,' such as at present exist in Wellington and are being inaugurated here, it is difficult to suggest how these abuses of fair trade can be effectually remedied, unless, or course, those interested in the 'cheap' craze remedy the matter themselves. We believe many of those who of late have been agitating for prices being cut down, have not seriously thought of the consequences. Of course, the root of the trouble lies in human nature, which buys in the cheapest market and asks no questions. The consumer demands cheap goods, the tradesman must sell as cheaply as the cheapest, or he won't sell at all. The inevitable competition comes in, which is simply an aspect of the great battle of life, in which the fittest survive. Thousands are miserably crushed to death every year as a consequence. But is this living? Is that what was contemplated by he who wrote - 'The world is wide, there's land beside, there's room enough for all.' Do those who are ever on the alert for 'cheap goods' realise what they are bringing upon themselves and children? We think not. Quality and cheapness hold the market against all other considerations. The Christchurch Press at a recent date says:- 'Among the workers, the majority, who are strong and expert, can bear the pressure well and get a living wage. But the weak, the slow, the dull and the inexpert find that they cannot produce fast enough to earn a livelihood. Their bitter cry is therefore heard, and many kind people who know nothing of factory prices and of the rapidity with which articles are made by experts, join in the cry and in angry denunciations. They see the weak thrust hard against the wall, and they abuse the man who leans against them. Thus the stout lady in the crowd abuses the person next to her for jostling her so rudely. The good soul is oblivious of the fact that her neighbour is simply helplessly transmitting the pressure and surging of a thousand others. Indeed, the indignation of the respectable and kind-hearted public over low wages is still more ridiculous; for they themselves have, by their love of cheapness, helped to give the finger thrusts of the million, which are focussed upon the unfortunates who are being crushed against the wall."*

The second article, titled *"ITS EFFECTS"*, cited several Australian examples of "sweating" and asked whether such privations are endured in New Zealand. *"We say unhesitatingly 'yes', though to a lesser extent. And even in Wanganui cases are not wanting where women who at one time earned a fair livelihood with the needle have had to work longer hours in consequence of their employers having to meet the craze for cheapness and cut down prices. So with other trades. Ask our cabinet makers what is the result of the craze for cheapness, and there will be no need to ask what will be the result if the 'War on Prices' continues. The effect will very soon become apparent. We hope our readers will give the matter a little consideration, and we feel certain they will see that nothing but harm will be the inevitable result of such competition."*

A flutter among the grocers?

Did Mark Twain do his homework?

It's true Mark Twain criticised the *"fanaticism and barbarism"* wording on the Moutoa monument as reported in the *Chronicle* last week - *"Weeping woman gets makeover"* (14 June, 2017) – but did he get his facts right?

Mr Twain embarked on a world-wide speaking tour in 1895, commendably choosing to pay off creditors rather than accept bankruptcy following a series of failed financial investments. His itinerary included Wanganui, where the eagerly awaited author and raconteur held two meetings in the Oddfellows' Hall, Ridgway Street. *"No time should be lost in booking seats or securing tickets to avoid disappointment,"* advised the *Chronicle* (28 November, 1895) *"as throughout the tour hundreds were nightly unable to gain admission."*

Twain received a rapturous reception both here and throughout the country but when asked for impressions about New Zealand, declined to be drawn. *"He showed a sensible objection to people hurrying through a place and venturing an opinion on the nature of the country and the characteristics of the people of which they know nothing. Mark shows better judgment in this matter than many people who have seen less of New Zealand than he did,"* declared the *Herald* (4 January, 1896).

Yet the great man seemingly failed to heed his own advice, making the common mistake of many a whistle-stop tourist by drawing conclusions about matters he had little time to assimilate. Or did he just have trouble deciphering his own notes? Twain railed against *"a couple of curious war monuments here in Wanganui. One is in honour of white men who 'fell in defence of law and order against fanaticism and barbarism'."* He criticised the wording and referred to the Englishmen who lie beneath it (of whom there aren't any), so it seems he mistakenly attributed the *"fanaticism and barbarism"* inscription of the Moutoa Monument to the "Sleeping Lion" monument at Queens Park, beneath which fallen soldiers *do* lie. He then describes the Moutoa Monument as having been erected, *"to Maoris who fell fighting with the whites and against their own people,"* (the Hau Hau), all of which suggests he got his facts seriously muddled, falling into the same trap he warned others to steer clear of.

That the Hau Hau were patriots as also stated by Twain is beyond question, but how valid is his denunciation of the *"fanaticism and barbarism"* inscription? Is it really *"archaic"* and *"of its time"* as suggested in the *Chronicle* article? Or does it remain an apt description of the Hau Hau (Pai Marire) movement, of which little is known today?

Pai Marire (goodness and peace) was founded as an anti-European movement by Te Ua Haumene, whose mental stability was questioned by his own people. Te Ua, taught as a child by missionaries, wove Maori and Christian beliefs into his new doctrine which was designed to see Israel (Maori) restored as the rightful inhabitants of the land of Caanan (New Zealand) and the unrighteous (Pakeha) held accountable on the Day of Judgment. By the time of the Battle of Moutoa on 14 May, 1864 Te Ua was losing his grip, Pai Marire was taking a more warlike direction and the Archangel Gabriel, the movement's inaugural patron saint was replaced by the more aggressive Archangel Michael. (Gabriel may have been useful in explaining visions to virgins and other menial tasks, but a more warlike image was now required). White men's heads were mounted on poles and used as a means of invoking the war gods – Captain Thomas Lloyd and Wanganui farmer James Hewett were among the victims – and adherents were promised deliverance from pakeha bullets by raising their right hand and shouting "Hau!" - practices which surely come under the definition of fanaticism.

And barbarism? The ovens had been prepared by the Hau Hau for post-Moutoa Battle celebrations. Thankfully they remained empty but a later leader, Titokowaru, openly boasted of eating human flesh, as evidenced by his letter now held in the Alexander Turnbull Library. The memoirs of Hau Hau slave Kimble Bent also testify to the reintroduction of this practice, as do those of one of Titokowaru's right hand men Tutange Waionui, who in later years would say, *"the Pakeha and Maori were now one and it was no use harrowing the Pakeha's tender feelings with tales of slaughter and cannibalism."* (*Hawera & Normanby Star:* 12 January, 1915). So the colonials and indeed many Maori had good reason to fear Hau Hau *"fanaticism and barbarism"*, which was used as a terror tactic with the sole aim of driving the white man back home to Merrie Olde Englande.

Much is made of the belief of settlers that local Maori were protecting the settlement of Wanganui at the time of the Battle of Moutoa, when their primary motive was to protect the mana of their river by opposing the Hau Hau invader. But there was also resistance by Maori to the rising militancy of Hau Hauism, because of fears of loss of tribal governance among a people who fiercely guarded their independence. They also had no desire to return to a savage practice they had long since renounced.

Te Keepa Te Rangihiwinui's (Major Kemp's) memorial stands a stone's throw from the Moutoa Monument. He also vehemently opposed the Hau Hau and with good reason – both personally and politically. During the 1868 Battle of Moturoa he called out Titokowaru for a "one on one" but the wily leader, although not lacking in courage, wisely declined.

The *Evening Post* (27 December, 1865) had this to say on the unveiling of the Moutoa Monument. *"The brave men who last year fell at Moutoa ….. were led by chiefs who were fully alive to the importance of the decided step which they took in supporting British authority within these districts. They were aware that persistent rebellion would eventually exterminate the Maori race and that whilst they fought to maintain law and order, they were by that course displaying a true patriotism to their own countrymen."* Which sounds like a good dose of colonial propaganda, except for the fact that around 600 Maori from as far away as Wellington had gathered for the unveiling and contributed a fierce and earth-shaking war dance to underline their support. Plainly, they knew the consequences of Hau Hau dominance and were determined to prevent it. (The statue which became the Moutoa Monument had caught the eye of Superintendent of Wellington Dr Isaac Featherston while on an Australian visit, when he spotted it in a Melbourne mason's yard. The superintendent, wanting something suitable to commemorate the Putiki Maori's victory over the Hau Hau in 1864, decided it was fit for purpose and had it shipped over to Wanganui).

However, the Battle of Moutoa did not bring peace, the Hau Hau mantle being taken up by the aforementioned Titokowaru, who had also benefited from a missionary upbringing and who has been described by some as the most astute military leader from either side of the New Zealand Wars. In June 1868 he raised the stakes. His men killed Trooper Tom Smith, took half his body away and reduced it to soup which was, *"partaken of by every member of the tribe who afterwards declared that they had never tasted such excellent fare."* (*Taranaki Herald:* 18 July, 1868). Then came Titokowaru's letter proclaiming this new tactic, followed by attacks on isolated settlers which led to a year of intense fighting in Taranaki, with a number of convincing victories to Titokowaru which caused confusion and panic among the European community. And while his demise was eventually due to the oldest downfall known to man, (*"He wahine he whenua, ngaro ai te tangata"*), he remained undefeated on the battlefield.

Atrocities were committed by both sides of the conflict, but history tells us that the Hau Hau warrior was a committed *"fanatic and barbarian"* as stated on the monument and Titokowaru and his followers would have scoffed at suggestions they were anything but. However, their hard-fought reputation is now in peril. Whereas Government forces led by celebrated names such as Cameron, Chute, Kemp,

McDonnell, von Tempsky and Whitmore failed, it seems the old warrior may soon be emasculated by today's cultural apologists who plan to install an "interpretation panel" on the monument.

But will it accurately reflect events as they were or will it be aimed merely at humouring our modern day sensitivities, a trend which threatens to suppress our historical past merely to accommodate a desire to avoid causing offence and thereby trivialising the trials, tribulations and tragedies faced by our forebears, both Maori and European. It is one thing to correct historical inaccuracies and bias. It is quite another to reinterpret our history according to how we would prefer it to have been.

Did Mark muddle his monuments?

The baubles of office

Our new Mayor Hamish has now been kitted out in his official neckwear bling and robes, although it's refreshing to see him perform many mayoral duties in a more relaxed sartorial style – casual jacket, jeans and open-necked shirt (hanging out). It must be said that the informal trend was set by Mayor Laws, but those whose memories stretch a little further back will remember the more formal baubles of office being regularly wheeled out for all occasions, be they important or otherwise, although it was a long time before Wanganui acquired such gimcrackery.

At a 1905 meeting of the Wanganui Town Council, Councillor Liffiton asked Mayor Arthur Bignell whether a suggestion of former mayor Alexander Hatrick had been lost sight of. (Mr Hatrick had proposed that a mayoral robe and chain of office be procured, together with a corporate seal and coat of arms for the borough). Mr Bignell replied that the idea had not been shelved and that he had all the details except for the sanction of Lord Petre's family for permission to use the Petre crest.

This was expected in the next mail, after which it would be referred again to council. But a year later the retiring mayor told his successor (Charles Mackay) that he was sorry there was not a mayoral chain to hand over to him as the occasion would have marked adding an additional link to it. But he did hand over the only civic possession available to him – the key to the mayor's room.

At a Borough Council meeting in 1912 the question of mayoral insignia and a borough coat of arms again surfaced. Cr Liffiton recalled the previous council's approach to his lordship asking if he had any objection to Wanganui adopting his coat of arms but that *"no reply had been vouchsafed."* Mayor Mackay then told the meeting that Lord Petre's coat of arms had already been installed above the Corporation Gas Office. Cr Muir thought coats of arms were absolute nonsense, a view not shared by Cr Liffiton. *"Wanganui should have them the same as other towns in the Empire,"* he declared and suggested, (perhaps as a compromise), *"a fern leaf or some other national symbol."* Cr Spurdle then proposed that any Wanganui coat of arms should include something to symbolise the borough overdraft! The matter was dropped.

Wanganui's coat of arms (including the Petre emblems) was finally presented to the city in 1955, by which time our First Citizen was clanking around with a glittering chain which grew link by link as each subsequent mayor came to office.

<u>Council chamber's poor acoustics ratified:</u>
It's not just in our present District Council chambers that listeners have been plagued with the problem of poor acoustics. A plague of a more sinister kind was once feared in the Borough Council's rooms, though caused by the same problem.

The *Wanganui Herald* (7 March, 1906) in its report of the council's monthly meeting stated, *"Several councillors exclaimed in tones of alarm, 'A rat? A rat? Where?'"* But as the article went on to explain, *"The acoustic properties of the Chamber were evidently at fault."*

The alarm had been triggered by Councillor Williams who had actually said, *"For the last two meetings I have seen a* wreck *in the Council Chambers,"* and (again probably because of the poor acoustics) had to repeat his remark to set his fellow councillors' minds at rest.

"Williams allayed their fears by explaining that he had referred to some broken chairs under one of the side tables, which visitors might think offered a poor contrast to the elaborate Mayoral chair," the *Herald's* readers were informed.

Cr Williams then bemoaned the fact that his own chair had no cushion. *"The missing cushion was promptly discovered*

252

reposing on the floor beside the Town Clerk's chair," reported the *Herald's* intrepid investigative journalist, *"and it was resolved to replace the 'wreck' with new furniture."*

Judging by the prominence given the story by the *Herald,* we may safely assume that no business of any significance was dealt with at the meeting.

<u>Council Capers:</u>
If our present day drink-driving laws had applied in the 1870s, it's likely many a Borough Councillor of the time would have spent a night in the cells. A council meeting in 1875 dealt with several mundane matters – appointing an Inspector of Nuisances (Mr Jas. Gabriel being the successful candidate), consenting to the construction of a weigh-bridge and responding to concerns by the Fire Inspector (J.W. Robinson) that Mr Beauchamp's saw-mill chimney was in a dangerous state. But inexplicably the meeting began to get a little heated over the next item on the agenda, a petition by residents of Bolton Row (now Urquhart St) that a footpath be formed or drains installed to allow run-off, with Cr Chadwick reporting that sometimes residents could not go out of their houses without encountering water up to their knees. He recommended instant action.

Cr Duthie: Proposed adjourning the matter to the next meeting to allow cost estimates by the Foreman of Works.

Cr Howe: Said the road was in a bad state and if left for another fortnight it would be a month before anything was done.

C Nathan: Said if it was left to the Foreman of Works, it would *never* be done.

Both Cr Duthie's amendment, then Cr Chadwick's original motion were voted on, with the mayor declaring the original carried. Duthie called his Worship's attention to the fact that he (the mayor) had not voted. Cr Duigan said that as the original motion had been carried, it could not be reconsidered.

The mayor said that because he had omitted to vote he would now do so, with Duthie responding that that would make it a tie. Nathan declared that if things were going to be done in that fashion he would retire, which he did, accompanied by Chadwick. His Worship then announced that he would put the question to the meeting again, to which Duigan said there was no point as the mayor only needed to declare which side he intended to vote for. Cr Laird wondered why Duigan was quibbling over such a trifling matter. Duigan replied that he had no desire to quibble, but wanted to know the reasons for his Worship's peculiar mode of procedure. At this point Nathan and Chadwick re-entered the chamber, with the former asking the mayor what had been decided.

Cr Duthie then rose and accused "certain members" of being drunk, that they didn't know what they were saying or doing and wondered why his Worship condescended to preside over such meetings. Cr Bamber recalled that the previous Borough Council meeting had fallen through for want of a quorum and had seen a member of the council staggering around drunk.

Cr Chadwick: *"Name him! Name him!"*

Cr Duthie: Recommended the meeting be dissolved as members turn up night after night drunk.

"The meeting here broke up in the utmost confusion – one Cr squaring at another, and threatening to 'give him a clip under the ear' - to which the other replied that the age of the aggressor was his protection. The angry disputants were eventually separated and the members dispersed." (*Chronicle*: 26 June, 1875).

<u>Mismanagement</u>: *"We have been shown the large pecuniary loss to which the borough has been subjected by the unbusiness-like proceedings in the matter of the water works plant."*

<u>Overworked</u>: *"It is contemplated to close the council office one day in every week so as to allow the clerk time to perform his duties."*

<u>Proposed mayoral salary</u>: *"Councillor Nathan protested this wholesale and unprincipled way of disposing of ratepayers' money. It was, he considered, the thin end of the wedge for the establishment of a salary for Mayors of Wanganui. Ratepayers had surely burdens enough now with Property Tax, general, special and water rates without any extra imposition."*

<u>Mayoral health up-date</u>: *"His Worship the Mayor is, we are glad to say, better; and now is on a fair way to recovery from his recent bad attack of gout."*

<u>Road works</u>: *"The question arose at the Town Board meeting as to whether a certain street crossing should be constructed of asphalt or of jarrah blocks. 'Let us,' suggested a certain councillor, 'make our town up-to-date. Let us put our heads together and make a wooden pavement.'"*

<u>Meeting under urgency</u>: *"The Town Council will hold their fortnightly meeting this evening. It is not expected that any business of importance will be brought under consideration."*

<u>New broom</u>: *"The apartment formerly used as the Borough Council Chambers has been cleaned, there being taken out therefrom, of honest dirt, seven buckets full."*

<u>Town Board meeting</u>: *"All at once, with an eccentricity in keeping with their previous acts, the whole meeting rose* en masse *and left the hall, and so ended the most incomprehensible and useless meeting we have ever been present at."*

<u>Ratepayers' meeting</u>: *"A meeting of ratepayers will be held to reconsider the report of the Town Board and to express a vote of no confidence or want of confidence in the board. It is to be hoped that the ratepayers will make it convenient to attend and keep in mind the responsibility that rests with them. We cannot suppose that any*

great numbers of ratepayers would imitate the conduct of those who brought everything into ridicule at the last meeting."

Coat of Arms, Wanganui City

256

Bike wise

With the invention and improvement of the bicycle, cycling became a very popular activity. By the end of the nineteenth century there was in Wanganui a sizable number of enthusiasts who had taken to the new craze, as this *Chronicle* article of 7 December, 1895 reveals.

"Thursday afternoon's procession of wheelmen afforded a pretty good idea that bicycling has caught on in Wanganui. The forty male riders who put in an appearance did not, however, exhaust the total number of the devotees of the wheel in the town and district. The ladies were not represented at all and there must be a full dozen who are either already proficient or are in course of training for bicycle riding, while several gentleman riders were absent, either from inability or indisposition to take part. The turnout suggests the enquiry as to whether this new means of locomotion is likely to be permanent. We are inclined to think that it is. It will not always be fashionable, but fashion having 'boomed', it will be found too healthy and convenient and enjoyable ever to be dropped. At the present prices of the machine in the colony, bicycling must of course continue as a luxury to working people. A man with a salary of a hundred pounds a year, if he has any family obligations, will think twice before he spends a quarter of his year's salary on a 'bike' when he reflects upon the probable cost of repairs and the limited life of a steel horse. It may be supposed, however, that bicycles will come down to half the present cost before many years are over. The query as to whether whirling on wheels is likely to be permanent is being answered in America, where it is catching on at the schools."

The *Herald's* account of the same cycle ride (5 December) foregoes its contemporary's speculation, but provides more detail about the event itself, which seems to have been such a novelty that many of the locals turned out to watch: *"No less than 40 cyclists took part in the inaugural run this afternoon under the auspices of the Wanganui Amateur Athletic and Cycling Club. The procession started from the Fountain about 2.45, headed by Mr*

A.D. Willis, M.H.R., followed by Mr J. Goss (Club captain) and H. Henderson (vice-captain), Mr Harold Watt on a gallant ordinary bringing up the rear. The cyclists left the Fountain in single file as far as the Bridge, where they turned round and went up the Avenue to the St John's Club. From there they proceeded along Glasgow Street to Kennedy's, (Upokongaro) *and intend returning on the other side of the river. There were a good number of the general public to watch the start, and previous to the procession moving off Mr Hobbs, one of our local amateur photographers and also a member of the Cycling Club, took a photo of the cyclists."*

By this time, as the *Chronicle's* report suggests, matters of propriety, health, fashion and benefits to health for the "weaker sex" had been thrashed out and women were finding new freedoms by tentatively taking to the streets on these new-fangled machines, after overcoming initial fears that cycling was unsuitable for women because leg movements and pressure placed on the pelvis by the saddle *"would arouse feelings hitherto unrealised by the young maiden."*

Another critic thought that arguments about whether knickerbockers were more suitable for women cyclists than skirts were of no consequence. *"What is really important,"* declared Mr Francisque Sarcey, *"is whether cycling may not take up too large a proportion of women's time and prove destructive to the individual, the home and the state."* But this did not stop two enterprising local women from opening an agency for the sale and hire of ladies' bicycles: *"Misses Statham and Rigg personally superintend the instruction of would-be cyclistes* (presumably the female term for their male counterpart) *and tell them how to ride and what to wear."*

But there were concerns over safety, with reports coming in from overseas of serious accidents, some proving fatal, as well as several cases of ladies being fined for *"furious riding."* However, a new innovation promised to mitigate the injury statistics. *"Eyes at their backs for cyclists is now provided by a new invention,"* reported the *Herald* (7 July, 1896). *"A mirror fixed on the handle-bar enables the rider to see behind him."* And in Wanganui the new cycling craze gave rise to a disturbing new form of law-breaking as this *Chronicle* report reveals: *"A number of leading residents including a doctor, a bank manager and the editor of one of the local papers have been fined in the Magistrate's Court for riding their bicycles on the footpath."*

<u>Cycling snippets:</u>

"The first bicycle that has been imported into Wanganui was brought by the Ahuriri yesterday. It was imported by Messrs Anderson Bros., Taupo Quay, at whose place it is now to be seen." (*Herald:* 22 September, 1869).

"We are informed that the new woman has made her appearance in Wanganui in the shape of an up-to-date lady cyclist in 'bloomers'." (*Herald:* 5 December, 1895).

"The first tandem 'bike' arrived yesterday to the order of Mr J.H. Watt, for a well-known Wanganui gentleman. The makers appear to have spared no pains in turning out a thorough machine. The 'trial trip' was made this morning and proved quite satisfactory." (*Herald:* 27 February, 1896).

"Complaint has again been made of the habit some cyclists have of riding on the footpaths to the danger of pedestrians. We had thought this practice was dying out, but it appears not to be the case."

<u>Cycling advertisements:</u>
"A DOUBLE-BARRELED BLESSING:
Jack Spratt, hale hearty and fat,
His wife dyspeptic and lean;
Each riding a Columbia bike,
In the Avenue often are seen.
Jack rides to lessen his weight,
His wife to increase hers;
And so you see the Columbia bike,
A blessing on both confers."

William Bruce of Guyton Street, Wanganui Representative.

****

"A really particular man knows better than to buy a startling bargain in the shape of a bicycle. A poor price means a poor machine. We sell only the best!" REYNOLDS, Guyton Street.

****

"For cycling to business,
For cycling for pleasure,
For cycling on wet, dry or boisterous weather.
For cycling to any known place on the earth,
Take Will Draffin's advice,
Ride the best; Rudge Whitworth!"
      W. Draffin & Co., Agents, Guyton Street.

****

"One man, one bike,
Big stone, hard strike;
Buckled rim, naughty swears,
W. Draffin, for repairs."

Correct riding attire was essential for cyclistes

St Peter's Church – 150 not out

Wooden buildings in colonial New Zealand did not have a great life expectancy. "Permanent" public edifices would quickly fall victim to the ravages of dry rot, wet rot, borer or all three, not to mention the ever-threatening Great Destroyer – fire.

So it was with an eye to the future that sometime about 1874 Wanganui Anglicans commissioned an architect to ascertain the projected life span of their church (now St Peter's) which then occupied a site in Victoria Avenue. After all, the building was already nearly a decade old, having been consecrated on 17 July, 1866 and their previous church hadn't lasted much beyond 20 years, so we can imagine parishioners' delight when the architect presented his findings.

"With proper maintenance," he announced, "it should last another thirty years!" That it had been constructed with heart native timbers including kauri, matai and totara no doubt contributed to its anticipated longevity.

Since early days the church has withstood threats of annihilation during the Taranaki Wars, a whiff of scandal, crippling debt – even the destruction of its boundary fences by squatters from the nearby "Rookery" according to the *Evening Herald* (7 November, 1870): *"It is said that the wave of immorality has rolled down to the Church of England fence and borne a portion of it away."*

Then there was the dismantling and removal in 1921 to its present site in Gonville, where it survived a storm during the rebuild so severe that workmen had to tie themselves to the structure to avoid being blown away, and the building had to be repositioned on its foundations after having shifted several inches. (Curiously the foundation stone, laid 16 October, 1865, along with details of the ceremony sealed in a bottle, was never found).

The contractor, Mr G.F. Benge, was a practised hand at moving churches, having shifted Collegiate School's former chapel across the old Town Bridge in 1911, where it became All Saints in Wanganui East, which in its turn has given way to the present church. The following account of the shifting of Christ Church to Gonville comes from *A Visitor's Guide to St Peter's Anglican Church:* "*The sections of the building were loaded on to motor lorries for the journey to the new site. However, at that time, parts of Koromiko Road had a sand surface and it was found that the lorries could not negotiate the hill. This necessitated using flat-topped drays drawn by horses under the direction of a Mr Snow for the purpose, and as well, a traction engine was employed to move some of the larger sections up the hill.*"

The church was saved from demolition in the 1950s when funds raised for a planned replacement were instead used for restoration, and those who admire the building's Carpenter Gothic architecture, should they peruse the architect's plans, would be forever grateful that the project never went ahead. The church then survived the Wahine Storm (just), which led to major strengthening work, making it now the oldest Whanganui building still in public use – and probably one of the safest, while the church which succeeded it is up for a $30,000-plus earthquake compliance assessment and likely major upgrading.

On its original site the church had sat among the graves of early settlers although a ban on further burials took effect in 1855 due to the unsuitability of the swampy ground. Church records list the sins of some burial candidates - "*Drowned while intoxicated*", "*Deserter from 80th Regiment*" and "*Drowned on the Lord's Day while bathing during the time of Divine Service.*"

The first vicar Rev Nicholls, unpopular with many, was eventually transferred to another parish under a cloud of scandal due to unsubstantiated rumours and gossip of drunkenness, but to his credit he several times waived substantial unpaid portions of his stipend, in spite of ongoing attempts to balance the books by means of bazaars, lectures, readings and organ recitals, which were regular features on the ecclesiastical calendar.

Church matters were often played out in the *"Letters to the Editor"* columns, most signed with *noms de plume* and dealing with such matters as the standard of music, lazy "bellows boys" and why couldn't the police, instead of maintaining order in the pubs, prevent unruly larrikins from making unseemly commotions while services were in progress.

Now, in its reincarnation as St Peter's, the church has notched up a further 95 years serving the Gonville and wider community. Many alive today, including the writer, remember with affection the school and kindergarten run by Miss Hylton, several vice-regal visits as well as the numerous happy and solemn ceremonies which have taken place within its sacred walls; also the dedicated clergy and lay people who have served during that time, many now nameless but whose contribution is immeasureable.

However declining parishioner numbers citywide led to the decision by church leaders to centralise most activities at Christ Church in Wicksteed Street. The final regular Sunday service at St Peter's will be held on May 8 at 9.30am. While that means services will then be curtailed to Wednesday worship services, weddings, funerals and community use of its hall, the church is secure in its Heritage NZ: Category 2 rating, which lists it as a building of historical significance.

Now retained as a "back-up option" if renovations at Christ Church go ahead, it may once again be fully utilised, but in the meantime a special service is being planned to celebrate its sesqui-centennial. This will be held on Sunday 28 August at 10.00am followed by a luncheon, to which past and present parishioners and members of the community are invited.

****

(This article was written in 2016 to commemorate the 150th anniversary of the church's original consecration. An outcome of the reunion held at the time was the formation of *"Friends of St Peter's Church"*, a group dedicated to preserving the church's rich historical and spiritual heritage. Since then the church has regained much of its vibrancy as a community centre with activities such as working bees, garage sales, craft and book sales, social evenings and Christmas carol services, as well as special church services. The Battle of Britain remembrance service also continues as an annual event).

Christ Church dismantled before resurrection as St Peter's

Baby sitters, tram fares, light bulbs and virgins

Sifting through old records is not as boring as it may seem. While researching the history of St Peter's Church for its sesqui-centennial, I came across some curious items from former times. The first is an appeal from organisers of the church's 100th anniversary (1966) for baby-sitters, to enable parishioners to attend the centennial dinner. Mrs Elizabeth Connell, secretary of the Wanganui Home Makers' Circle, was pleased to inform the committee that 14 members of her group would be available for baby-sitting duties.

A 1920s newspaper article, lamenting the fact that few men attended church, criticised those who did for reaching to the "tram-fare" pocket of their waistcoats when finding money for the offering and encouraged them to be more generous. And an excerpt from the July, 1942 St Peter's newsletter states: *"It goes against the grain to gather people together and not take up a collection."*

The same newsletter offered an innovative idea for church heating. *"It has been suggested that if the lights are left on during Evensong the church will not be quite as cold. The experiment has been tried, but with a very small congregation, and whether they were less cold than they would otherwise have been I cannot say."* The writer noted that the extra illumination made it harder for worshippers to drop off to sleep, *"but let no-one imagine that that is why it is being done!"* Conversely, the writer added that if the church *was* in darkness a parishioner could sleep without troubling the preacher – as long as he didn't snore.

Also quoted were the words of an Irish Protestant church-warden who vehemently declared, *"There'll be no saints or virgins in this parish while I'm on the vestry!"*

The curious case of the disappearing cornerstone

Will a ninety-five year old mystery be solved now that contractors are about to redevelop the Selwyn Buildings site in Victoria Avenue? (2017) The site contained our first public burial ground and was formerly occupied by Christ Church before it was dismantled and rededicated the following year as St Peter's in Gonville. But church records contain this intriguing statement.

"Strangely enough, when the church building was dismantled, a search was made for the foundation stone originally laid in 1865 but it was never found by the contractor – only a hole in the ground."

So what happened to it? Foundation/cornerstones by that time had outgrown their significance of being integral to a building's structure and were largely ceremonial, signalling the start of a project and looking forward to its completion. So if no cornerstone was found, the question must be asked, "Was it ever laid in the first place?"

The answer is a most definite "yes". The photographic record shows a large crowd of church adherents kitted out in all their finery gathered at the site. In the foreground is a stack of bricks ready for the project to commence and in the centre a tripod from which the stone is suspended. A newspaper account (*Wellington Independent:* 26 October, 1865), quoting an earlier *Wanganui Times* story under the headline, *"LAYING THE FOUNDATION STONE OF CHRIST CHURCH"* states: *"At one p.m. yesterday, the cornerstone of the above church was laid by the Right Rev. Charles John, Lord Bishop of Wellington, in the presence of a large and respectable assemblage of the inhabitants. The Bishop, attended by the Rev. Charles H.S. Nichols [sic], the Rev. Richard Taylor, and the Rev. Basil Taylor, with the Churchwardens and Building Committee, proceeded from the old church to the site of the proposed building where the choir, on their arrival, chanted the 132nd psalm."*

The Bishop then preached a short sermon and said a prayer before the laying ceremony after which, *"a small bottle, containing the following inscription was laid beneath, in a place prepared for it:- 'The foundation stone of a Parish Church, erected for the Worship of Almighty God, by the Parishioners of Christ Church, Wanganui, was laid by the Right Rev. Charles John, Lord Bishop of Wellington, October 16th, 1865.'"* Also listed were churchwardens, vestry and members of the building committee including the architect, Henry C. Field.

At the time of the church's dismantling fifty-five years later, the Borough Council asked churchwardens what they proposed to do with *"two memorial stones on Christ Church property commemorating two important phases in the town's history,"* (*Herald:* 28 September, 1921) but it's unlikely the cornerstone was one of them. If the council had acquired it, why would the contractor have looked for it? But why was there a hole in the ground?

Does the answer lie in the nature of the land on which the church stood? Burials had long since been discontinued there because of the unsuitability of the swampy ground and when the first Church of England (1844-1866) was erected it took some time to locate a suitably firm site. But it was a shocking tragedy which really showed up the instability of the ground and it occurred just a few yards from the foundation stone, the day after the laying ceremony. *"A dreadful accident has just occurred in Victoria Avenue. Dr Gibson has lately had a quantity of sand removed from the sand hill behind his house and had employed Mr W. Aiken to erect a substantial fence along the foot of the excavation. While Mr Aiken and three men were so engaged, a little earth fell and jammed the legs of one of the men and while his comrades were assisting him, fifteen or twenty tons more came down, burying three of the party and hurling the other a distance of several yards. Mr Aiken's head and arm were left free and he succeeded in uncovering the head of the man next to him, but in spite of the eager efforts of a number of persons who rushed to the spot, more than twenty minutes elapsed before the man first jammed could be extricated, and he was then to all appearance dead."* (*Chronicle:* 18 October, 1865).

A common practice to prevent heavy objects such as water barrels from sinking into unstable ground was to set them on a foundation of solid materials such as up-ended bottles. Did the church's elusive cornerstone, no doubt lacking any form of foundation, simply sink under its own weight? The Whanganui District Heritage Inventory lists the site as pre-1900 and of archaeological and historic interest. Is there something of archaeological and historical interest still there, patiently awaiting discovery?

Laying of the Christ Church cornerstone - 16 October, 1865

More archaeological treasures yet to be discovered?

The *Chronicle's* recent article on the archaeological dig at the present Farmers' site highlights the vast amount of knowledge which can be gleaned from such studies.

I have to admit that when I heard the dig was in progress, along with all the legal wrangling which accompanied it, I questioned its value. Why spend all that time, effort and money on a project which would yield the same as any other pre-1900 colonial building site – fragments of pottery, clay pipes, broken bottles and a few rusty horse-shoes among other detritus.

But my opinion was drastically altered after attending the first of Naomi Woods' lectures on the result of the dig when, by combining findings at the site with contemporary newspaper articles, she built up a picture of the Byrnes family who had lived there in the mid to late 19th century, thus adding considerably to the early history of the town. The second lecture centred around a better known family – the Chavannes, who operated a stable and later a motor garage from the same spot.

So what other sites around Whanganui are ripe for archaeological exploration? (Unfortunately the opportunity to explore one prime heritage site has been lost with the redevelopment in Victoria Avenue at the site (Selwyn Buildings) of the first two Churches of England, although it may be argued that the area would have been well dug over when bodies from the burial ground were exhumed early in the 20th century and again when more bones were discovered during World War II trench digging activities.

I am aware that archaeologists in New Zealand are a rare species but there are two city sites which may yield interesting results, both of which are now vacant and both were last built on over 150 years ago.

The first is in Plymouth Street, a few metres up from Spooners Dry Cleaners in the Avenue. Until last year a quaint, pretty little cottage (Russell House) sat there, one I admired every time I walked past it as a young lad. It had been altered internally and housed various community groups over the years so was not original inside, but it was likely built around the same time as Sandridge Hall, a grand mansion erected across the road for Mayor Watt in 1869 and (to use modern terminology) "deconstructed" in 1979. Then suddenly one day the cottage was gone and the section has remained empty ever since.

The second site is in Campbell Street, next to the former Plunket Rooms and opposite the Davis Library. Most locals remember the building which occupied it as the Palm Lounge, but the restaurant was merely an addition to what already existed – Sandown, a retirement home built in 1873 for the famous missionary, peace-maker, explorer, historian, botanist, zoologist, geologist, ethnologist and author, Richard Taylor. Unfortunately Rev Taylor only lived in it for a few months, dying in October of the same year, although his wife Caroline remained there until her death in 1884 and their daughter Laura until her death in 1887. Both the restaurant and homestead burned down in a suspicious fire in 1999.

An advertisement in the 22 May, 1889 edition of the *Wanganui Herald* helps to picture the house and grounds. *"TO LET – Sandown Villa, Queen's Park, Wanganui. The house contains 14 rooms with commodious outbuildings, including stable and coach-house. The grounds are half-an-acre in extent, including orchard and vegetable garden. Very healthy situated and commanding a magnificent view. To a desirable tenant the rent will be very moderate. Apply to JOHN NOTMAN, Taupo Quay."*

This is a prime building site and while there may be a good reason for it to have been vacant for nearly twenty years, there is no guarantee it always will be. What treasures lie beneath the surface, both there and in Plymouth Street?

Sandown Villa, from a painting by Cranleigh Barton

Wanganui – the garden city

In the early years of the 20th century the Wanganui Scenery Preservation & Beautifying Society was established. It comprised a number of branches incorporating participating suburbs, with the St John's Hill branch featuring prominently by making improvements to Virginia Lake. The *Chronicle's* editor announced (2 May, 1903), that in response to Mayor Alexander Hatrick's proposal to turn the Virginia Lake Reserve into a public park, he had written to two prominent nurserymen to obtain their views on its feasibility. Mr A. Laird was of the opinion that with judicious management, Virginia Lake (formerly Virginia Waters), had the potential to become one of the prettiest spots in New Zealand, while Mr W.T. Benefield proposed a carriage drive around the entire perimeter of the lake so that visitors could enjoy their excursion without having to leave their seats. He also suggested revenue-producing activities such as boating, tennis, croquet and bowls. Both men advised that the acquisition of a strip of land one or two chains wide on the town side of the lake to improve access was essential for the scheme's viablity as a tourist attraction, and that failure to do so would be regretted by residents and visitors for all time.

Once the land had been procured the Borough Council put up a prize for the best design for a layout of the reserve. This was won by a trio of prominent Wanganui people – Mr and Mrs H. Sarjeant and Mr J.T. Stewart, who entered the competition under a *nom de plume*. Ornamental gates were made and hung at a cost of £60, a couple of lion ornaments carved and donated by a Mr Caddy were installed as entrance guardians, a Coronation Band Rotunda was built overlooking shelter rooms for picnic parties, flag-staffs were erected at various points and Mrs Watt donated two cannon in memory of her late husband, former mayor W.H. Watt.

The editor marvelled that so much had been accomplished with plants worth just £50 and labour worth £150, declaring, *"The visitor will realise that not half of the beauties of the reserve have been told and he will gladly send his donations to the St John's Hill Beautifying Society."*

Not everyone was happy with the society's achievements. A *Chronicle* correspondent calling himself *"An Active Member"* questioned what he alleged was the misuse of funds spent on Wanganui East gardens which would be washed away in the first flood, predicted the new band rotunda would be seldom used and declared the fancy gates as being the most amusing part of all. *"Such an elaborate affair,"* he scoffed, *"more particularly considering the rough and wild state of the grounds."*

Before matters got to this point Virginia Lake had been more than just a potential visitor attraction. It was the source of water for a time (once an ongoing dispute between the owner and the Town Council had been settled) and attempts had been made to stock it with various species of fish. Australian perch were introduced in 1877, but when a proposal to add carp was made in 1882 the secretary of the local Acclimatisation Society objected. He pointed out that he had personally introduced 300 brown trout which he had bred in his own back yard and added, *"We do not want future generations to revile us for propagating worthless fish."* English carp were bad enough, but the proposed variety were, in his opinion, fit only for manure and pig food. *"Let us get salmon, trout, perch and tench, but for Heaven's sake preserve us from the worthless Prussian carp."*

But while the Beautifying Society was improving the parks and reserves around the city, it encouraged its members to put some work into their own properties. *"Not only do the streets want beautifying,"* said Mr Hope Gibbons, *"but also the private gardens."* Another member was less diplomatic. *"While the society is busy beautifying the town,"* he huffed, *"some of the fences in the Avenue, which are owned by wealthy people, are *hideous things, usually patched up with pieces of tin."*

Others were doing their bit to undo the endeavours of the society by vandalising plantings and tearing out trees. Letters regularly appeared in the daily papers warning perpetrators of dire consequences if they were caught and urging parents to keep a close eye on their children. Illegal shooting in the Virginia Lake Reserve was also a problem for a time and the St John's Hill branch chairman warned that prosecution would follow the apprehension of any offenders. *"The society has gone to a great deal of trouble and expense in procuring birds to add to the attractiveness of the lake,"* he declared and did not want the pleasure of citizens spoiled by the actions of a few.

In April 1910 volunteers were called to plant out the area around the newly installed Durie Hill steps. A local firm had kindly donated kerosene tins fitted with handles for the conveyance of manure and ropes were provided *"for the safety of those workers who may be allocated duties to the dangerous places."* Volunteers were requested to be at the site in time to make a start punctually at 2.30. A photograph of the occasion shows about seventy people working up the hillside, the men wearing long trousers and waistcoats with ladies modestly attired in long-sleeved blouses, ankle-length dresses and hats. Other areas targeted by the society included Laird's Park, both banks of the Wanganui River and Castlecliff. Shakespeare's Cliff came in for particular attention for obvious reasons. Native shrubs and trees were recommended for their soil-binding propensity, although Alexander Hatrick (at that time president of the society), promised to donate Canadian Mountain Ash trees for planting along the cliff frontage. He had recently returned from Vancouver and was impressed by the beauty of the trees, declaring that in full bloom they were a mass of scarlet flowers and berries and were one of the sights of the city. Sightseers today would be hard-pressed to see any evidence of Canadian Mountain Ash trees, so it must be assumed the donation for some reason never eventuated, or the trees failed to flourish.

Energetic and enthusiastic Castlecliff members, under the supervision of the Borough gardener, planted out 875 trees especially chosen for their suitability during one working bee, and had another 250 cabbage trees lined up for the following Saturday. And just as in more recent times our hanging baskets caught the eye of other centres around New Zealand, so the society's early efforts were becoming famous throughout the colony. In July, 1912 the Wanganui Town Clerk received a letter from the Blenheim Beautifying Society asking for particulars of the work being done here. *"I know your city well,"* wrote its secretary, *"and have been forcibly struck with the manner in which either your Borough Council or some private society had added to the beauty of the place."*

A letter was also received from the Onehunga society asking for details of what had been achieved in Wanganui, noting that one of its objects was, *"to promote a harmonious scheme for beautifying the town which not only attracts attention and compels admiration, but helps considerably to send the town ahead, attract population and add to the general prosperity of everyone."*

However, Dunedin was the beautification Mecca for New Zealand in those early days and in 1918, having turned down a request the previous year, that city's Superintendent of Gardens & Reserves arrived in Wanganui to advise the local society on how best to plant out reserves and waste grounds around the city. He was Mr David Tannock, described as *"a gentleman of great experience in horticulture and afforestation."* He had been trained at Kew Gardens and had wide experience in various tropical gardens before settling in Dunedin, where his work earned him wide renown.

Mr Tannock was treated to tours of the city's reserves which included Virginia Lake, Peat's Park, Matipo Park, Aramoho Cemetery, Queen's Park, Laird's Park, the Borough Nursery, Kowhai Park, Victoria Park, Durie Hill and Castlecliff. After spending a week on inspection Mr Tannock addressed a public meeting in which he expressed high praise for Wanganui's beautifying society, pointing out that while Dunedin's group was now seeing the mature fruits of thirty years' hard work, judging from what he had seen, Wanganui would soon be known as one of the garden cities of New Zealand.

He noted that while outer areas were being attended to, those closer to town required attention, particularly Queen's Park, which would soon become a centre of attraction once the Sarjeant Gallery was completed. *"Melancholy and ever-the-same pines,"* he advised, should be uprooted and replaced and unneccesary fences removed, questioning why fences – which are designed to keep people out – should be installed in places where people are encouraged to come in. He went so far as to suggest that citizens should do away with fences around their private gardens, *"as they do in America."* He also urged the formation of a Town Planning Branch, to avoid streets and buildings being placed in all sorts of positions and places and crowded together. Home owners were encouraged to establish gardens, for even those who did not appreciate beauty's intrinsic value recognised what an asset it was to a town from a business point of view or when selling one's home.

Hoardings were ugly things, he declared and the Wanganui Council might manage to get along without them if citizens nagged long enough and hard enough. Grass berms should be laid down with a good sole, so that *"a man could use his lawn mower with some degree of pleasure."* The building of children's playgrounds was also encouraged (see separate story) although the mayor noted that *"we've already done something for the children."*

Mr Tannock encouraged Wanganui residents to adopt another Dunedin innovation - the model cottage garden, in which locals could learn how to plant out their own back yards in vegetables and fruit. Afforestation was another

Dunedin project, implemented with the aim of one day paying off the entire Dominion's debt. He considered Wanganui's reserves to be suitable for such a project. Cemeteries should be *"as attractive and neat and bright and possible."* and it was advisable to provide a caretaker's cottage in places such as the Virginia Lake Reserve.

"Wanganui is very fortunate in having such a thoroughly enthusiastic and practical Borough Gardener as Mr Tucker, who works harmoniously with the different societies," concluded Mr Tannock, adding, *"It is essential that all work together and sink any little differences."* (Applause).

The meeting ended with much effusive hand-clapping and thanks for Mr Tannock's address, along with the hope that a juvenile branch of the society would soon be established. Society members obviously took heed of Mr Tannock's recommendations. A deputation to the Borough Council the following year requested that a dwelling be erected at Virginia Lake, *"of a size suitable for a Borough gardener and of a design in keeping with the surroundings,"* that unsightly hoardings around the town be taken down and that the fence near Cook's Gardens be removed.

David Tannock

Redirecting mischief

"Mothers should supervise their children's games and where possible, join in with them. Far better than gossiping over the back fence or gadding about town."
We can imagine what response that statement would receive should it be made today, but in 1918 the Dunedin Superintendent of Gardens & Reserves got away with it. As well as giving advice on enhancing our gardens and reserves (and sorting out errant housewives), Mr Tannock did not forget the needs of children and provided the beautifying society with a report, *"dealing essentially with the well-being of children so far as it relates to the need of providing an outlet in play for their limitless energy."* (This in spite of Mayor Mackay's assertion that *"we've already done something for the children."*)
The report had special reference to Kowhai Park, for which improvement plans had already been drawn up and the inevitability of a children's playground being included had been accepted. It noted that in developing towns there were plenty of vacant lots and open paddocks in which children could play but as the towns grew, children were crowded into the streets or into their only-too-limited back yards.
"To play in the streets and gutters is unsanitary and undesirable. They dirty their clothes, hurt themselves if they fall on the hard asphalt and seriously impede traffic." Therefore every community with any interest in the proper physical and moral development of its young people had an obligation to make plenty of provision for play areas which, besides benefiting children, would serve to keep buildings apart, provide breathing spaces and afford a welcome break in the rows of houses. Such play areas should be no more than half a mile from each home, although a quarter mile was more desirable. Mothers should accompany their children, supervise their games, and where possible, enter into them. (Refer to opening

278

sentence).

"Many people are inclined to look upon the modern playground as a fad taken up by busy-bodies for their own aggrandisement and to say, 'Why, there was nothing like that in my young days,'" continued Mr Tannock.

But it was his opinion that it was unlikely there was the same need in the critics' young days, but in any case the world had advanced since then and it was up to adults to make the children as happy and healthy as they could and for them to be a pleasure, not a burden, to their parents. He described initial opposition to providing playgrounds at reserves and schools in Dunedin, but said prejudices were finally overcome and a successful playground was established where swings, see-saws, a sand-pit and seats were installed. Mr Tannock then listed the various items of equipment, along with safety features and any problems associated with each, which could be adapted for any town in New Zealand.

<u>Swings:</u> Erected in pairs with seats constructed of stout blue-gum; dressed with sharp corners eliminated. Designed to be dismantled each evening, *"to prevent a certain class of youth, too big to be a boy and too undeveloped to be a man,"* from loutish behaviour. To be inspected regularly in the interests of safety.
<u>See-saws:</u> A different activity from that of today. One child sat on the end to keep it down, while others crawled up the plank then slid down the other side. Must be constructed from non-splintering timber.
<u>Sandpits:</u> Should be filled with material which would not dirty their clothes.
<u>Playing lawns:</u> Considered essential whenever there was sufficient space, *"for the very wee ones to creep and roll about."*
<u>Wading pool:</u> Six inches at one end, nine to twelve at the other. Concrete bottom covered with layer of sand.
<u>Shelter shed:</u> To provide shelter from rain, but cheap structures should be hidden with creepers or shrubs.

Sanitary conveniences also necessary.

<u>Drinking fountain:</u> Bubble type. Also penny-in-the-slot gas rings were desirable, plus water tap for washing.

<u>Other playground fixtures:</u> Slides, horizontal bars, open-air gymnasium and *"giant strides"*, now a largely obsolete item (due to safety concerns) it resembled a maypole but allowed the children to run around in circles, taking giant strides as their feet left the ground.

The report states that all these facilities would provide the necessary exercise young children require and ensure they would not have to wait until they were old enough to play cricket, football or hockey. The author includes a few pointers on the value of play. (1) It secures the best kind of physical activity because it is pleasant exercise. (2) It requires frequent judgment of time, distance, mode of action etc and these train the mind. (3) It develops social spirit, because all play is with groups of two or more children. (4) The child learns the meaning of fairness. Later he will apply this to work, so that play is the beginning of the development of moral character.

Mr Tannock concludes with a very good reason to provide the aforementioned activities: *"We should remember that Satan finds mischief for idle hands to do and when children are swinging etc., they are not breaking trees or destroying shrubs and flowers."*

Providing children's playgrounds would prevent this

Granny Dalton (Part 1): Was Granny a murderer?

"Behave yourself, or Granny Dalton will get you!"

That was the threat used by parents to keep many a young colonial on the straight and narrow, although it seems Granny's influence extended long after her death and well into the 20th century, both as the town's bogey woman and by lending her name to an obscure Springvale walkway. She was also well known for burning down her little shacks on a regular basis.

Bridget Walsh was born in Ireland in 1823 and was married by the time she was 20. Under the name Bridget Dalton she arrived in Wellington on the *Woodlark* in March 1874 after a three and a half month voyage from London, along with other "Emigrant and Colonial Aid" passengers. The ship's passenger list shows she was accompanied by Ellen (24, dairymaid), Catherine (30, servant) and Johanna (14, servant), most likely daughters as one of her daughters (Ellen) played a dubious part in Granny Dalton's colourful life in Wanganui, where Granny settled soon after her arrival in New Zealand. Bridget Dalton's county of origin is not listed, but her headstone records it as Kilkenny. Ellen's birthplace is also listed as Kilkenny and Johanna and Catherine's is given as nearby Waterford.

The *Woodlark* flew the yellow flag on entry to Port Nicholson due to scarlet fever having broken out ten days after leaving London, resulting in 39 cases of the disease – 18 of which were fatal, along with ten deaths due to other causes. There is no record of a spouse accompanying Mrs Dalton. However, in the early 1880s a Bridget Dalton lived with her husband John in a little workman's cottage on the corner of Harrison Street and Bolton Row (now Urquhart Street). The street was in an area known by the unflattering sobriquet of Poverty Flats, a label which accurately described it according to the report of a meeting of the Borough Council in 1875. On the agenda was a petition from Bolton Row residents asking that the council *"take some steps in the direction of forming a footpath, or cut some drains to allow the water to run off, as in wet weather the Row is nearly under water."* Cr Chadwick supported the request, having visited the locality the previous week and found that several residents could not leave their houses without getting up to their knees in water. A proposal to comply with the request was carried, then councillors were mired in points of order before the meeting broke up in confusion amid accusations of drunkenness and threats of violence. However three years later improvements were being carried out and in 1879 water mains were installed.

A Mrs Dalton appears several times in the diaries of Laura Harper (nee Taylor) daughter of missionary Richard Taylor. The entries are for 1877. Mrs Dalton carried out washing and cleaning duties at the Taylor's residence, Sandown, in Campbell Street, just up the hill from Bolton Row.

The Daltons came to the notice of the authorities in 1883 when John Dalton went missing: *"The police have had their attention directed since Saturday last to a man named John Dalton, who has not been seen nor heard of since that date. We learn that he always went home regularly at night, and his wife has never known him to be absent from home before, which makes his absence most remarkable. He was last seen at half-past nine on Saturday last, in the Masonic Hotel, and no one has seen him since, and his wife entertains an idea that some harm must have happened to him, though there was no reason to believe that he would have any thoughts against his own life. He was a man advanced in years,* (meaning he was probably at least 50 years of age) *and obtained his living by working on the wharf, his home being in Bolton Row."* (*Herald:* 25 October, 1883).

The Masonic Hotel was situated at what was then known as River Bank at the end of Plymouth Street, so was conveniently placed to be the pub of choice for Dalton. The next day the

Chronicle added that shortly before his disappearance he had left his companions, announcing that he would soon return, but no more was seen of him. *"It is said that he had been drinking, but was quite capable of taking care of himself .... It is supposed by some that Dalton fell into the river and was drowned, but others think he has left the town."*

The convenience of a nearby river was always appreciated by drinkers wanting to attend to the calls of nature, but unfortunately this often led to the sad result suspected in this case, for drink and slippery riverbanks are a lethal combination. The evidence of opened trouser buttons on a recovered body would aid the coroner in coming to an obvious conclusion.

Ten days after Dalton disappeared the *Chronicle* (5 November) reported that the police had exhausted every effort and plan to discover the whereabouts, dead or alive, of the missing man. *"The river has been carefully dragged by Detective Benjamin and Constables Looney and McClenaghan, but, even supposing the poor fellow had fallen a victim to a watery grave, the fresh of the past few days would probably have carried his body out to sea."*

But more misfortune was to come Mrs Dalton's way. A year later (6 September, 1884) the *Chronicle* carried the following story: *"A MEAN THIEF.- Mrs Dalton, a widow woman residing in Harrison Street, whose husband died about a year ago, has ever since been working hard to earn her own living and save a few pounds for a rainy day. She succeeded in accumulating the sum of £9, which she had carefully put away in her house. On looking for it in the accustomed place a day or two ago not a shilling of it was to be found. Some mean, petty thief had discovered the poor woman's secret, and did not stand upon ceremony about robbing a lonesome widow. Mrs Dalton has her suspicions, but no sufficient clue has yet been found as to the identity of the thief."*

Three months after the theft police received a disturbing report - that the bones of John Dalton lay beneath the house he formerly resided in at Bolton Row. Tongues must have been wagging, for how could Mrs Dalton not know that her husband's body had been concealed there? Mrs Dalton no longer occupied the house, no doubt having been forced to leave due to the theft of her life's savings. It was now tenanted by a Mr Eastbury, who had complained that he could not live there because of the smell. On checking beneath the house, he claimed to have seen John Dalton's boots full of bones.

But the Herald labelled the story a rumour and dismissed it, following a thorough search by two policemen. It seems that when Mr Eastbury made his report, he had been *"in a state of liquor"*, which for him was not unusual judging from court records of the time.

"It is hardly probable that a body could have lain for over fifteen months under the house unknown to anyone, and that it should just now be detected by its smell." (Herald: 31 December, 1884). *"The house is situated some height from the ground, and can easily be examined underneath, besides which it is close to the footpath, along which there is considerable traffic, and from which any smell would be detected."*

So Mrs Dalton was in the clear.

Bridget "Granny" Dalton

Granny Dalton (Part 2): Will the real Granny "D" please stand up

Curiously, just six days after the theft which likely forced the eviction of Mrs Dalton from her Bolton Row home, a letter from Bridget Dalton appeared in the *Chronicle,* pleading for help to prevent her eviction from her home – but this Bridget Dalton did not live in Bolton Row. She lived in a little community which had sprung up on Rutland Hill (Queen's Park) after the military moved out and had been there for some time. The authorities had signalled their intention to move the lady on, as reported in the *Herald* (10 September, 1884). *"The Domain Board held a short meeting last evening to consider what steps should be taken to remove an old woman named Mrs Dalton from the Queen's Reserve. It was stated by the foreman that the works could not be completed till her house was shifted, and the Mayor stated that he would take the matter in hand and see to it."*

Mrs Dalton plainly thought that she also should take the matter in hand, hence the letter to the *Chronicle* (12 September) from her which read: *"SIR,- May I ask you to give me space in your valuable paper to call public attention to what I am sure you cannot but acknowledge is a great wrong to me. I have lived on the Rutland Hill for many many years with full permission of the Government authorities, and without any objection to my residence there – and I am now told that I am to be turned off, my home destroyed, and without any compensation to me. If that was all I would not mind so much, but I see stables and other buildings being erected on the very same land which I am told is wanted for public purposes only. This is very plain to me that there is no justice or right in the matter. If stables and other buildings can be erected on the land for another party, why cannot I be allowed to remain in my humble little cot for the remainder of my days. Does this not seem to perpetuate the old saying, 'There is one law for the rich and another for the poor.' - I am, &c., BRIDGET DALTON."*

Beneath her letter was a short note from the editor which reads: *"We imagine Mrs Dalton's amanuensis must have been misinformed."* It's unlikely Mrs Dalton was able to read or write, hence her need for an amanuensis, probably a Mr Tom Bishop who was a cook at Chavannes' Hotel and who provided leftovers for the old lady and her pets, of which we shall learn more in due course. The "misinformation" referred to by the *Chronicle's* editor related to the incorrect assumption that the stable extensions mentioned (James Smiley's, Ridgway Street, who featured in our Red Lion fire story), encroached onto the Queen's Reserve. But as already indicated, this letter from a Bridget Dalton claiming to have lived in her Rutland Hill home for *"many, many years"*, came just a week after the report of the Bolton Row Bridget Dalton losing her life's savings to a thief. Previous accounts about Granny Dalton have assumed the Bolton Row Bridget Dalton was her, but the confusion was obviously the result of two women of the same name living in close proximity to one another. A later newspaper entry, (*Herald:* 16 September, 1887) records the death at the Colonial Hospital of Bridget Dalton, although certainly not "Granny" Dalton from Rutland Hill, as the deceased's age is given as just 51, (although it should be noted that ages and dates can sometimes be notoriously unreliable). The death notice also states that she was a relation of Granny Dalton, who by that time was making a name for herself, further indicating the existence of two Bridget Daltons. However, a follow-up notice the next day not only refuted any connection between the two, but identified the deceased as the widow of the man who had disappeared and was presumed drowned four years previously.

So having established that Mrs Dalton of Bolton Row has drawn a very large "red herring" across our path, let us now get back on the trail of the real Granny Dalton, who emigrated to New Zealand on the *Woodlark* and who had made her home on Rutland Hill. What was she doing there?

After the military withdrew from the Rutland Stockade, which stood on the brow of the Queen's Reserve hill overlooking the town, squatters moved into the soldier's whares. These primitive dwellings, which stood outside the stockade's perimeter, had been constructed of materials such as raupo and toi toi. Although illegal under the Raupo House Ordinance Act of 1842 due to fire risks and attracting a £20 fine for non-compliance, an ammendment to the act in 1853 specifically allowed their use for Her Majesty's soldiers stationed at Wanganui. But when the soldiers moved out, the squatters (or "exquisites" as the *Herald* so colourfully labelled them) moved in. This situation lasted only as long as the township could tolerate it, with calls from the newspapers to evict those who were alleged to be causing so much revelry and debauchery, and from citizens crying foul over having to pay rates while those on the hill paid none. The following blast from the *Herald* (7 November, 1870) seems to be the catalyst which was needed to provoke the authorities into action:

"Frequent complaints have been made lately to the police, who are powerless in the matter, about the class of people who have assembled on the Rutland Hill adjoining the Stockade. The soldiers when stationed there, had erected a number of toetoe whares, in which their families resided, and when they left Wanganui, those whares were left standing and were gradually taken possession of and occupied by a number of exquisites who have obtained for their locale the suggestive name of the 'Rookery'. There is, we believe, an act or ordinance which forbids the existence of toetoe whares within the boundaries of the town. While the military remained an exception was formed, but there is no occasion why the law should not now be enforced. It is said that the wave of immorality has rolled down to the Church of England fence which encloses the church grounds, and borne a portion of it away. If the place is such a rendezvous for questionable characters as the police positively affirm, the authorities

should put whatever law does exist in force to burn or destroy the 'Rookery'."

It is not the author's task to speculate on the nature of the *"wave of immorality"* which was said to have rolled down the hill taking away a portion of the Church of England fence. However the reader, without too much cerebral exertion, should quite easily be able to fill in the blanks.

But it wasn't long before the "exquisites" began to return and a new community was established on Rutland Hill. Little shacks appeared with yards fenced off for pigs, goats, and chickens as well as the odd vegetable garden. And as the community grew, so the stockade diminished – a door here, a few windows there, perhaps a sizeable number of roofing shingles, although the usefulness of corrugated iron meant that the boundary fences were soon found wanting in performing the task they were designed for. The stockade's well and water pump, left intact by the departing military, were also of great benefit to the new residents. So it was to this established community that Granny Dalton attached herself and to which the mayor, (*Chronicle* proprietor and editor Gilbert Carson) ventured to interview Granny. The *Chronicle* (24 September, 1884) reports that Mr Carson had seen the old lady and arranged for her transference to a site near the cemetery, although the *Herald* of the same date adds a little colour to the story.

"The second chapter in the Mrs Dalton business seems to have had a happy conclusion. The Mayor reported last night that he had visited 'Granny,' and that the old lady had consented to being shifted. He told her that a site would be chosen for her on the Town Belt, and that there was little chance of her being disturbed by the Council after that. The old lady was left in a grand humour, and as jolly as possible, though she pulled a face at first at the thought of leaving 'me poor plants.'"

Now that Granny (and all the other residents) had been shifted, the Domain Board was able to redevelop Rutland Hill into a public reserve.

Rutland Hill – Granny's address for many years

Granny Dalton (Part 3): Who stole Granny's ducks?

After being evicted from her former home on Rutland Hill, Granny Dalton was resettled into a little shack near the town's gaol, (now site of the Whanganui Resource Recovery Centre), along with an assurance from the council that she would not be disturbed again.

Granny's next recorded adventure occurred the following year. Under the heading *"WHO STOLE THE DUCKS?"* the *Wanganui Herald* reported, *"Bridget Dalton charged C.H. Von Kaisenberg with killing certain ducks belonging to her."* (22 October, 1885). Granny was known for her rag-tag menagerie of Noah's Ark cast-offs which followed her round and which she fed with handouts from sympathetic hotel kitchen staff.

Mr Von Kaisenberg pleaded *"not guilty"*, but he had been spotted by a prison warder holding two ducks and chasing others. Warder Meehan, who was in charge of a gang of prisoners at the time, identified not only Mr Von Kaisenberg, but also Granny's ducks.

"Saw the accused come out of the corner of the enclosure, he was then chasing the ducks. He had also two ducks in his left hand .... When accused noticed witness he bent himself down and tried to hide his face. He did not drop the ducks, but went off towards the cricket ground and got through a gap. Recognised the prisoner by his dress as being the person that he saw with the ducks."

When challenged, the accused asked, *"Do you think it likely that a man could catch two ducks in one run out of a flock?"*

"I don't know," replied the witness. *"I have had no experience in catching ducks. All I know is that you had them."*

Several other witnesses gave evidence including Ellen Dalton, *"daughter of the prosecutrix,"* who stated that her mother ran ducks on the reserve and that a dead duck exhibited in court was one of hers, *"to all appearances."* Inspector James (to Mrs Dalton): *"Did you give any authority to*

accused to take any of your ducks?"
Granny: *"Oh no, Your Worship."*
Inspector James: *"What was the value of the duck?"*
Granny: *"The duck that was killed I would not give for 5s."*
Inspector James: *"How many ducks are there missing?"*
Granny: *"There are four missing. One went home wounded."*

When the prisoner tried questioning Granny she replied, *"Don't spake to me,"* then accused him of lying, told him that she didn't like him and would kill him if she got the chance! Of Granny's flock of 37 ducks, *"33 or 32"* remained. Prisoner continued to deny the charges and called witnesses in an effort to establish an alibi, but to no avail.

"His Worship said that he believed accused guilty of the offence, but for the sake of his wife and children he would not send him to prison, but would inflict a penalty of 20s and costs." (Herald). However Mr Von Kaisenberg, perhaps leaping at the chance of a break from Mrs Von Kaisenberg, opted for the alternative – seven days in prison!

Six years later Granny's feathered friends were again targeted. Four boys, *"amused themselves by pelting stones at Granny Dalton's ducks and succeeded in killing and wounding 15 of them, to the value of 45 shillings."* (Herald: 19 June 1891). The boys pleaded guilty and were let off with a caution, the Bench, *"taking into consideration the fact that 'Granny's' claims had been satisfied. When asked if she was satisfied with the £2/5s compensation, she replied in a loud voice, 'No, I am not! I wouldn't part with me ducks! I love me ducks; I love me ducks!'"*

Granny not satisfied with abduction payout

Granny Dalton (Part 4): No peace for Granny

We have seen that Granny Dalton, who had lived undisturbed on Rutland Hill for many years, was moved to a new location to help pave the way for the demolition of the Rutland Stockade, thus freeing the area to be transformed into a public reserve. Granny, adoptive mother to a large menagerie of strays, was given an assurance from the authorities that she would be allowed to see out her remaining years in her new home near the town gaol in peace. But it was not to be. On December 2, 1886 the *Chronicle* reported that the fence surrounding the Rutland Stockade (which at that point was still standing), would be taken down and the materials used to enclose the new gaol.

"We regret to hear that 'Granny Dalton', who some two or three years ago was induced to submit to the removal of her belongings from Queen's Park, on which she had for a long time squatted, is about to be interfered with again. It appears that her present domicile is located within the boundary of the land granted for the purpose of the new gaol, and as the whole section is about to be fenced, 'Granny' will have to shift, as she does not possess the qualifications requisite to ensure her residence within the gaol walls."

The Inspector of Prisons wrote to the Borough Council requesting that Mrs Dalton be shifted from the Prison Reserve as it was now occupied. In true bureaucratic fashion the matter was referred to the Works Committee who, it was thought, *"might, in their peregrinations, find some spot for her to reside."* (*Chronicle:* 2 February, 1887).

The inspector was informed that the matter was in hand but after two months of inaction he wrote again. Cr Bennie thought that as the land on which Granny resided did not belong to the council, they could not shift her, but Cr Austin pointed out that it was the council that put her there in the first place. It was decided to write to the Inspector of Prisons

292

informing him that the council had no ground available and that application should be made to the Charitable Aid Board on Granny's behalf.

It would be six months before the slowly turning wheels of officialdom began to see results: *"'Granny Dalton' has received notice from the Gaol Department that she must quit the site on the Gaol Reserve near the cemetery on which she at present resides. Her case having been represented to the Mayor* (by this time James Laird), *that gentleman has suggested another site on which Mrs Dalton may be permitted to locate herself."* (*Chronicle*: 11 August, 1887).

On the 31st of August the *Chronicle* informed its readers that because she had received notice to move, Mrs Dalton had asked to be allowed to reside on some other unoccupied portion of land and had applied to have her little house shifted to the new site, *"so that she might end her days in peace."* The mayor said that the Leaseholds Committee was in favour of letting her have a piece of land that was now available and that Mrs Dalton was quite willing to move to *"a site near Mitchell's paddock on the sandhill."*

The Herald identified the site as being *"behind the racecourse,"* and said that Granny was willing to accept it as *"she showed a spirit of independence and was not desirous of going on the Charitable Aid Board."* Two councillors had inspected the spot and considered it was suitable for the purpose intended.

Several articles indicate that Granny's new home was situated in Asylum Road, but as the facility intended to validate the name was never built, the road was given a new name – Purnell Street.

Purnell House today occupies the site intended for the asylum which gave Granny's street its original name

Granny Dalton (Part 5): Some mothers do 'ave 'em

While Granny was battling authorities seemingly intent on moving her from place to place, she was also having family troubles. It seems the problem of stay-at-home adult children is not a modern trend.

Readers will recall that three daughters accompanied Bridget Dalton on her voyage to New Zealand – one of them Ellen, with her occupation given as dairymaid. Under the surname Cotter, Ellen found herself behind bars one night due to being under the influence of liquor and assaulting her mother with a plate.

"Both were injured in the fray, as the parent returned the affectionate advances of her offspring with a fire shovel; but the plate fared worst of all." (*Chronicle*: 16 May, 1881). The *Herald* noted that Ellen's action during the fray was as the result of her *"unduly whipping Bacchus."* Just a week later she was again facing charges of being drunk and disorderly with a friend who had been engaged in a noisy quarrel with her husband. *"Having been admonished in a fatherly manner by the Bench, they were fined 5s each."* (*Chronicle*: 20 May, 1881).

Ellen appeared regularly before his Honour, usually on drunkenness and vagrancy charges and was once back in court within 24 hours of a previous offence. On another occasion she was charged with *"being in a Harrison-street house by night without lawful excuse."* (*Chronicle*: 23 March, 1881). Police had gone to the house after complaints that there were *"men and women killing each other in the house."*

The prisoners, Ellen Cotter and a man named Richard Hartshorn, claimed they had permission to be there, but that was refuted by the owner who said she had *"met the prisoners at the Courthouse when the band was playing. The woman was the worse of liquor, and the man was pulling her about. They came to the house and went in, and commenced kicking up a row."* Both prisoners were sentenced to a week's imprisonment with hard labour.

It was six years before Ellen again appeared in the court reports. She was charged with stealing a pocket-book, knife, photographs, locket and a half-sovereign from the guest of the Ship Hotel while he was sleeping. Three witnesses testified against her. She was sentenced to a month in prison with hard labour and cautioned not to repeat the offence.

But while Granny Dalton may once have fended off Ellen with a fire shovel, she had no hesitation in going in to bat for her daughter when she was allegedly assaulted by one John Chandler: *"Complainant* (Ellen, back to her maiden name) *stated that defendant came to the house where she and her mother lived, and as she was passing out about 5.30 o'clock he used very abusive language and struck her several times. She pushed him, and he fell down, but before that never gave him any provocation. The plaintiff's mother* (Granny) *gave corroborative evidence in a graphic and emphatic manner, which caused much amusement in court."* (*Chronicle:* 16 August, 1887).

The defendant said that he had quite civilly asked to be repaid 25 shillings the complainant owed him, but was knocked down. The Resident Magistrate sided with Ellen and fined Chandler 10s with costs, or in default seven days' imprisonment.

Four months later Ellen, back to the name Cotter, was again before the R.M, this time in her more accustomed role of defendant. Perhaps there were not many opportunities in Wanganui for dairymaids, for by this time she'd had a change of occupation, as this court report reveals. (*Chronicle:* 15 December, 1887).

"Ellen Cotter was charged with being an idle person, having no visible means of support. Prisoner pleaded not guilty, stating that she had means of support. Constable Mackle stated that he had known prisoner for about three years. He had arrested her at 3.30 yesterday morning in the Girl's High School reserve. She was with a man, and appeared to be sleeping. The man bolted, but she was too

drunk to do so. Prisoner was in the habit of going into fishermen's huts with men and lived by prostitution. Sergeant Bisset had known prisoner for seven or eight years and had known her to be a common prostitute. She had been convicted of vagrancy and drunkenness. Prisoner stated that she earned money by going into service and when not so employed lived with her mother, who had means to keep her. She had, when with her mother, taken in washing. In answer to the Bench, she stated that she had earned no money during the last three months. She was sentenced to one months's [sic] imprisonment, with hard labour."

A year later Ellen Cotter (alias Duncan) was charged with being a rogue and vagabond with no visible means of support. Pleading guilty, she said she had been looking for a place and had found employment as a general servant. *"She asked to be let off and promised not to give the police any trouble again. Sergeant Anderson stated that there were previous convictions against the prisoner for larceny and vagrancy and she had been in the habit of keeping bad company and getting drunk."* (*Chronicle:* 25 October, 1888). She was sentenced to a further month's imprisonment in the Wanganui Gaol.

Two years later, back to her maiden name, Ellen was again behind bars after a bout of Christmas revelry. *"Though the amount of drunkenness has not been large during the holidays, still one or two over-thirsty individuals have spent part of the time in the lock-up. Yesterday morning, Ellen Dalton, an old offender, was fined 10s or 48 hours."* (*Herald:* 27 December, 1889).

This is the last reference to Ellen by name in the Wanganui newspapers. No doubt much to the relief of local police and the judiciary she moved to Masterton where she lived with a new husband and where she was eventually joined by her mother in 1902. A funeral notice in the Wairarapa Daily Times announced her death in the common style of the times by not mentioning her name, only her husband's: *"The friends of Mr Stephen Maskrey are respectfully invited to attend the funeral of his late wife, which will leave his residence, 52 Bannister Street, on*

WEDNESDAY, December 3rd, at 3.30pm, for the Masterton Cemetery. HOAR & PERMAIN, Sanitary Undertakers. 'Phone 11." Ellen is buried with Granny at the Archer Street Cemetery in Masterton. Her plaque reads: *"In loving memory of Ellen Maskrey. Died 1 December, 1913 aged 52 years. R.I.P."*

Wanganui Courthouse - familiar to Granny and her daughter

Granny Dalton (Part 6): Granny keeps the home fires burning

At the time of the other Bridget Dalton's death in 1887, Granny Dalton would have been about 65 years of age (and from all accounts, yet to form an intimate acquaintance with soap and water). By Victorian standards she would have been considered "of advanced years". She was also, as we saw in the previous episode, burdened with the drunken antics of a delinquent adult daughter. But her troubles continued. Having been moved twice by the authorities she lost her home again – this time by fire.

"The cottage in Asylum Road which has been occupied by Granny Dalton for some years past was, we regret to say, burnt down yesterday. The poor old lady will have the sympathy of one and all in her misfortune and we trust some means will be found to assist her in her trouble." (*Chronicle:* 15 November, 1890).

It was six months before Granny was rehoused, although the indomitable "old" hermit no doubt fended well for herself and her extended family of pets in the meantime. *"It was decided, on the motion of Mr Carson, to allow Mrs ('Granny') Dalton the use of an unoccupied house near the Racecourse at the pleasure of Council."* (*Herald:* 6 May, 1891).

But even though the authorities kept a paternal eye out for Granny, it did not stop local larrikins from tormenting her and it was just a month after she moved into her new home that the four boys mentioned in Part 3 of this series killed some of her ducks. And it did not stop another disaster from overtaking her.

"The house belonging to the Borough at the back of the Racecourse and occupied by Granny Dalton was burned down yesterday morning. The house, which contained four rooms, was, we believe, insured for £75." (*Chronicle:* 25 October, 1892).

The *Herald* (25 October) considered the fire was accidental, *"owing its origin to a foul chimney, the soot from which had fallen down and communicated with the boards."*

The *Chronicle*, impressed with the promptitude in which the Standard Fire Office paid out the insurance claim (within five days), declared it *"sufficient almost to make a record."*

Granny, perhaps confident in the knowledge that the faulty chimney would have been council's responsibility, asked what assistance could now be given her. *"Mrs Dalton waited on the Council to point out that owing to the fire in her house, she was rendered homeless, and to ask what assistance could be given her. The Mayor and Cr Carson were asked to make enquiries to do the best in the matter they could."*

Her request must have been granted, for next we hear she is beseeching councillors *"with the modest request that they undertake the erection of an additional room to her already palatial residence."* (*Chronicle:* 31 May, 1893.

"The council, however, were inhumane enough to imagine that they had already done as much as possible for the old lady and her application was not entertained," was the *Chronicle's* sardonic response. A wise decision, as it turned out.

Granny Dalton outside one of her "palatial residences"

Granny Dalton (Part 7): Granny missing – feared dead

Having hit the headlines for over a decade, Granny Dalton seems to have lived in relative obscurity for a couple of years, but that suddenly changed in early 1895, when fears for her safety were raised.

"Granny Dalton has been missing from her home since Monday last. The police would be glad to hear from any person knowing anything as to the whereabouts of this old identity." (Herald: 6 February).

Two days later the *Herald* reported that Granny had last been seen near the Castlecliff school-house, where she told someone she had lost her way but refused to be put on the right track. *"Sgt Cullen sent down a couple of constables yesterday and they together with a search party of about 20, searched all the sandhills in the vicinity, but without success. It is now considered that the old woman has perished, probably in one of the swamps, in trying to find her way home unaided."* (Herald: 8 February).

But soon there was good news! *"All fears as to the safety of old Granny Dalton were set at rest yesterday afternoon, for she was driven in from Kai Iwi having been found on Mr D. Blair's place there in the morning in a very bad plight. The old woman having been kindly cared for was brought in as stated and taken to the Police Station, after which she was received into the Hospital. 'G' must have had a very rough experience through the gorse, fern etc., but she stuck to her bundle of sticks for all that."* (Herald: 11 February).

The *Chronicle* added that "G" had been found in the Blair's wool-shed in a very weak state and taken into their home, where her wet clothing was removed and she was given some nourishing food. After a time of recuperation at the Colonial Hospital she returned to her cottage in Asylum Road – probably fairly promptly, for hospital fees were £1/1s a week for those who could afford it, while those who couldn't were expected to work for their keep.

No doubt Granny's menagerie of scruffy hangers-on was as concerned about their carer's absence as was the local constabulary, but they were probably well looked after by those people who were concerned for her well-being. For despite shunning main-stream society, Granny had her friends within the community.

"Charity never faileth," announced the *Herald* (8 May 1895), *"but when it is dispensed in an unostentatious manner it is all the more deserving of commendation and we are pleased to recall such an act by several members of the Salvation Army to one looked upon almost as an outcast. Some few days ago a surprise visit was paid to Granny Dalton, and the wretched tenement inhabited by her and her pets – dogs, cats, fowls, ducks etc., - was thoroughly renovated and cleaned, (no small matter as our readers may suppose), and the wants of Granny, who was sadly in need of assistance, attended."*

The article informed readers that Granny had previously resisted attempts to admit her into the *"Old Men's Home"*, instead preferring to eke out an existence for herself in her little shack near the racecourse.

"But of late," continued the *Herald, "she has become so much more feeble, and scarce able to attend to her own wants. It cannot be wondered at that visitors to Granny should not be very many, considering her dishevelled appearance and still more uninviting abode. But fortunately for 'G' all are not phariasical* [sic] *and no doubt the kindness of the members of the Army was much appreciated."*

But again disaster struck. Granny's house (which readers will recall she had unsuccessfully petitioned council to add another room to) burned to the ground. *"The poor old woman whose figure is very familiar in Wanganui, was kindly taken care of by Mrs T. Dickson till the police were communicated with and Constable Shearman afterwards removed her to the Jubilee Home. This is the 3rd or 4th occasion 'G' has been burned out, the outbreaks probably being due to burning logs falling from the fireplace. She would be much more comfortable at the 'Home', of which however, she has no desire of becoming an inmate."* (*Herald:* 2 March, 1898).

Sally Annes to Granny's rescue

Granny Dalton (Part 8): Wanganui's first council house tenant?

Is the council's present day provision of pensioner units directly attributable to Granny Dalton's dire housing needs of over a century ago? A postman would have found it a considerable challenge to keep up with Granny's constant changes of address due to a seemingly endless series of evictions and house fires, but she was always able to attract the attention of kindly mayors and borough councillors, who never failed to ensure she had a roof (albeit very basic) over her head.

That concern for our heroine also had spin-offs for the wider deprived community (or lower socio-economic sector to use today's terminology), according to an article in the *Wanganui Herald* (17 January, 1900), which reported that Mayor Alexander Hatrick had given permission, subject to council approval, *"for the erection of a cottage on the Borough reserve, near the Cemetery, for a family in distressed circumstances in Wanganui, the money for which had been raised by subscription."*

Cr Peat immediately announced his intention of objecting to the mayor's action and Cr Richardson, while sympathetic to the mayor's efforts to assist a deserving family, *"thought the council might err in establishing a precedent."* But Cr Bell pointed out that there was already a precedent for such a step, *"in that the Council had allowed Granny Dalton to occupy a piece of a borough reserve and he had never heard anyone raise an objection to this."*

Cr Perrett was all for helping the unfortunate family and thought no great harm would result. Cr Liffiton also had no objection provided a document was drawn up declaring that the occupants had no vested interests in the property. *"He pointed out that in the past the council had had great difficulty in getting rid of persons who lived on the reserves now known as*

Queen's Park and Cook's Gardens." (Granny Dalton herself, as we have seen, being one of them).

Cr Bassett expressed sympathy for the unfortunate family and commended those who were doing something about it, but *"thought it was most unfortunate that they had in the town an institution specially established to provide for such cases, in such a state that people of this sort were practically excluded from it."* (He was talking about Jubilee Home in Aramoho, which at the time was the subject of council and public scrutiny because of alleged mismanagement). *"He* (Cr Bassett) *did not undertake to criticise the gentlemen who had control of it; but there was the fact that the public generally were dissatisfied with the conduct of it, as also the old people themselves. It was a lamentable state of affairs that they could not send the family to the Home and make them comfortable."* As for the proposed cottage itself he was concerned, not about setting a precedent but *"being desirous of guarding the Avenue to the Hospital. The locality between the town and the Heads was fast being built on, and he thought that in time the Borough reserves would be taken up for residential sites."* Mayor Hatrick gave an assurance that, *"he had no doubt the cottage would not be unsightly and might be erected back from the road."*

In light of the above, if a future council ever has occasion to name or rename a block of pensioner units, why not honour the incorrigible old lady who badgered councillors into providing them in the first place?

But later that year Jubilee Home featured again in the local press – all because of Granny Dalton. It began with a story in the *Chronicle* (30 October, 1900), which surely would have sent distraught borough councillors straight to the liquor cabinet. *"Granny Dalton was yesterday morning unfortunate enough to have had her cottage burned down. It appears that 'G', after cooking her breakfast, went outside and on her return found the place in flames. It will be remembered that this identity met with a similar loss some time ago and that the Collegiate boys very generously collected sufficient money to build the cottage just burned down. 'G' was admitted to the Jubilee Home yesterday afternoon."*

(As readers will recall, this cottage was one of many which suffered a similar fate and was indeed built by Collegiate students from a special offertory of £3/12s which was raised in 1898 and recorded in the school's Chapel Account). But Granny did not stay long at Jubilee. The *Chronicle* (30 November, 1900) records that while she appeared very contented there, she was one day granted permission to go to town, on the understanding she would return in the evening. *"As she did not put in an appearance the police were communicated with and found the old lady living among the ruins of her cottage. She was brought before the Court next day, and on being asked if she would go back to the Home she replied that she would be delighted to do so. On that condition she was discharged, but after a cab had been brought and everything was in readiness, she changed her mind and expressed her intention of going to see the 'old place' once more, stating that she would go to the Home 'to-morrow'. With 'Granny', however, to-morrow never came and yesterday morning she was again brought before the Court. On being asked by Mr Kettle if she would stay at the Home if sent there, Granny replied, 'Perhaps I will; perhaps I won't,' remarking at the same time that it touched her pride to be sent there. 'But,' said Mr Kettle, 'if you won't stay at the Home, you will have to go to gaol; you can't stay in the sandhills without a house.' Granny said that the gaol would be as good as the Home to her. The old lady evidently being of the opinion (in common with the majority of mankind), that 'be it ever so humble there's no place like home,' said that she wanted her own little home rebuilt, where she would be quite happy."* When Mr Kettle informed her that he would try to have that done, Granny consented to go into the home in the meantime.

But the call of the sandhills was too strong for Granny Dalton, according to an article which appeared two months later, (*Chronicle:* 27 December, 1900). *"A case which has taxed the ingenuity of the authorities to provide for has recently again come before the Court. Granny Dalton finds that she is quite unable to sacrifice even so much of her liberty as is implied in being an inmate of the Old Men's Home. It will be remembered that some time ago the small house given to her by the Collegiate School was burnt down. Since then she has haunted the same spot except when removed by the police. It seems clear now that she must exist near her old home if at all. In consequence of this we are informed that the Rev. J.M. Marshall has ordered another whare to be built for the old lady on behalf of the Collegiate School. Messrs Britten and Purnell have already got the contract in hand."*

Several days later (31 December) the *Herald* reported that Granny had been remanded for a week in custody until her cottage could be built, although her incarceration should not be interpreted as a punitive measure by the authorities. In fact it was quite the opposite; rather a means of keeping her safe until her new house was ready for occupation. *"Mr Kettle SM told Granny that she was only detained in the gaol until the building for her could be erected and that she must not think of herself as a prisoner, such detention being for her own benefit."*

Granny's new residence must have been erected with astonishing speed, for just a few days later the following appeared in the *Herald* (3 January, 1901). *"'Granny' Dalton was brought before Mr Kettle this morning to be formally discharged. His Worship told the old soul that her cottage had been rebuilt and handed her the key, whereupon 'Granny' remarked with much emphasis, 'God bless you,' and 'God bless ye all.' Mr Kettle then cautioned 'Granny' to be very careful and not burn down her place again and to expend some portion of her available cash in the purchase of blankets and cooking utensils and deposit the balance of her money with some public official. 'Granny' was most profuse in her promises to do as directed and left the Court calling for blessings on all and sundry."*

By now Granny Dalton's notoriety was spreading – at least as far as Masterton where her daughter Ellen was now living. *"Poor old Granny Dalton is once more in the little house which the charitable public have built for her. Let us hope she will be spared a few more years to enjoy her new possession." (Wairarapa Daily Times:* 5 January, 1901).

Which she did for the following fifteen months and continued to be a familiar sight on her daily treks to town, accompanied by her menagerie of pets who seemed quite happy to risk catching something from their beloved benefactor, knowing she would share with them the food scraps scrounged from sympathetic hotel cooks. And a story passed on to me recently, although mentioning no names, sounds so "Granny Dalton-ish" I shall include it here. Apparently train drivers, if they spotted a particular "old Wanganui identity" waiting at a certain location by the lines, would "accidentally" drop a few lumps of coal beside the track.

Granny Dalton's final Wanganui home probably stood somewhere on the land now occupied by Riding for the Disabled and a track which began at about the present location of the High School gates and emerged at London Street was, (at least until the 1970s), known unofficially as "Granny Dalton's Lane." But it appears she had neighbour problems, according to the *Historical Record* (Journal of the Whanganui Historical Society Inc., Vol 21: No 1, May 1990). Part of her old burnt-out home remained and was occupied by a man dubbed, "The Lodger". (The building material for this shack had been predominantly kerosene tins and was once affectionately referred to by Granny as *"Sphlendid, but rayther narrer."*) The Lodger tried to break into Granny's house one day, *"T' get me shillin's,"* she complained. *"The ould bla'guard. He was a bad ould man the ould vagabond, an' sure I was very kind to 'im I was. Many th' bits o' t'bacca I give 'im."*

The Lodger, of course, was evicted from his kerosene tin home. But Granny Dalton's celebrity days were almost over.

Jubilee Home - as good as a gaol for Granny

Granny Dalton (Part 9): The final years

"Granny Dalton, who has been a familiar figure in Wanganui for many years, has changed her place of residence. She left by the mail train last week for a town down the line where she intends to reside." (*Chronicle*: 8 April, 1902).

An article in the April, 1902 edition of the *Wanganui Collegian* reads: *"The gaiety of the school was considerably eclipsed by the news that 'Granny' Dalton had abandoned the mansion erected for her by the school some year or two ago, and had been seen in a special carriage in the train on her way no one knows whither. The game in the park appears to have disappeared, if this is not an Irishism; since her departure the drive is uncared for, the Hot Houses are in ruins, the 'moated garage' stands empty. It is really rather sad that such an old identity should have vanished from the scene but nothing would surprise us less than to see at the beginning of the term the old lady installed once again in her wide domains."*

And so Bridget Dalton, whose independence and lifestyle were a constant challenge to the goodwill and ingenuity of our city fathers for over 25 years, would no longer be seen trudging the streets of Wanganui. Or would she? It certainly seemed the town had seen the last of her and after several months of no sightings the *Herald* (26 August), reprinting an article from the *Wanganui Collegian*, appealed to the community for any knowledge of her: *"Great mystery seems to surround the whereabouts of Granny Dalton. If anyone hears of her in the holidays, the editor will be glad to receive information."*

Later that year the *Herald* (16 December), again quoting the *Wanganui Collegian* ran this item: *"As there are no signs or prospect of the return of Granny Dalton, her mansion has been sold for £1. This, together with the balance in hand in her favour amounting to £1/14s, will be given to the first charitable object that presents itself."* But then – a little snippet tagged on which must have been received by the *Collegian* editor in time for the print deadline. *"We may add that 'Granny' has again returned to Wanganui and yesterday she looked quite 'spick and span', as compared with her former garb."*

Perhaps her daughter Ellen, with whom she was now living, was trying to make up for all the grief she had caused her mother in former years. But Granny Dalton's sojourn back in her old stamping grounds must have been short-lived, for the next reference to her appeared in the form of an obituary in the *Wanganui Herald* (6 April, 1903).

"The death is announced at Masterton of an old lady, whose figure for the last thirty years was as familiar to residents of Wanganui as her dress of later years was quaint. We refer to old 'Grannie' Dalton, who passed away at the residence of her daughter, at the advanced age of 80. 'Grannie' possessed many peculiar characteristics, none perhaps more striking than her love of liberty and independence. She preferred a life of solitude and freedom in a rude cabin among the sandhills and toi tois and fern to the more hospitable refuge afforded in the Old People's Home at Aramoho. 'Grannie' had many kind friends in Wanganui, and always had a good word to say for the College boys - 'Gad bless 'em'! – who erected a hut for her after she was burned out. Some of the Convent Sisters were equally solicitious [sic] for the old body's welfare, and paid regular weekly visits to her abode, which they tidied and cleaned up, as 'Grannie' seemed to have a particular aversion to the look of water and soap – about her only failing. She was of remarkable physique, and up to quite recently carried loads on her back in her long tramp through the sand that would have staggered many a strong man. Requiescat in pace!"

Buried under the name Margaret, her headstone reads: *"In loving memory of Bridget Dalton. Born Kilkenny, Ireland. Died 4 April, 1903 aged 80. R.I.P. Erected by her daughter Ellen Maskrey."* The most well-known photograph of Granny (refer to "Granny Dalton: Part 1") is listed as unattributed. However, an article in the 1 November, 1906 edition of the *Wanganui Chronicle* features a report on the Manawatu A&P Show. Listed in the photography section is the statement: *"In the class *for genre or figure studies, Mr T.W. Downes won first prize with his somewhat overdone subject, Granny Dalton."*

And so Granny Dalton was dead. But lurking in the shadows, at least in the minds of many frightened young children, was the apparition of a scary old woman who would seize them and carry them away if ever they misbehaved.

Granny Dalton – happy in her sandhills home

Christmas spirit alive and well in 1907

The flying machine is in its infancy, the super-liner *Titanic* is yet to progress from the drawing board and Gallipoli is an obscure location known only to geographers. Elvis Presley's grandfather is a teenager, young women are expected to remain in the family home until married and the nearest thing to takeaways is raiding the neighbour's orchard.

Our mayor is the popular, but yet-to-be outed Charles Mackay, the Watt Fountain has recently been moved to make way for our new tram system, the Waimarie is barely run in and the latest number to be added to our Telephone Exchange is 540.

It's 1907 – one hundred and ten years ago and all boys and girls are trying (or pretending) to be good, for the *Herald* has just announced that Santa has again chosen the Economic as his Wanganui headquarters.

The great man will arrive on the 3.00pm mail train, then proceed in his *"famous motor car"* to his destination where he will demonstrate his chimney-descending skills. All good children are promised a present.

While they are distracted, mother can choose from the Economic's vast array of gloves, reliable hosiery, coloured sunshades, collars, costume fronts, ribbons, handkerchiefs, summer costumes and aprons.

McGruer's have specials on Christmas ties and the DIC has men's and boys' clothing at holiday prices. J Williams & Co Jewellers are advertising "beautiful and artistic" items, while Dr Williams' (no relation to the jeweller) Pink Pills guarantee a cure for post-Christmas indigestion, headaches, nausea, vomiting, anaemia, influenza, eczema, rheumatism, sciatica, St Vitus' Dance, nervous disorders, paralysis and ladies' ailments. Three shillings a box, please.

Miss K.C., a local lass, has just scored a useful Christmas

bonus of one guinea, winning a national competition by poetically extolling the virtues of the Universal Cold Cure.

"Out hiking I caught a bad cold,
Of that I am perfectly sure.
I was soon put all right,
I was cured in one night,
By the great Universal Cold Cure."

(There's no record of Miss K.C. going on to achieve further literary fame).

Rain fell on Christmas Eve, but did nothing to dampen the enthusiasm of citizens who promenaded up and down the Avenue. The City Band commenced caroling but had to abandon it – at 8.00pm according to the *Herald,* but not until 8 o'clock the next morning said the *Chronicle* – due to bad weather.

However rain could not dampen the cheer at Jubilee Old Men's Home. *"The rain came down and the sky was grey, but the spirits of the old men who have their home at Upper Aramoho rose higher and higher until the hour of dinner arrived and then the excitement grew intense. The dinner gong was sounded and the vets walked and tottered into the hall. Those who were deaf were unable to hear the tables groaning under the weight of Christmas cheer, but the strain was soon lifted! After the meal they rested and prepared for high tea. If comfort adds to one's happiness, then the old men of Jubilee Home ought to be extremely happy."* (*Wanganui Chronicle:* 27 December).

Hospital patients were also well looked after, according to the *Chronicle.* *"Were ill-health not the qualification for residence at Wanganui Hospital, one would almost be tempted to wish oneself an inmate of the institution at Christmas time. At that season the visitor finds it difficult to believe he is surrounded by suffering humanity, so bright and happy are the faces and so cheerful the general atmosphere. The Christmas which has just passed was no exception to the rule. In fact it may be safely said there were few happier Christmas parties than that at the Hospital. How could it be*

314

otherwise? There was practically a 'full ship' ......, but fortunately there were few so seriously ill as to be debarred from participation in the good things provided for their entertainment ...... The whole staff, from the Matron (Miss McKenny) to the most junior officer, had gone to work with a determination to make the Christmas celebrations memorable, and if the enthusiastic demonstrations of appreciation by the patients may be taken as a criterion, they succeeded admirably. The wards were pictures. They were decorated artistically with flowers, palms, coloured paper and various devices and when the electric lights were switched on the effect was charming. Each ward had its own favourite colour and the tastefulness shown in its display says much for the artistic nature of the nurses who were the guiding spirits. Each nurse had a loyal kingdom, for her subjects (after critical examination of the other wards) were perfectly satisfied that theirs was the best of all."

After the traditional carol singing by the nurses *"sleep then claimed attention, the children of the Hospital first making sure that their stockings were hung where they could not fail to catch the eye of Father Christmas as he passed through the building on his midnight journey."*

Patients eagerly opened their gifts the next morning. Not one had been missed! A party of carol singers from various churches arrived, followed by breakfast. *"Then came the wait for the great event of the day – Christmas dinner. This was laid out in the convalescent room, which, like the wards, was very nicely decorated. The dinner was a triumph of Christmas cheer, there being abundance of everything which kindness and culinary skill could suggest."*

After all the moveable patients had taken their places and grace sung, *"an onslaught was made upon the eatables, which apparently afforded comfort and pleasure. Those who could not leave their beds were waited upon by the nurses. Evening brought the crowning event of the year, for Santa Claus kindly paid a special visit in order to distribute the wondrous gifts displayed on the Christmas tree. This function took place in the women's ward, the end of which looked very picturesque. Pride of place was given to the handsome Christmas tree laden with presents for old and young, and around it were gathered all the patients who could be safely moved, members of the visiting medical staff, nurses and friends. The ward looked very gay and each and all were highly interested in the proceedings that followed. After a number of musical items had been rendered, Father Christmas appeared, and, to the amusement of spectators, handed out the prizes according to the tickets which had been previously drawn by the audience. The appropriateness and inappropriateness of gifts caused much laughter and it is safe to predict that no small amount of bartering was done when the play was over. After the tree had been denuded of its hangings, another very enjoyable programme was given. Then a happy Christmas party separated, the patients being tucked into their beds and the visitors entertained at supper. The Matron and the nurses are worthy of warm commendation for the amount of labour they must have devoted in order to make their patients spend a day which, we venture to think, will ever remain one of their pleasantest memories."*

At what seems like an anti-climax in comparison, a large audience at the Opera House was enthralled by the *"exceedingly interesting"* and *"excruciatingly humorous"* kinemato-graphic colour pictures shown by means of a Cooper's Opera-scope.

Merry Christmas everyone – from 1907.

Father Christmas motors to the Economic

An extended New Year for *Chronicle* staffers

Good news, all you hard-working *Chronicle* staffers - management has decided to give you an extended new year holiday.

It's true! Read on. *"In order to afford the whole of our staff with a complete holiday, without the inevitably pleasure-restricting stipulation of an enforced return on Monday night, we have decided to issue the Chronicle on New Year's Day, but not on the following morning."*

The statement expresses the hope that readers and the public will, *"fall in with this arrangement and thus contribute to the relaxation and enjoyment of our staff, with whom hard work and no play is the customary form of existence, and to whom holidays are normally like angels' visits – few and far between."*

Unfortunately it's dated 30 December, 1876 – but, coincidentally, the dates align exactly with the days of this year (2017), so although publishing deadlines now differ, this could be a great opportunity to negotiate the same benefits your predecessors enjoyed over 140 years ago.

Naturally, any form of employment over the festive season is to be avoided whenever possible but there are some, particularly those engaged in medical or emergency services, who must be on call while the rest of us relax. It seems this was not always the case.

"The new year was ushered in with the customary rejoicings," declared the *Chronicle* (2 January, 1879). *"At some of the churches devotional services were held; while throughout the town bells were rung, guns discharged and fireworks exhibited, the main streets being paraded by companies of noisy, though in most cases harmless, revellers. There were, however, some disgraceful exceptions. Two or three low scoundrels, not satisfied with the 'fun' derivable from inconveniencing people by shifting their gates, and the perpetration of other similarly absurd pieces of mischief,*

wantonly hurled stones through the windows of the Chronicle office, the Post Office and the new Bank of Australasia. Such disgraceful proceedings should not have been possible. Knowing the predelictions of some of our Wanganui youth on such occasions, the whole police force ought to have been on duty from twelve till two o'clock on New Year's morning. Although it is too late to remedy the mischief, we trust Mr Inspector Goodall will do his best to bring the scoundrels to justice."

Two days later, under the headline *"The Window Smashing Business"*, the *Chronicle* reported that the main offender had been apprehended and *"may have to pay dearly for his folly."* But three days after that the Chronicle affirmed, *"The hero of the window breaking business on New Year's morning has made himself scarce, having left for Wellington by steamer on Sunday with the view, it is said, of proceeding to Melbourne."*

This was not the first time such vandalism had occurred in Wanganui. *"It appears that the Colonial way of bringing in the new year is by smashing the windows of any public house that refuses to open its doors and supply the wakeful spirits with beer; at least this was the practice yesterday morning, when Mr Hackett had nearly every window in his house broken, together with sundry articles of household furniture."* (*Evening Herald*: 2 January, 1868).

Outlying towns were not immune from such activities, as Turakina residents discovered throughout the 1870s. *"This horrible nuisance, unless dealt with very effectively, will soon become perfectly unbearable to the more sober portion of the community,"* complained a *Chronicle* subscriber (4 January, 1875. *"A band of these worthies on New Year's eve paraded Turakina in the most disorderly and riotous manner – throwing stones on the roofs of houses, boxes thrown against people's doors, gardens trampled and other things that border on still greater mischief. In addition to the horrible noise made by twenty or thirty tin cans, together with as many discordant voices, there is a new feature introduced – the discharge of firearms."*

The writer alleged that the disturbance was not the work of

mere boys, but that the ringleaders were, *"a good deal on the shady side of thirty."* Two years later *"larrikinism and tin-kettling"* again hit the town, this time with the addition of rolling iron tanks, chalking doors, removing gates and pulling down fences. *"The protector of the public peace bravely tried to quell the hubbub single-handed, but his excited vociferations were totally disregarded and he was treated to a double-distilled agony of crackers, kettles and drums. What a blessing it is, Mr Editor, that New Year's Day comes but once in twelve months."*

Perhaps the last word should go to *"Mr Editor"* (*Chronicle:* 25 December, 1874). *"We again wish for all our friends, (we don't think we have any enemies in the world) and hope for ourselves, 'A Merry Christmas and a Happy New Year'."*

Epilogue

What better way to conclude our look into the past than to return to the words of *"Marksman"*, whose lighthearted speculation on the subject of the first European to discover Wanganui kicked off this selection of whimsical tales. Marksman, who wrote a number of articles for the *Herald*, and who admitted that his object had been to *"blend fact and fiction so as to make a readable groundwork,"* had apparently been chastened for his approach by an offended readership which was not yet ready for his style of satire. *"I understand that exception has been taken to the past history of Wanganui being burlesqued,"* he acknowledged, *"and as my object has always been to avoid giving offence where possible, I will for the present drop both humour and fiction, and confine myself solely with facts."* Under the title, *"SKETCHES OF WANGANUI: PAST, PRESENT & FUTURE,"* he gives his impressions of Wanganui as it was in 1856 and how it had developed up until the time of his article which was written in 1891.

"Although considerable progress had then been made, the town still presented a very rude and uncivilised appearance, many of the houses being built with clay walls and other primitive material, the banks of the river being dotted with tents, whilst a stockade on the heights and a number of block houses, with sentries on guard, gave a military aspect to the scene. The population appears also to have been a strange mixture of soldiers, whalers, shepherds and farmers, in which the Scotch nationality seems to have largely predominated. Provisions were also extremely high (in price) *with the exception of a few ordinary articles, which fortunately happened to be amongst the necessaries of life. A good description of the aspect of the town has been given by Mr C. Burnett, who describes the various buildings in detail, from which it appears that on the site of the present Post Office, at that time stood a school, store and circulating libraary* [sic]. *Scattered up the present Avenue, which seems to have been a very wet and boggy place, there were a few straggling houses*

320

and cottages, leading up to a sand hill, the site of the present Weslyan Church. There were no other dwellings between this sand hill and St John's Bush, with the exception of a small farm house and a school and parsonage. A few ugly little churches stood on almost the same sites as are now occupied by the fine buildings representing the English, Presbyterian and Catholic denominations. A wheelwright's and blacksmith's establishment represented what is now Hallenstein's Clothing Factory, (now vacated site of Anderson's For Men) *whilst a small dwelling house stood where* Paul's fine drapery premises now are, (now Foster's Hotel).

The Quay would appear, however, to have been the principal business locality and boasted of two hotels, a general store, auction mart, butcher's shop and lock-up. From this very imperfect description it will however be seen that the Wanganui of today is a vastly different place from what it was then, and as one gazes on the now busy thoroughfares and handsome business establishments, it is hard to realise the rude aspect that the township then presented, together with the struggles and privations of the early settlers. Like a moving panorama however, the scene gradually changed. One by one the old familiar landmarks disappeared, and as advancing civilisation rolled on in its endless course, a magical transformation took place in the aspect of the town and its environs. The swamps were drained and beautiful streets laid out and formed. The rude dwellings of the pioneer settlers were replaced by the present handsome and commodious buildings. The unsightly sand hills were covered with a verdant carpet and were formed into parks and beautified with trees and flowers. A noble bridge spanned the waters of the river, whilst elegant villa residences adorned the banks. Schools, colleges, churches, reading rooms and every modern luxury and convenience that our present civilisation demands, were added from time to time, until Wanganui now stands one of the prettiest, best equipped and picturesque townships in the colony." (Herald: 16 May, 1891).

Which returns us full circle to our introductory comments quoting the Chamber of Commerce's pamphlet which lauded the many wonderful attributes of the River City and assured us that the man who had travelled the world and seen its wonders would settle in Wanganui's welcoming embrace, never again to be seduced by the charms of fickle temptresses on faraway shores.

A romanticised view of early Wanganui, with the unremarkable first Church of England enhanced to cathedral status